Teaching Transatlanticism

Teaching Transatlanticism

Resources for Teaching Nineteenth-Century
Anglo-American Print Culture

Edited by Linda K. Hughes and Sarah R. Robbins

EDINBURGH
University Press

Edinburgh University Press Ltd
The Tun – Holyrood Road, 12(2f) Jackson's Entry, Edinburgh EH8 8PJ

www.euppublishing.com

Typeset in 11/13 Ehrhardt by
Servis Filmsetting Ltd, Stockport, Cheshire,
and printed and bound in the United States of America

A CIP record for this book is available from the British Library

ISBN 978 0 7486 9445 7 (hardback)
ISBN 978 0 7486 9447 1 (webready PDF)
ISBN 978 0 7486 9446 4 (paperback)
ISBN 978 0 7486 9448 8 (epub)

Contents

Acknowledgements

If all writing is collaborative, certainly a project focused on transatlantic culture would need to be. This book has been collaborative from the start – both in spirit and in practice. To offer a complete record of thanks due to our numerous partners would require far more space than we have available. So we hope the many members of our talented, committed *Teaching Transatlanticism* network will know that we gratefully carry detailed knowledge of their generous contributions far beyond what we say here, where we highlight key examples of the assistance that made this project possible.

A book needs a publisher. A publisher that provides a welcoming home and related intellectual projects is a gift indeed. Our first thanks, therefore, must go to the entire team at Edinburgh University Press, and especially to Jackie Jones, who guided this project from its inception. The press's prior publications on transatlantic culture, led by innovators of transatlanticism as a field, have been inspirational models for scholarship and teaching. Susan Manning's influence has been at the heart of this work, and her impact lives on beyond her too-early passing. The lively community of *Symbiosis* – both the journal and its regular biennial conferences – has been a model for us as well. Looking ahead to future work in transatlantic studies, we are grateful to be launching a project of anthology-making with Andrew Taylor, again with thanks to Jackie Jones's leadership.

In the end, a collection is only as strong as its contributing authors. Ours has benefitted enormously from the deep knowledge of transatlanticism and of engaged teaching that our contributors bring to their work. They have also demonstrated a special willingness to share their work and their writing processes in ways atypical of much academic publishing. In an online workspace, they allowed us to post their drafts, opening up the stages of their essay-making to the examination of our students at TCU and the students of others who joined this project's Teaching Transatlanticism network. With grace and a liberal pedagogical spirit, they also opened up their editing steps to those enrolled in our 2013 team-taught seminar; each student had the unique opportunity to work as an early reader and copyeditor with one of our chapter authors. We hope that it gave our authors a productive connection with a reader similar to many who will be coming to the book in the future: emerging teacher-scholars, eager to learn about transatlanticism and teaching from the very best practitioners.

The teaching focus and scholarly framework that undergird this project have been achievable in large part because we are privileged to work together at TCU. TCU's teacher-scholar model is an authentic, deep-seated commitment. It allows for out-of-the-ordinary enterprises like our own initial team-teaching of a transatlantic graduate seminar in 2010 – the inspiration for this book. TCU regularly provides faculty with resources for enhancing their pedagogy; that 2010 seminar drew on funds from the university's Instructional Development Grant programme, which enabled us to bring Barbara McCaskill, Meredith McGill, and Kate Flint to campus to share their transatlantic scholarship and model the best teaching in the field for our first group of graduate students. In 2013, we secured a second Instructional Development Grant, this time to support the building of an online workspace to connect our students with this collection's authors and to enable the start-up development of the Teaching Transatlanticism website linked to this book. The AddRan College of Liberal Arts, led by Dean Andrew Schoolmaster, further contributed to the website's launch through the 'Creativity and Innovation in Learning' grant programme, as did our partnership with TCU's Mary Couts Burnett Library, including Dean June Koelker and energetic staff members Ammie Harrison and Jacob Brown. Complementing the enthusiastic support of English Department chairs (Brad Lucas in 2010, Karen Steele in 2013) and the Director of Graduate Studies (Mona Narain), who helped us navigate the logistics of mounting a team-taught course, these TCU grants and cross-campus partnerships have been indispensable to our work.

All the students in our 2010 and 2013 graduate seminars have made significant contributions to this book. While we are especially pleased to have the voices of four of our 2010 students directly represented in the collection, we are grateful for the engagement of both groups throughout this project, in print and online. The Teaching Transatlanticism website (<teachingtransatlanticism.tcu.edu>) – including the reading guides linked to each week's focus on the 2013 syllabus – gives some indication of the richness of our ongoing conversations in seminar meetings. In addition to serving as initial copyeditors of a chapter, students in that second offering of the course also read and responded to draft versions of the collection's essays, thereby contributing to our own shared editorial vision.

Several graduate student research assistants made vital contributions beyond the framework of the seminars. Full partners – indeed, leaders – in the design, building, and refining of the Teaching Transatlanticism website, Tyler Branson and Marie Martinez have been invaluable colleagues as the four of us sought to envision new possibilities for linking print and online publishing. Carrie Tippen (Lorraine Sherley Research Fellow for 2013–14), Mary McCulley (Addie Levy Research Fellow for 2013–14 and alumna of the 2010 seminar), and Larisa Asaeli (Graduate Research Assistant and another alumna of the 2010 course) all assisted in a range of tasks in the final stages of manuscript preparation, bringing both good cheer and attentive care to their work.

Finally, we thank Johns Hopkins University Press for permission to reproduce parts of the essay by Sandra A. Zagarell, '*The Portrait of a Lady*: "no intention of deamericanising"', *Henry James Review*, 35: 1 (Winter 2014), 23–33.

Note on Companion Website

In addition to the rich and exciting materials presented in *Teaching Transatlanticism: Resources for Teaching Nineteenth-Century Anglo-American Print Culture*, we invite readers to visit and contribute to our companion website, teachingtransatlanticism.tcu.edu. The materials on this interactive site both complement and supplement the chapters in the collection. We hope our readers will continue the conversation on our discussion boards, view the digital appendices to the book, and access our collection of 'Teaching Resources', which contains transatlantic lesson plans, stories of teaching, primary and secondary readings, information about academic programmes, and doctoral exam lists. To foster even more collaboration and innovation among transatlantic teacher-scholars across the globe, we invite visitors to submit their own resources to our growing collection. We anticipate that this website will serve as an ongoing extension of the printed text – and a space where collaborative learning about teaching in this growing field can continue for years to come.

Notes on Contributors

Larisa S. Asaeli is a doctoral candidate at Texas Christian University, where she also teaches composition and literature classes. Her research interests include long nineteenth-century transatlantic literature (especially periodicals), reform literature, and social activism. In her composition and literature classes she focuses on the rhetoric of activism and social change in oral and printed texts. Her dissertation research is on women, citizenship, and social activism in nineteenth-century American periodicals, with special emphasis on the temperance, abolition, and suffrage movements. She is especially interested in how these movements were transatlantic exchanges. You can read more about Larisa's work by visiting <http://www.larisaasaeli.net/>.

John Cyril Barton is Associate Professor of English at the University of Missouri-Kansas City. He is author of *Literary Executions: Capital Punishment and American Culture, 1820–1925* (Johns Hopkins University Press, 2014) and co-editor of *Transatlantic Sensations* (Ashgate, 2012). His essays have appeared in *Nineteenth-Century Literature*, *Arizona Quarterly*, *Law-and-Literature*, *REAL: Research in English and American Literature*, *Studies in American Fiction*, *Critical Horizons* and the MLA volume, *Integrating Literature*. In addition to team teaching a course on transatlantic sensation fiction, he uses transatlantic contexts in both his American Literature and African American Literature survey courses and has framed recent graduate courses on crime fiction in terms of the international campaign to abolish capital punishment.

Susan David Bernstein is a professor in the Department of English, University of Wisconsin-Madison. Since 2008 she has taught four courses about transatlantic literary studies: 'Transatlantic Print Culture and Popular Literature' (graduate seminar); 'Transatlantic Reading and Rights' (undergraduate upper-level course); 'Transatlantic Jewish Literature' (undergraduate course cross-listed with the Center for Jewish Studies); and 'Transatlantic Networks' (graduate seminar). Recently she has published *Roomscape: Women Writers in the British Museum from George Eliot to Virginia Woolf* and two articles on transatlantic reading: 'Transatlantic Sympathies and Nineteenth-Century Women Writing' (in *The Cambridge History of American Women's Writing*, edited by Dale Bauer) and 'Transatlantic Magnetism: Eliot's *The Lifted Veil* and Alcott's Sensation Stories' (in *Transatlantic Sensations* edited by John Barton and Jennifer Phegley).

Tyler Branson, PhD candidate at Texas Christian University, is the leader and co-editor of the digital design team for the Teaching Transatlanticism project. His primary research interests are in public sphere theory, composition theory, civic engagement, writing pedagogy, and new media writing. Winner of several awards at TCU, including the Tate Prize in Composition Studies, Branson is the former holder of the Radford Fellowship, president of the Winifred Bryan Horner Rhetoric Society, and currently serves as the Lorraine Sherley Research Fellow at TCU. In spring 2015, Branson is slated to defend his dissertation, which investigates how writing and public narratives about writing are shaped and contested.

Scott Challener studies comparative modernisms at Rutgers University.

Alison Chapman (University of Victoria, Canada) has taught numerous undergraduate and graduate courses in the UK and Canada, many of which incorporated transatlantic poetry (and this is often despite overt and implicit institutional pressures to leave American literature to the Americanists). She is completing *Networking the Nation: British and American Women's Poetry in Italy, 1840–1870*, which partly aims to bring transatlanticism back to the centre of 'Victorian' poetry. The essay appearing in this collection is an attempt to ask why so much teaching and research on Victorian poetry and print culture has transatlanticism as its critical blind spot.

Isaac Cowell is working on a dissertation in British Romanticism at Rutgers University.

Bakary Diaby works on eighteenth- and nineteenth-century Anglophone literature and philosophy at Rutgers University.

Kate Flint is Provost Professor of English and Art History at the University of Southern California. Author of *The Woman Reader 1837–1914* (1993) and *The Victorians and the Visual Imagination* (2000), her last book, *The Transatlantic Indian 1776–1930* (2009) explicitly addressed the importance of Canada to the developing dialogue about the transatlantic. Her current research, on the cultural history of flash photography, is concerned, in part, with how aesthetic and technological information and opinion concerning photography circulated in the transatlantic world in the nineteenth century.

Linda Freedman is a Lecturer in British and American literature at University College London. She is the author of *Emily Dickinson and the Religious Imagination* (Cambridge University Press, 2011) and is completing a book on William Blake and America. She has published widely on nineteenth- and twentieth-century English and American literature and has an ongoing interest in teaching and researching transatlantic and interdisciplinary connections.

Christopher Gair is Head of English Literature and Associate Director of the Andrew Hook Centre for American Studies at the University of Glasgow, Scotland. He is the author of *Complicity and Resistance in Jack London's Novels* (Edwin Mellen, 1997), *The American Counterculture* (Edinburgh University Press, 2007), and *The Beat Generation* (Oneworld, 2008) and is the editor of *Beyond Boundaries: C. L. R. James and Postnational Studies* (Pluto, 2006). He edited editions of Stephen Crane's *Maggie: A Girl of the Streets* (Trent Publications, 2000) and Jack London's *South Sea Tales* (Random House, 2002). He has published essays in journals including *Modern Fiction Studies*, *Journal of American Studies*, *Western American Literature*, *Studies in the Novel*, and *Studies in American Literature* and is founding editor of *Symbiosis: A Journal of Anglo-American Literary Relations*.

Susan M. Griffin is Professor and Distinguished University Scholar at the University of Louisville. She is the editor of the *Henry James Review* (Johns Hopkins University Press) and has published widely on James and on Anglo-American fiction and culture, including *Anti-Catholicism and Nineteenth-Century Fiction* (Cambridge University Press, 2004) and, most recently, co-edited *Henry James and Alfred Hitchcock: The Men Who Knew Too Much* (Oxford University Press, 2011). She is currently co-editing two volumes of the forthcoming Cambridge edition of Henry James's fiction. Recent transatlantic seminars include: Scenes of Reading; Hawthorne, Eliot, James; Victorian Ghost Fiction; Nineteenth-Century Things; Fantastic Metamorphoses.

Daniel Hack is Associate Professor of English at the University of Michigan. Author of *The Material Interests of the Victorian Novel* (2005), he is currently writing a book on the uses of Victorian literature in nineteenth- and early twentieth-century African American literature and print culture. Work related to this project has appeared or is forthcoming in the journals *Critical Inquiry*,

Novel: A Forum on Fiction, and *Victorian Studies*, and in several books: *The Blackwell Companion to George Eliot*, *Early African American Print Culture in Theory and Practice*, and *The Oxford Handbook of the Victorian Novel*. Hack has taught transatlantic courses at both the undergraduate and graduate levels, including a graduate seminar on 'Race and Transatlantic Print Culture' and an undergraduate course on 'Prejudice and the Nineteenth-Century Novel'. His essay on teaching Dickens in a transatlantic context appeared in *Approaches to Teaching Dickens's* Bleak House (MLA, 2009).

Linda K. Hughes, Addie Levy Professor of Literature at Texas Christian University, was led to transatlanticism by her interests in nineteenth-century periodicals, gender, and publishing history, as well as by teaching an undergraduate course in British literature entitled 'Imagining America'. Her transatlantic publications include 'Between Politics and Deer Stalking: Browning's Periodical Poetry' (*Victorian Poetry*, 52: 1 (Spring 2014)); *A Feminist Reader: Feminist Thought from Sappho to Satrapi* (4 vols, Cambridge University Press, 2013), co-edited with Sharon M. Harris; 'Reluctant Lions: Michael Field and the Transatlantic Literary Salon of Louise Chandler Moulton' (in *Michael Field and Their World*, eds Margaret D. Stetz and Cheryl A. Wilson, Rivendale Press, 2007); and *Graham R.: Rosamund Marriott Watson, Woman of Letters* (2005, winner of the Colby Prize). She is the co-author, with Michael Lund, of *The Victorian Serial* (1991) and *Victorian Publishing and Mrs. Gaskell's Work* (1999), and author/(co-)editor of six other books and over one hundred book chapters and articles. Serving on numerous editorial boards, she is the recipient of National Endowment for the Humanities grants, the biennial British Women Writers Association Award for contributions to scholarship and mentoring (2012), and several teaching awards at TCU.

Kristin Huston is a doctoral candidate at the University of Missouri-Kansas City, where she also teaches composition and literature classes. Her research interests include gender and sexuality studies, the history of the body, nineteenth-century transatlantic literature and art, and periodical studies. In her women's literature classes she encourages students to examine the exchange of ideas across the Atlantic as a means to create a richer context for their study of literature, culture, and women's history. Her dissertation involves the study of representations of Creole women in previously unexamined British and American periodicals of the nineteenth century. She is also co-editor of *Transatlantic Sensations* (2012).

Rachel Johnston is a PhD Student at Texas Christian University, where she has taught first- and second-year composition, introduction to literature, and mythology. She is currently working on her dissertation tentatively entitled 'Unions in Crisis: British and American Marriage Anxiety and Nation-Building in Art and Novels, 1660–1860'. This project explores the portrayal of failed marriages in eighteenth- and nineteenth-century transatlantic art and novels and the ways these failed relationships both influence and challenge emerging gender expectations and British and American national identities. Rachel has presented at CCCC and SWTX APC/PCA, including a paper entitled 'From Bluebeard to Darwin: Sexual Selection and the Dangerous Bearded Man in British and American Fiction' and has recently published a collaborative tribute for *Legacy*: 'Reading Frances Smith Foster'.

Lauren Kimball is working on a dissertation on the role of verse traditions in nineteenth-century American literary experimentation at Rutgers University.

Chris Koenig-Woodyard is an award-winning teacher, who read for Master of Studies and Doctor of Philosophy at Oxford University. A former Doctoral Fellow (Oxford University) and Post-Doctoral Fellow (University of Toronto) of the Social Sciences and Humanities Council of Canada, he teaches at the University of Toronto, and has taught and lectured at Oxford, the University of Western Ontario, Trent University, the University of Guelph, Morgan State University (Baltimore, Maryland), and Wilfrid Laurier University. He is co-editor of *Transatlantic Romanticism: An Anthology of American, British, and Canadian Literature, 1767–1867* (Longman, 2006); *'Sullen Fires across the Atlantic': Essays in British and American Romanticism* (Romantic Circles); and *Romantic Poetry in America: A Bibliography* (forthcoming). He is a contributing editor to *The Broadview Anthology of British Literature: Concise Volume B*; and is managing editor of the *Jackson Bibliography of Romantic Poetry* (at <http://jacksonbibliography.library.utoronto.ca>). His work has appeared in *The Wordsworth Circle* and *Romanticism and Victorianism on the Net*. In 2006, he was a recipient of an Undergraduate Teaching Award, Students' Administrative Council-Association of Part-Time Undergraduate Studies, University of Toronto.

Molly Knox Leverenz is an English Studies doctoral candidate at Texas Christian University. Her essay, which was largely inspired by Robbins and Hughes's graduate transatlanticism course, 'Illustrating *The Moonstone* in America: *Harper's Weekly* and Transatlantic Introspection', was recently published in *American Periodicals*. Leverenz focuses on print culture and reading communities in her research. She is currently working on her dissertation, which examines narratives of beauty and romance in contemporary Young Adult Fiction.

Meredith L. McGill edited and wrote the introduction to *The Traffic in Poems: 19th C Poetry and Transatlantic Exchange* (Rutgers University Press, 2008), a collection of eleven essays that trace the ways in which the transatlantic crossing of people and goods shaped Anglo-American poetry. She is also author of *American Literature and the Culture of Reprinting, 1834–1853* (University of Pennsylvania Press, 2007 reprint). She teaches American literature and advises graduate students working on transatlantic projects at Rutgers University.

Marie Martinez, lead manager of the 'Commons Workspace' and member of the digital design team for the Teaching Transatlanticism project, is a PhD candidate at Texas Christian University. Her primary research areas include British literature in the nineteenth century and Victorian periodicals. Marie is particularly interested in transatlantic discourses and networks of nineteenth-century periodicals and other literatures as they intersect with and complicate Victorian theories of contagion, travel, industrialisation, and sensation fiction. Her dissertation project is entitled 'Victorian Outbreak Narratives: The Influence of Cholera on the Nineteenth-Century Literary Imagination', while Marie's teaching includes a variety of composition and literature courses. Currently, she is teaching a course entitled '19th-century Contagion' which examines the ways a selection of American and British novels, poems, and short stories represent and conceive of literal and metaphorical contagion.

Michael Monescalchi studies Early American literature and culture at Rutgers University.

Melissa Parrish studies twentieth-century American literature at Rutgers University.

Jennifer Phegley, Professor of English at the University of Missouri-Kansas City, is the author of *Educating the Proper Woman Reader: Victorian Family Literary Magazines and the Cultural Health of the Nation* (2004) and *Courtship and Marriage in Victorian England* (2011). She has also co-edited *Reading Women: Literary Figures and Cultural Icons from the Victorian Age to the Present* (2005), *Teaching Nineteenth-Century Fiction* (2010), and *Transatlantic Sensations* (2012). In addition to team teaching a course on transatlantic sensation fiction, she has taught a graduate seminar on transatlantic authorship, organised a course around the pairing of Charles Dickens's *Bleak House* and Harriet Beecher Stowe's *Uncle Tom's Cabin*, and incorporated transatlantic themes in both American and British literature surveys.

Alan Rice is Professor in English and American Studies at the University of Central Lancashire. He was awarded a National Teaching Fellow from the Higher Education Academy in 2007 and holds a PhD in American Studies from Keele University (1997), an MA in American Cultural Studies from Bowling Green State University, Ohio (1990), and an MA in English Literature and History from the University of Edinburgh (1984). He has worked on the interdisciplinary study of the Black Atlantic for the past two decades including publishing *Radical Narratives of the Black Atlantic* (Continuum, 2003). Alan was academic advisor to the Slave Trade Arts Memorial Project in Lancaster, was editor in chief of Manchester's Revealing Histories Website and a co-curator of the Whitworth Art Gallery Manchester's 2007–8 exhibition 'Trade and Empire: Remembering Slavery'. His latest monograph is *Creating Memorials, Building Identities: The Politics of Memory in the Black Atlantic* (Liverpool University Press, 2010) and his latest edited collection is a special issue of *Atlantic Studies* on the 'Slave Trade's Dissonant Heritage' edited with Johanna Kardux (2012). He is also continuing the work on black abolitionists in Britain started in his co-edited *Liberating Sojourn: Frederick Douglass and Transatlantic Reform* (Georgia, 1999) with a new collection in *Slavery and Abolition* (2012) with Fionnghuala Sweeney. He has given keynote presentations in Britain, Germany, the United States, and France and has contributed to documentaries for the BBC, Border Television and public broadcasting in America as well as appearing on BBC's *The One Show*. He is an advisor to museums in Liverpool, Lancaster, and Manchester.

Jarrod Roark researches crime, punishment, and gender performance in nineteenth-century American literature and culture, and specifically in the works of Mark Twain and antebellum writers. He earned a PhD in this field in spring 2013. Jarrod has taught at the University of Missouri-Kansas City, the Art Institute of Kansas City, and the Barstow School, where he currently teaches in the Department of English and serves as a Dean of Student Life and Coordinator of the Barstow Speaker Series. Jarrod has presented research at national and international conferences, including the *American Literature Association Annual Conference*, *The Mark Twain Conference* in Hannibal, Missouri, the *Missouri Conference on History*, the *Pop Culture Association/American Culture Association National Conference*, and most recently at *The Seventh International Conference on the State of Mark Twain Studies*. His work has been published in *New Letters Literary Magazine*, *Directions*, *Proceedings: The Image of the Outlaw in Literature, Media, and Society*, and the *Mark Twain Annual*. Currently, Jarrod is revising a book manuscript – a process that was influenced by his dissertation *Beneath Mark Twain: Justice and Gender in Twain's Early Western Writing, 1861–1873* and the collaborative chapter in this collection, 'Teaching "Transatlantic Sensations"'.

Sarah R. Robbins is Lorraine Sherley Professor of Literature at TCU, where she teaches nineteenth- and twentieth-century American literature, gender studies, popular literature, writing, and transatlantic and cross-cultural studies. She is author of *The Cambridge Introduction to Harriet Beecher Stowe* and of *Managing Literacy, Mothering America*, winner of a Choice Book Award. With historian Ann Pullen, she prepared the award-winning critical edition of *Nellie Arnott's Writings on Angola, 1905–1913: Missionary Narratives Linking Africa and America*. She also co-edited *Bridging Cultures: International Women Faculty Transforming the US Academy*. Before coming to TCU, she served for over a decade as founding director of the Kennesaw Mountain Writing Project, a National Writing Project site in northwest Georgia, where she earned the Governor's Award in the humanities for leading numerous programmes in curriculum development. Drawing on those initiatives, she co-edited essay collections on civic engagement, including *Writing Our Communities* and *Writing America*. As co-director of the multi-year NEH project on 'Making American Literatures', she collaborated with teachers from around the US to create new frameworks for teaching. Prior to helping envision *Teaching Transatlanticism*'s online presence, her earlier collaborative work on humanities-oriented websites includes 'Keeping and Creating American Communities' and 'Women's Work in the Long Nineteenth Century'.

Erik Simpson is Professor of English at Grinnell College. He is the author of *Literary Minstrelsy, 1770–1830: Minstrels and Improvisers in British, Irish, and American Literature* (2008) and *Mercenaries in British and American Literature, 1790–1830: Writing, Fighting, and Marrying for Money* (2010), in addition to articles on British literature, transatlantic literature, and the use of digital technologies in undergraduate teaching. His current work focuses on the theory and practice of digital pedagogy, as well as developing the physical, institutional, and inter-institutional structures to support such practice.

Marjorie Stone, McCulloch Chair in English, Dalhousie University, Halifax, Canada, has published on Elizabeth Barrett Browning, Robert Browning, literary collaboration, Tennyson, Dickens, Gaskell, Christina Rossetti, Toni Morrison, sex trafficking, cultural citizenship, 'retooling the humanities', and other subjects. Most recently, she was Volume Co-Editor for three of five volumes in *The Works of Elizabeth Barrett Browning* (2010), and recipient of a National Humanities Center Fellowship (2011) for a project on nineteenth-century literary transnationalism and the cosmopolitan citizenship formations arising out of a number of intersecting or linked movements from the 1830s to the 1880s: abolitionism, the Italian liberation movement, the peace and free-trade movement, the proto-Zionist movement, and the anti-trafficking movement often referred to as the 'white slave trade' controversy. Phase one of a digital archive of resources on Elizabeth Barrett Browning that she is constructing with Keith Lawson can be found at <http://www.ebbarchive.org>.

Andrew Taylor is a Senior Lecturer in English Literature at the University of Edinburgh. He is the author of *Henry James and the Father Question* (2002) and *Thinking America: New England Intellectuals and the Varieties of American Identity* (2010), and the co-author of *Thomas Pynchon* (2013). He has co-edited *The Afterlife of John Brown* (2005), *Transatlantic Literary Studies: A Reader* (2007), *Stanley Cavell: Philosophy, Literature and Criticism* (2012) and *Stanley Cavell, Literature, and Film: The Idea of America* (2013).

Tom F. Wright is a Lecturer in American Literature at the University of Sussex. He is the editor of *The Cosmopolitan Lyceum: Lecture Culture and the Globe in Nineteenth-Century America* (2013), and has published essays on Ralph Waldo Emerson, Thomas Carlyle, Bayard Taylor, and the painter Richard Caton Woodville. He is currently completing a book on the transatlantic dimensions to nineteenth-century public lecturing.

Sandra A. Zagarell, Donald R. Longman Professor of English at Oberlin College, holds a BA from the City College of New York and an MA and PhD from Columbia University. She has taught American literature and British literature for many years and now also offers an advanced course in transatlantic literature. Her scholarship focuses primarily on nineteenth-century American literature, most recently on formal and rhetorical dimensions of narrative and on intersections between the history of the book and the study of imaginative writing. A senior editor of the *Heath Anthology of American Literature*, she is responsible for Volume C which covers the period 1865–1910.

CHAPTER I

Introduction: Tracing Currents and Joining Conversations

Linda K. Hughes and Sarah R. Robbins

The actuality of transatlantic literary exchanges is as old as ships carrying persons, enslaved and free, along routes propelled by Atlantic Ocean currents. Cargoes of print followed in due course, penned by multinational writers such as Frederick Douglass, Phyllis Wheatley, Alexis de Tocqueville, and Mary Wollstonecraft. Transatlantic literary history has long been associated with Henry James and T. S. Eliot, American-born writers who ended their lives as British citizens. But bidirectional literary exchanges between British and American authors began much earlier. Ralph Waldo Emerson was indebted to the transcendental thought of Samuel Taylor Coleridge, who at one point planned to emigrate to the United States, and to Thomas Carlyle's *Sartor Resartus*. *Sartor* had failed miserably when serialised in *Fraser's Magazine* in 1833–4 in Britain, yet the serialised *Sartor* inspired Emerson to oversee its first publication as a book in Boston. *Sartor* then returned to Britain via Harriet Martineau, who, visiting the US in preparation for *Society in America* (1837), took back twenty-five copies of the 1836 American edition to Britain, selling them from her London home until *Sartor Resartus* was republished as a British book in 1838. Only then did it become extraordinarily influential on both sides of the Atlantic.[1] Earlier still, Washington Irving's indelible impression on Charles Dickens helped inspire the invention of a Dickens Christmas. Irving's *Sketch Book of Geoffrey Crayon, Gent.* was quickly pirated in British periodicals after its initial American publication in May 1819, leading to British publication of the book in 1820. Irving's series of Christmas sketches set at Bracebridge Hall (written when he was living in Birmingham, England) lovingly recall old games such as hot cockles, invoke a brimming wassail bowl, and feature a benevolent squire who joins in his guests' festive dancing. Dickens's reviewers recognised the influence of Irving on the Dingley Dell episode in *Pickwick Papers*; as the October 1837 *Quarterly Review* asserted, 'The only writer who appears to have exercised any marked influence on his style is Washington Irving . . . Wardle's Manor House, with its merry doings at Christmas-time, is neither more nor less than *Bracebridge Hall* at second hand.'[2] The many Americans who attend annual stagings of *A Christmas Carol* are testifying not only to the transatlantic influence of Dickens on US culture, but also, indirectly, of the American author on whose foundation Dickens made Christmas peculiarly his own.

Nor were such exchanges confined to male writers. Anna Laetitia Barbauld never travelled in person to America, but her poetry and children's literature did, with the latter emerging in both reprintings and reconfigurations, serving as models for the domestic teaching narratives of US women writers ranging from Lydia Sigourney to Catharine Maria Sedgwick, who corresponded enthusiastically with Barbauld and celebrated with clear pride when a letter from the English authoress praised one of the American's new novels.[3] Harriet Beecher Stowe had a similarly productive correspondence with Harriet Martineau and George Eliot (Marian Evans) around shared experiences of authorship – and a personal bond with Lady Byron that led to Stowe's controversial 'defense' of her friend in print.[4] Whether solely through epistolary dialogues, or via connections strengthened in travel-enabled personal meetings, nineteenth-century authors rode the currents of transatlantic exchange.

Despite this longstanding tradition of boundary-crossing literary conversation, ideologies of nationhood dating back to Hegel made literature a crucial part of formulating distinct national identities. Nationally-based pedagogies have played at least as important a role in covering over or simply ignoring transatlantic currents of thought and print dating back hundreds of years. Narratives of the rise of English and American literary studies, including D. J. Palmer's *The Rise of English Studies* (1965), the chapter on American literature in Gerald Graff's *Professing Literature* (1987), or David Shumway's *Creating American Civilization: A Genealogy of American Literature as an Academic Discipline* (1994), have shown that numerous institutional, historical, and cultural factors were at play in helping to enforce English (more recently, British) and American literature as separate subfields. For example, the ostensibly 'scientific' methods of philologists helped align the study of English literature with the prestige of Classics at Oxbridge, and US universities' embrace of American literature was supported by literary theorists of the 1930s and 1940s who sought to identify themes and structures specific to the national literature and culture (such as F. O. Matthiessen in *American Renaissance*, 1941). In British studies, the Beowulf-to-Virginia-Woolf surveys on both sides of the Atlantic did not readily admit the notion of American influence, and British precedent was not often welcome in classrooms that sought to restage America's attainment of independence in terms of its literary heritage – even in the UK, where interest in American studies led to the founding of the British Association for American Studies in 1955. Of course, individual professors might depart from majority positions, as Susan Griffin's essay in this collection demonstrates (and Sarah Robbins's experience of classes taught by Richard Fogle at the University of North Carolina in the mid-1970s and Julie Ellison at the University of Michigan in the early 1990s also attests). Still, influential, widely adopted anthologies tied to periodisation or surveys in the UK and US reinforced strong concepts of coherent national literatures. The first *Norton Anthology of English Literature* was issued in 1962, the first *Norton Anthology of American Literature* in 1979, and both hefty tomes underscored the evidently self-contained, separate literary traditions of distinct nations.[5]

If the impulse to safeguard national identity has been one factor reinforcing separate curricular formations for British and American literature, scholarship has also influenced pedagogical practice. Long before the efflorescence of 'transatlantic studies' at the turn into the twenty-first century, individual books and articles found their way into print. Walter Allen took up two interests that remain compelling today, travel and cultural exchange, in *Transatlantic Crossing: American Visitors to Britain and British Visitors to America in the Nineteenth Century*, published in 1971. The majority of transatlantic commentary for the next two decades, however, focused on Modernism, and only occasional articles on major nineteenth-century authors or on publishing history in transatlantic context appeared.[6] In the 1990s a more deliberate, self-aware approach to transatlantic studies of literature quickened, aided by a newer hermeneutic that interrogated fixed boundaries and canonical literature.[7]

In 1990 Susan Manning published *The Puritan-Provincial Vision: Scottish and American Literature in the Nineteenth Century*, asserting a distinctive transatlantic Anglophone literature separate from English literature and culture. Paul Gilroy's *Black Atlantic* (1993) excavated an Atlantic culture drawing all at once from African, American, British, and Caribbean exponents. Then, in 1997, *Symbiosis: A Journal of Anglo-American Literary Relations* was founded, providing a forum for historical and theoretical criticism from within a principally American studies framework. With a grant from the Carnegie Trust for the Universities of Scotland, the STAR (Scotland's Transatlantic Relations) Project began in 2002 under the leadership of Susan Manning through the Institute for Advanced Studies in the Humanities at the University of Edinburgh. Although STAR's mission focused on circum-Atlantic research with a Scottish emphasis, the project's seminars, workshops, and publications (particularly the *Edinburgh Studies in Transatlantic Literature*) soon supported transatlantic research and teaching far beyond its home institution while expanding from a small group of collaborating scholars to establish numerous international affiliations and launch an innovative degree programme in Literature and Transatlanticism.

In part because one element of the avowed identity of the US is as a nation of immigrants whose influx led to complex reformations of national identity,

American studies was the first locus of systematic studies of transatlantic culture. Accordingly, in introducing *Transatlantic Literary Studies: A Reader*, Susan Manning and Andrew Taylor begin with 'American Studies'; while offering a compelling call for transnational approaches, their introduction simultaneously affirms the continued value of comparative studies of national ideologies by critiquing the narrow, post-World Second War conception of the American Studies field that associated it with visions of US exceptionalism.[8] Similarly, the ongoing significance of such cross-Atlantic analyses is evident in the 1999 founding of the online journal *49th Parallel: An Interdisciplinary Journal of North American Studies*, co-sponsored by the Universities of Birmingham and Nottingham.[9] A key dimension of these new lines of activity has involved resisting the tendency evident in some early forays into transatlantic studies: studying 'influence' (especially British culture shaping its American counterpart) more than conceptualising transatlantic relations as interactive.[10]

Meanwhile, theoretical work by Paul Giles has been a crucial intervention in transatlanticism, beginning with *Transatlantic Insurrections: British Culture and the Formation of American Literature, 1730–1860* (2001), followed by *Virtual Americas: Transnational Fictions and the Transatlantic Imaginary* (2002) and *The Global Remapping of American Literature* (2010). Giles's *Transatlantic Insurrections* posited an essential interchange between British and American literature and culture in the very formation of what was seen as distinctively 'American' – a project shared by Meredith McGill in *American Literature and the Culture of Reprinting, 1834–1853* (2002). Giles has also been a key figure in transatlantic British studies, arguing in *Atlantic Republic: The American Tradition in English Literature* (2006) that a shared dissenting culture helped form both American literature and an important strand of British literature. In turn Amanda Claybaugh, in *The Novel of Purpose: Literature and Social Reform in the Anglo-American World* (2007), has linked Great Britain and the US not only through a shared literary marketplace (as McGill argues) but also through an interactive social reform agenda underwritten by a commitment to realism.

As this brief encapsulation indicates, scholarship has increasingly admitted and probed the dynamic currents of literary production and exchange that drifted (and sometimes raced) in multiple directions across the Atlantic, opening up ever-larger questions about where, exactly, the boundaries of transatlanticism start and stop (the Caribbean? South America? Africa? Newfoundland? the North American Pacific coast? the English Channel?) and the multiple ethnic, linguistic, and literary streams pouring into the mix. As Kevin Hutchings and Julia M. Wright have observed, 'the heuristic value of the transatlantic' has become increasingly clear, especially as a lens for highlighting 'liminal and fluid inter-national spaces' and demonstrating how particular 'transnational subjects . . . resist the interpellative pull of the modern nation-state'.[11]

If the opening of boundaries reveals a complex, vast new geographic and cultural area to explore, how might such exciting new perspectives be imported into the classroom? If awareness of transatlantic currents opens up immense new teaching possibilities, how is this very immensity to be cogently contained within a single syllabus? And how are appropriate instructors to be recruited to reinvent literary studies within a transatlantic lens when most (if by no means all) faculty are products of academic training premised on separate national cultures of British and American literature, with geographic or ethnic addenda such as Native American, Commonwealth, or Caribbean literatures? This was the dilemma we faced when, already convinced by our prior work that literary production on either side of the Atlantic (at any latitude) was always already interactive and multi-sourced, we decided to offer the first graduate seminar in transatlanticism at our institution, Texas Christian University (TCU), in the fall of 2010.

ENVISIONING A TRANSATLANTIC SEMINAR

If the growth of scholarship on transatlantic literary culture represents one highly positive impetus for teaching within this burgeoning tradition, another factor encouraging such work goes beyond the humanities disciplines to the shift in mission so evident in many institutions of higher education today – that is, the call for universities to align their curricula with a 'global' vision. In the US, universities have increasingly moved toward 'global learning' as a key goal for higher education. Steve O. Michael, Provost at Arcadia University in the US, has pointed to 'global leadership' as one of three student learning outcomes most likely to be affirmed in US universities' mission statements now.[12] In the UK, Regenia Gagnier, who was awarded a British Academy Research Development Award for a Global Circulation Project, comments in a special 2013 issue of *Critical Quarterly*, 'Academics will have noticed the increasing demand over the last decade on the part of students, professional organisations, funders, HE administrators, and publishers for work that we might call global, international, or worldly.'[13] And the most recent report of the British Association of American Studies on the discipline from 2000–10 emphasises transnationalism as the most important emergent trend, one that decouples American studies from the US.[14] Meanwhile, movements such as the Bologna Process, launched in 1999 and involving over forty nations, are signalling an increasing commitment to a collaborative, shared vision for intercultural education, at least within the EU community. Ulla Kriebernegg has pointed to connections between this movement and the adoption of pedagogical strategies associated with the 'Americanisation' of university teaching in European settings.[15] Whether homogenisation or international-level collaboration in higher education is being invoked, the blurring (or breakdown?) of distinctions between curricular models as delivered within different national settings may be, some scholars have suggested, more a consequence of interrelated socio-political trends – the decline of the nation-state and the rise of international corporations – than it is a product of enlightened revision for traditional fields of study.[16]

Considering such tensions around the place of nationally oriented fields within 'globalised' higher education actually highlights potential benefits to literary study that operates within a framework emphasising historical context. More specifically, we would argue, one step toward understanding the ongoing shifts from nationally oriented curricular formations to transnational ones involves looking closely at a period, specifically the nineteenth century, when particular cultural practices linked to strengthened national identities – especially British and American literature-making enterprises – were forcefully asserting themselves in those terms. Significantly, that same period represents an era of intense intercultural, transnational exchange. An awareness of these seemingly contradictory yet interactive processes is part of what led us to develop a team-taught transatlantic literature course with a nineteenth-century focus.

Though one of us works in American (Sarah Robbins) and the other in British studies (Linda Hughes), we both recognised that the nineteenth century represents an especially crucial era for the study of transatlanticism. Benedict Anderson has emphasised how the rise of print culture during this century facilitated the 'imagined communities' of national identity formation,[17] but this same ongoing force simultaneously promoted cross-national affiliations. Social causes ranging from abolition to women's suffrage generated and helped sustain international networks. Advances in travel and communication – such as steamships and telegraphs – made transatlantic travel and sustained transnational correspondence easier.[18] Thus, though this was clearly an age when national identity flourished, it was simultaneously a time of increased intercultural exchange. Accordingly, while appreciating the call Wai Chee Dimock has made for transnational literary culture across 'deep time', we find that the admittedly 'artificial' period of the nineteenth century offers a particularly rich time frame for teaching.[19]

Space is also a crucial consideration for literary study, whether a course is organised around a national or an international rubric. In planning our first seminar, we recognised that international enterprises throughout the nineteenth century were certainly not limited to the currents linking North America and the Caribbean with the British Isles.[20] Still, we would argue, this particular pathway remains worthy of singular attention. Since they share the English language as a major medium of communication and cultural production, the US, Canada, and/or the Caribbean, on one side, and Britain, on the other, offer a body of rich, complex material which, though massive in scale, is relatively accessible to today's students. Further, English language texts passing along the various Atlantic currents and cross-currents of the nineteenth century very often devoted intense attention to examining social value systems – whether capitalising on those held in common or highlighting differences bound up in the very efforts to define national distinctions referenced above. Often, in fact, a single nineteenth-century author writing in English for a transatlantic audience would use a combination of affiliation and distancing rhetoric within the same work to mark, simultaneously, both intercultural connections and cross-cultural differences.

In personal terms, our own backgrounds as British and American literature specialists, respectively, made team teaching a course on nineteenth-century transatlantic print culture both appealing and pragmatic. Each of us would bring expertise from one nationally oriented tradition, while both of us shared an interest in the same historical period, in the history of print culture, broadly defined, and in intersections between literary culture and broader social movements of the nineteenth century, including shifts in literacy practices. Leavening our enthusiasm with an awareness that we were entering challenging new territory, we proposed our team-taught class to the administration and, after promising to draw an enrolment beyond the number of students for a typical seminar, secured approval for our pilot, to be offered in the fall semester of 2010.

Once we began brainstorming ideas for our syllabus, we contacted colleagues who had taught courses (or modules within courses) with content similar to the one we were planning. We also sought books and articles on teaching nineteenth-century transatlantic culture. On the first count, our professional networks did garner several energising examples.[21] On the second, despite the growing range of scholarship defining/describing the field of transatlantic studies, and even more individual essays and books modelling various methods for transatlantic research, we found few publications specifically addressing pedagogy.

Given the limited resources to guide our curricular planning, we submitted a proposal to our home institution's Instructional Development Grant programme to bring to campus three influential scholars who also had experience teaching from a transatlantic perspective: Meredith McGill (Rutgers; *American Literature and the Culture of Reprinting, 1834–1853*), Barbara McCaskill (University of Georgia; editor of *Running a Thousand Miles for Freedom*), and Kate Flint (University of Southern California; *The Transatlantic Indian 1776–1930*). Besides facilitating one session apiece of our seminar, each consultant also gave a public lecture based on her in-progress research and spent time with the two of us evaluating our course. Admittedly, it was challenging to carve out adequate class time for students to hear from both of us during most weekly sessions, and from our consultants in the different sessions each of them attended. It was equally difficult to find a balance between primary and secondary readings, between 'American' and 'British' texts, between discussion and project-based activities. Some of these challenges are typical of any graduate course. Nonetheless, we found these factors exacerbated (in vexing if also exciting ways) due to our transatlantic agenda. While the final version of the 2010 syllabus pared down our readings considerably from earlier drafts, it still suffered from having too many individual readings for the students to absorb and reflect on fully.[22]

On a more conceptual basis, we also struggled to identify the most productive organising principles for the syllabus. Here we sought to balance attention to 'the literary' with an emphasis on cultural threads that could help provide coherence and context. We realise this is a question relevant to any literature course, but having a mix of students with more previous training in one nationalist tradition or the other (not to mention our own differences in this regard) heightened this challenge. Many in the class would be encountering individual authors and texts for the first time. How could we best build a shared context for productive conversations: through what blend of thematic strands, historical context, theoretical connections, and close reading? How could we achieve a productive balance between national and transnational dimensions of analysis, between comparative and interactive approaches, between a focus on influence and difference and one on shared culture?

At the same time, we wondered which particular writers and genres were essential to include. In specific terms, we sought to avoid selecting authors solely on the basis of celebrity or canonicity, even as we felt the perhaps predictable pull to include figures like Twain, Tennyson, Stowe, and Dickens. Meanwhile, we wanted to ensure that the syllabus would resist seeming to replace national canons of nineteenth-century literary studies with a new transatlantic one – via either authors or individual titles – and instead would convey both crucial questions to address in transatlantic studies and methods of inquiry. Accordingly, we adopted as sub-topics several movements that connected literary products and personages on both sides of the Atlantic (abolition, feminism, labour organising, imperialism), on exchanges flowing across such networks, on the means of intercultural dialogue (such as periodical culture's cross-Atlantic reach), and on new opportunities for travel and writers' records of those experiences. Our syllabus, available on the website associated with this volume, seemed to engage our students productively at the time. But neither the two of us nor the hard-working members of our class closed out the semester feeling that we had achieved a clear view of this still-emerging field or a confident grasp on its potential for future scholarship and teaching. With the benefit of some distance and more reading in transatlantic studies, by the fall of 2013, we were prepared to mount a 'new and improved' version of the course.

For our second syllabus, we made a number of changes. We decreased the number of primary texts and added more readings dedicated to theorising the transatlantic as a subject of scholarly inquiry and to providing a history of the field, particularly in relation to nationally oriented literary study. Because our 2010 students most readily grasped transatlanticism at a conceptual level in relation to specific examples of transatlantic exchange (such as the impact of Oscar Wilde's American tour on Frances Hodgson Burnett's *Little Lord Fauntleroy*), we selected several new primary texts that would highlight how individual writers and readers participated in larger transatlantic social trends over time. For instance, we replaced Equiano's autobiographical account with the *The History of Mary Prince*, enabling two productive comparative connections: one between the Susanna Strickland who edited Prince's narrative while in England and the Susanna Strickland (Moodie) who emigrated and settled in Canada; and another between Prince's autobiography as a participant in multiple genre traditions (including anti-slavery writing and narratives shaped by ethnic or class differences) and another new addition to the syllabus, *A Woman of Colour*.[23]

Perhaps most importantly, the second seminar was enhanced by our having joined a larger network of conversations about teaching transatlantic culture than we had in 2010. By early summer of 2013, for instance, we had received draft versions of this volume's chapters; connecting with authors in a range of diverse institutional settings and collaborating to organise the book manuscript helped refine our thinking. Our students capitalised on these connections by reading and responding to the draft essays, thereby witnessing – and even participating in – a new intervention into the field as it was unfolding.

OVERVIEW OF THE VOLUME

Many of the contributors to this collection write from the vantage point of years-long transatlantic pedagogy involving entire courses, individual modules, or a single literary figure. Others are drawing from their scholarship to envision how they and others might embark on new modes, methods, and frameworks of transatlantic teaching. We envision a similar mix among the readers of this collection, therefore we have sought to address both course-level frameworks for those delivering a term-long transatlantic course and more focused curricular elements for those considering how a single component (a particular author or text, a recurring theme, a methodological approach) in a course organised around another heuristic can be re-imagined transatlantically.

Given our international content, it has been vital to have sites from around the Atlantic basin represented among our contributors. Thus they come from eastern, southern, and western Canada, east and west central lowland Scotland, the north and south of England, and the northeastern, southern, Midwestern, and western US. We hope for a similar diversity within our audience, with readers coming from diverse locales, varying career stages, and different personal histories of prior study. We anticipate, too, that an array of voices will join our curricular conversations via the website associated with this volume.

In line with this multi-faceted agenda, the anthology opens with the first question a new (or newly interested) teacher of transatlanticism might have – what IS transatlanticism? – and then moves from designs for term-long courses to the teaching of major figures or individual genres. We end by looking ahead to the possibilities opened by digital humanities and the effects of transatlantic pedagogy on the evolving perspectives of graduate students, the 'rising generation' (in nineteenth-century terms), for teaching in the field.

Susan M. Griffin's moving professional memoir, 'On Not Knowing Any Better', opens Part I ('Curricular Histories and Key Trends') by retracing how she became transformed from a graduate student freed from the usual constraints of national disciplinary boundaries to a theoretically and professionally self-aware scholar and teacher of transatlanticism. Susan David Bernstein then deftly probes transatlantic pedagogical organisation at a theoretical level, emphasising the roles of genre, intertextuality, spatiality, and temporality in a chapter entitled 'Transatlantic Networks in the Nineteenth Century'. Christopher Gair, founding editor of the seminal journal *Symbiosis: A Journal of Anglo-American Literary Relations*, appropriately closes Part I by tracking the forces leading up to the 1995 founding of the publication which, he explains, was intended from the start both to examine 'Anglo-American Literary Relations' and to serve a 'doubly symbiotic purpose, also challenging the separation of research and teaching'. Revisiting key texts from as far back as Edgar Allan Poe's nineteenth-century literary criticism, Gair foregrounds a perspective represented in the mid-twentieth century by books like C. L. R. James's *Beyond a Boundary* (1963) to locate the work of *Symbiosis* in a long-standing tradition emphasising transatlantic interdependency and running counter to such forces as the Myth/Symbol exceptionalism stance dominating much of American Studies in the post-World War II era.

Part II ('Organising Curriculum through Transatlantic Lenses') presents materials and curricular designs for complete courses. In 'Anthologising and Teaching Transatlantic Literature' Chris Koenig-Woodyard recounts how pragmatic efforts to overcome barriers posed by nationally based literature anthologies led to the creation of *Transatlantic Romanticism* (2006) and his course drawing on concepts reflected in that anthology. Daniel Hack's ' "Flat Burglary?" ' explores how a graduate course emphasising print culture exchanges between African-American and British literature could be readapted to an undergraduate classroom that emphasised cultural mobility,

originality and appropriation, and canonicity. Alan Rice's innovative pedagogy
in 'Dramatising the Black Atlantic' merges local history, historiography, and
transnational scholarship with collaborative classroom performance to enhance
students' understanding of the human meaning and intricately interwoven elements of the triangular slave trade. His pedagogy has particular resonance
in his students' specific locale, since in Lancashire agents of the slave trade,
cotton manufacturers, and middle-class women consumers of sugar all had an
entrenched stake in the trade's continuance.

Parts III ('Teaching Transatlantic Figures') and IV ('Teaching Genres
in Transatlantic Context') offer a compendium of resources for teaching a
single classroom unit or assembling clusters of texts. Kate Flint, in 'The
Canadian Transatlantic: Susanna Moodie and Pauline Johnson', demonstrates
that teaching *Roughing It in the Bush* makes possible an examination of the
comparative transatlanticisms of Canada, the US, and Scotland; she also
suggests a range of generative contextual materials for such a unit. Rather
than comparative transatlanticisms, Marjorie Stone places three figures in
conversation within transatlantic abolitionism. 'Frederick Douglass, Maria
Weston Chapman, and Harriet Martineau' reveals how this grouping can
disrupt the binaries of race and gender, as well as the privileging of some print
forms over others, that threaten to re-enter even a pedagogy like transatlanticism, dedicated to blurring boundaries. In contrast, by re-reading a single text
transatlantically, as Andrew Taylor illustrates in a re-examination of Melville's
Israel Potter (1855), we can disrupt fixed categories of literary periodisation.
In ' "How did you get here? And where are you going?" ' Taylor ably demonstrates how Melville's historical novel of the US revolutionary era can be re-
theorised within a transatlantic framework. Sandra A. Zagarell's '*Americans*,
Abroad' recounts how working within the parameters of transatlanticism for
her undergraduate Transatlantic Currents course at Oberlin dramatically
affected the ways that she and her students understood Henry James's *The
Portrait of a Lady*.

Shifting from consideration of literary figures to the teaching of genres,
Part IV further expands the possibilities for adopting a transatlantic lens. In
'Making Anglo-American Oratory Resonate', Tom F. Wright reports on a
transatlantic literature classroom focused on oratory. Not only does such a
course introduce students to a major nineteenth-century genre still undergo-
ing recovery, but it also resituates major orators on either side of the Atlantic –
such as the Grimké sisters, Douglass, and Emerson on one side and Gladstone,
Ruskin, and Dickens on the other – in relation to each other. Part IV also
presents innovative approaches to textual transatlanticism. In 'Genre and
Nationality in Nineteenth-Century British and American Poetry' Meredith
L. McGill and her six student co-authors report how new literary histories
arose through nineteenth-century poetry studied in terms of circulation rather

than authorial or national origins. As the title implies, 'Teaching Transatlantic Sensations', another multi-vocal account blending teachers' and students' voices, presents revelations emerging from a graduate course examining American and British sensation fiction as interactive parts of a larger print culture whole. In addition to describing a group project on print culture, this chapter by Americanist John Cyril Barton, Victorianist Jennifer Phegley, and graduate students Kristin Huston and Jarrod Roark also details how transatlantic study reshaped Huston's and Roark's dissertation projects.

Teaching Transatlanticism continues the theme of new pedagogical directions through Part V's focus on 'Envisioning Digital Transatlanticism'. In 'Transatlantic Mediations', Alison Chapman describes how a graduate course initially designed to focus on Victorian poetry in the context of digitised nineteenth-century periodicals took a transatlantic turn when many of the students chose to work with publications that either featured transatlantic poetry or circulated transatlantically. In 'Digital Transatlanticism', Erik Simpson recounts the impact of building a database-backed website entitled 'The Transatlantic 1790s'. The digital project organised by Simpson mirrored the networked nodal points of transatlanticism itself, since students drew together writings originating in diverse, highly specific locales (just as the website drew upon students' individual and interactive efforts). Tyler Branson, who has served as the lead designer of the Teaching Transatlanticism website associated with our volume, closes this section with a chapter positioning digital humanities enterprises like our online project within the context of scholarship on public spheres, both in previous eras and today.

Our Part VI 'Afterword' continues this pattern of reflection blended with projections toward future work in transatlantic studies. In 'Looking Forward', four of our 2010 students – Larisa Asaeli, Rachel Johnston, Molly Leverenz, and Marie Martinez – describe how the experience of transatlantic pedagogy has led them in new directions in their teaching and research. Overall, our hope is that the diverse collective experiences recounted in *Teaching Transatlanticism* can serve as a starting place and ongoing resource for readers, inspiring further innovations in the classroom and in exchanges online.[24] With that in mind, we invite our readers to join now in transatlantic conversations.

NOTES

1. Later in the century, Jane Addams would recall her own and her classmates' fondness for quoting Carlyle while at Rockford Seminary ('Boarding School', *Twenty Years at Hull-House with Autobiographical Notes* (New York: Macmillan, 1910)) and describe her later re-reading

of Carlyle as a welcome break from medical school textbooks during her short stint at the Medical College of Philadelphia ('Snare', *Twenty Years*).

2. 'The Pickwick Papers', *Quarterly Review*, 59 (October 1837), 507. See Pierre Irving, *The Life and Letters of Washington Irving* (New York: G. P. Putnam/Hurd & Houghton, 1866), vol. 1, p. 417; Ernest Boll, 'Charles Dickens and Washington Irving', *Modern Language Quarterly*, 5 (1944), 466; and Richard Kelly (ed.), *A Christmas Carol, by Charles Dickens* (Peterloo: Broadview Press, 2003), pp. 20–1.

3. On Barbauld's writings crossing the Atlantic and being transformed, see Sarah Robbins's 'Re-making Barbauld's Primers: A Case Study of the "Americanization" of British Literary Pedagogy', *Children's Literature Association Quarterly*, 21: 4 (Winter 1996–7), 158–69; reprinted in Dana Ferguson (ed.), *Children's Literature Review*, 160 (Detroit: Gale, 2011), pp. 36–49.

4. On the enthusiastic British embrace of Stowe's anti-slavery writing, see Sarah Meer, *Uncle Tom Mania: Slavery, Minstrelsy, and Transatlantic Culture in the 1850s* (Athens, GA: University of Georgia Press, 2005). On Stowe's personal popularity in England, see Sarah Robbins, 'Harriet Beecher Stowe, Starring as Benevolent Celebrity Traveler', in Beth Lueck, Lucinda Damon-Bach and Brigitte Bailey (eds), *Transatlantic Women: Essays on Nineteenth-Century American Women Writers in Great Britain and Europe* (Durham, NH: University of New Hampshire Press, 2012), pp. 71–88.

5. Secondary schools circulated parallel visions of national literature as self-contained. For instance, an often-taught 1950 anthology for US students included this description of 'Contemporary American literature', which used a river-oriented water metaphor containing the field within continental boundaries: 'The stream of literature is a constantly widening river fed by a succession of new movements, points of view, and types of subject matter . . . [O]ld currents often continue along beside the new, though perhaps in modified or blended form. In colonial days, our literature was like the Mississippi River near its source in northern Minnesota – a little stream easily bridged. In the first half of the nineteenth century it resembled the Mississippi as it skirts southern Minnesota, Wisconsin, and Iowa – a majestic river edged by imposing bluffs, romantic in its beauty. In the last half of the century it looked more like the Mississippi after some of its great tributaries draining east and west have poured into it.' See Rewey Belle Inglis et al. (eds), *Adventures in American Literature*, Standard 3rd edn (New York: Harcourt, Brace, 1950), p. 739.

6. Robert Weisbuch's *Atlantic Double-Cross: American Literature and British Influence in the Age of Emerson* (Chicago: University of Chicago Press, 1989), though tracking sustained interrelationships, emphasised American

literature's efforts to distance itself from English cultural dominance as part of a nation-building agenda.

7. As Susan Manning and Andrew Taylor comment, 'Our current global patterns of connection and interrelation suggest that the autonomously secure national space – whether defined through tangible or imagined characteristics – is no longer a viable category of self-definition. In a borderless world, homogeneity and singularity increasingly give way to transnational spaces of relation and hybridity . . .' See 'Introduction: What Is Transatlantic Literary Studies?', in Susan Manning and Andrew Taylor (eds), *Transatlantic Literary Studies: A Reader* (Edinburgh: Edinburgh University Press, 2007), p. 3.

8. US-based scholars working in American Studies have critiqued the exceptionalist bent evident in the field's early days, while attributing that stance to a postwar victor's mentality. See, for example, Janice Radway, '"What's in a Name?" Presidential Address to the American Studies Association, November 20, 1998', *American Quarterly*, 51 (March, 1999), 1–32. Though much scholarship has focused on repositioning American Studies in a hemispheric perspective, as in *Hemispheric American Studies*, the founding of the *Journal of Transnational American Studies*, and calls for a post-nationalist practice in *The Futures of American Studies* point to an increasingly comparative, transnational commitment. See Caroline F. Levander and Robert S. Levine (eds), *Hemispheric American Studies* (New Brunswick, NJ: Rutgers University Press, 2007) and Donald E. Pease and Robyn Wiegman (eds), *The Futures of American Studies* (Durham, NC: Duke University Press, 2002).

9. The journal's self-description affirms slippage still lingering around the 'American' term: '*49th Parallel* is a peer-reviewed, interdisciplinary e-journal devoted to American and Canadian Studies' (available at <http://www.49thparallel.bham.ac.uk/> last accessed 9 May 2014).

10. We thank Brian Wall, a graduate student in the University of Edinburgh's programme who studied with Manning and Taylor, for reminding us of this important 'turn' in transatlantic studies. In fall 2013, Brian joined the private online workspace where our contributors and the 2013 seminar students read and responded to draft chapters for this volume.

11. Kevin Hutchings and Julia M. Wright, 'Introduction: Mobilizing Gender, Race and Nation', in Hutchings and Wright (eds), *Transatlantic Literary Exchanges, 1790–1870: Gender, Race, and Nation* (Farnham: Ashgate, 2011), p. 2.

12. At our own home institution of TCU, for instance, 'Learning to Change the World' is the tagline for promotional materials; the official mission is 'To educate individuals to think and act as ethical leaders and responsible citizens in the global community'. Stephen O. Michael asserts that 'most

university mission statements in the United States are becoming increasingly interchangeable', with 'global' learning joining academic excellence and diversity as regularly cited goals. See Michael, 'Response 4: In Pursuit of Excellence, Diversity and Globalization: The Art of Leveraging International Assets in Academia', in Sarah R. Robbins, Sabine H. Smith, and Federica Santini (eds), *Bridging Cultures: International Women Faculty Transforming the US Academy* (Lanham, MD: University Press of America, 2011), p. 138.

13. Regenia Gagnier, 'Introduction: Victorian Studies, World Literatures, and Globalisation', *Critical Quarterly*, 55: 1 (April 2013), 1. For the Global Circulation Project, see <http://literature-compass.com/global-circulation-project/>. Another instance of such globally based scholarship is *A Feminist Reader: Feminist Thought from Sappho to Satrapi* edited by Americanist Sharon M. Harris and Victorianist Linda K. Hughes. Rather than emphasising Anglo-American feminism, the four-volume reader situates feminist writing in a global context (Cambridge: Cambridge University Press, 2013).

14. The study by Richard Martin, which also notes a marked decline in American studies majors in the UK during the era of the Iraq war and the presidency associated with it, cites Susan Castillo: 'American Studies is no longer coterminous with US Studies.' Martin remarks further, 'One argument is that transnationalism superseded the more specific focus on transatlanticism at the turn of the millennium, as scholarship started to provide closer attention to critiques of the nation-state and global relations, and the study of Hispanic and Asian histories and cultures, both within and beyond the United States, received greater emphasis.' See Martin, *American Studies in the UK, 2000–2010*, a report commissioned by the British Association for American Studies in conjunction with the Fulbright Commission, July 2012 (available at <http://www.baas.ac.uk/images/stories/Download_docs/american%20studies%20in%20the%20uk%202000-2010.pdf> last accessed 12 May 2013).

15. While tracking 'the impact of the Bologna Process on the transatlantic dialogue on higher education' (p. 14), Kriebernegg has simultaneously noted the ironic lack of direct engagement with the Bologna vision on the part of US-based higher education (p. 13). See 'Introduction', *The Transatlantic Dialogue on Higher Education: An Analysis of Cultural Narratives* (Berlin: Logos Verlag Berlin, 2011). See also Kriebernegg's 'Alien Alliances', in Robbins et al. (eds), *Bridging Cultures*, pp. 129–37.

16. Masao Miyoshi, 'Borderless World? From Colonialism to Transnationalism and the Decline of the Nation State', *Critical Inquiry*, 19 (1993), 726–51. Miyoshi argues that the rise of transnational corporations in the 1990s (versus multinational ones earlier) promoted efforts to build a shared set

of transnational cultural products and practices. Amir Mufti similarly warns: 'More bluntly put, it is hard not to wonder if all this talk of world literature might not be an intellectual correlate of the happy talk that accompanied globalisation over the last couple of decades until the financial crash and its ongoing aftermath introduced a certain reality check into the public discourse.' See 'Orientalism and the Invention of World Literatures: Introduction', *boundary 2*, 39: 2 (2012), 71.

Following Miyoshi, Grantland S. Rice suggests that just as the rise of the nation-state promoted both a national consciousness and a commitment to disciplinary fields linked to national identity (such as 'American' literature), the rise of the global marketplace is helping to displace from higher education the disciplines most closely associated with nationhood. Posits Rice: 'Although the decline in importance of the nation-state has not threatened the existence of the English department per se, thanks in large part to the tangible economic value of rhetoric and composition training, it *has* divided and weakened the field of American literature' (emphasis in original); see 'New Origins of American Literature', *American Literary History*, 13: 4 (Winter 2001), 816. See also Manning and Taylor, 'Introduction', pp. 2–4.

17. See Benedict Anderson, *Imagined Communities: Reflections on the Origin and Spread of Nationalism*, 2nd edn (London: Verso, 2006), especially Chapter 3, where Anderson relates the rise of a national consciousness to print-capitalism (pp. 39–48).

18. Historian Aileen Fyfe links steam-driven travel and transatlantic print culture in her study of the Edinburgh-based publishing firm of William Chambers, devoting a chapter to 'Steamships and Transatlantic Business' in *Steam-Powered Knowledge: William Chambers and the Business of Publishing, 1820–1860* (Chicago: University of Chicago Press, 2012), pp. 173–252.

19. Dimock calls for a global vision of American literature, resisting traditional (national and regional) geographic boundaries. At the same time, she urges scholars and teachers to think beyond the lure of periodisation: 'The continuum of historical life does not grant the privilege of autonomy . . . to any temporal segment. Periodization, in this sense, is not more than a fiction: unavoidable to be sure, but also unavoidably artificial, naturalized only at our own peril' (Wai Chee Dimock, 'Deep Time: American Literature and World History', *American Literary History*, 13: 4 (Winter 2001), 757). See also Dimock, *Through Other Continents: American Literature Across Deep Time* (Princeton: Princeton University Press, 2006).

20. See, for instance, Joselyn M. Almeida, *Reimagining the Transatlantic, 1780–1890* (Burlington, VT: Ashgate, 2011) and Robert David Aguirre,

'Mexico, Independence, and Trans-Atlantic Exchange, 1822–24', *BRANCH: Britain, Representation and Nineteenth-Century History*, ed. Dino Franco Felluga, Extension of *Romanticism and Victorianism on the Net* (available at <http://www.branchcollective.org/?ps_art icles=robert-david-aguirre-mexico-independence-and-trans-atlantic-exc hange-1822-24> last accessed 9 May 2013). We have noted how terms such as 'international' and 'transnational', like 'cross-cultural' and 'inter-cultural', accrue and carry varying connotations as employed by scholars writing for a range of contexts. 'Transnational' is a relatively recent term which would not have been invoked by nineteenth-century writers and readers, who tend to use 'international' when referencing exchanges occurring during that earlier era. However, like Hutchings and Wright, we recognise the value of applying terms such as 'transnational' in today's analytical contexts, as in the opening sentence of their essay collection's introduction: 'Transatlantic scholarship is centrally interested in a trans-national view of the northern Atlantic region and the complex ways in which this region was significant to the individuals who passed over it . . .' ('Introduction', p. 1).

21. Thanks to these generous colleagues, whose syllabi significantly aided planning for our first seminar: Daniel Hack, University of Michigan; Peter Manning and Susan Scheckel, SUNY Stony Brook; Eliza Richards and Beverly Taylor, University of North Carolina, Chapel Hill; Jonathan Elmer and Mary Favret, Indiana University; Sandra Zagarell, Oberlin College.

22. See the syllabus for our 2010 course on the Teaching Transatlanticism website (available at <https://teachingtransatlanticism.tcu.edu/wp-con tent/uploads/2013/12/syl-2010-hughes-and-robbins.pdf> last accessed 7 May 2014).

23. Like our 2010 syllabus, the 2013 version is available via our website (available at <https://teachingtransatlanticism.tcu.edu/wp-content/ uploads/2014/04/syl-English-70583-updated-dec-19-2013-1.pdf> last accessed 7 May 2014).

24. The website includes additional information about contributors' reading lists, assignments, and course or lesson plans; it also hosts a discussion forum and invites further sharing of materials to which we hope our readers will contribute.

PART I

Curricular Histories and Key Trends

CHAPTER 2

On Not Knowing Any Better

Susan M. Griffin

M y disciplinary disposition is resolutely Anglo-American. This is true in my teaching, my reading, my research, and my writing. Yet in retrospect I realise that I began work in transatlantic studies because I didn't know any better. Really, it was a combination of naiveté and dumb luck. The personal and historical circumstances of my undergraduate education at Georgetown University (1971–5) and graduate school studies at the University of Chicago in the late 1970s and early 1980s (before graduate students were 'profession-alised', when women's studies began, as the job market tanked), the choice to write a dissertation on Henry James, my focus on nineteenth-century fiction, the various reading communities I joined and created over the years, the happenstances of my hiring – all worked to make reading American and British texts together seem, not a violation of disciplinary norms, but normal. Whether this is a story of blissful or stubborn ignorance I leave to others to judge. But this highly individual history does, I think, illuminate the structures and strictures – intellectual, economic, professional, pedagogical – of the field of English studies. And reflecting on the questions and assumptions about genre, reading practices, cultural communities, and literacies that we bring to syllabus design and classroom practice can perhaps suggest strategic alternatives to the often mechanical assessments of teaching and learning that we now face.

When I attended Georgetown, the requirements for an English major were few, and the orientation of virtually all of my classes was resolutely New Critical. (My freshman honours class used Allen Tate and Caroline Gordon's *House of Fiction* anthology.[1]) Not only that, but I was an honours English major, and the classes designed for that group tended to be more along the lines of what I now recognise as 'special topics'. My guess is that then, as now, honours classes were places for professors to try out new courses designed around their own scholarly interests. I loved it all. But, if the idea of 'coverage' was suspect in those days, the practice of literary history was virtually invisible. It was all close reading, with *Portrait of the Artist as a Young Man* as the sacred text. A further peculiarity of my undergraduate education is the fact that, aside from a contemporary American poetry course taught by a poet, I took no classes in American literature. This may have been a personal aversion, but I suspect that the offerings were sparse.

Having taken a year off after my BA, I ended up in the MA programme at the University of Chicago. (Why Chicago? It was the best place that I got into.) It happened that several people I knew from Georgetown had started at the University of Chicago directly after graduation the year before; they were in comparative literature and art history. Other college friends were living and working in the city. I knew no one in the English programme – hardly unusual. But having friends who had pioneered Chicago for me meant that the people I spent time with that first year were not in my department. That, in turn, meant that I wasn't tuned in to the constant, competitive gossip about who were the best people in the programme, what supposedly powerful professors one needed to cultivate to succeed, or how to strategise acceptance into the PhD programme. Not that I was or am above gossip – I just wasn't part of those particular discussions. I had some idea that I should learn English literature from its beginnings, so I signed up for Anglo-Saxon, not realising other students had already decided on areas of study and that this was a course for specialists in, well, Anglo-Saxon, or at least medieval literature. Another instance of not knowing any better. For an entirely different set of reasons, I also chose courses with young female professors because there had been only one or two women on the Georgetown faculty (Chicago had, as I remember, five or so). Looking back, I really cannot see or recall any kind of coherent plan to my coursework. Interestingly, I did actually take a class with Robert Streeter, a generous teacher and old-school Americanist, that paired American and British nineteenth-century novels.

The formative teacher of my graduate school years was William Veeder. I took several classes with him, including an independent study on Henry James. To say that Bill, a friend to this day, shaped my reading, writing, and teaching practices, is to understate the matter considerably. In this context, however, what is important is that Bill's work was and is consistently transatlantic. (It is, perhaps, significant that he began as a novelist.) For example, I took a course with him on nineteenth-century gothic that dealt with British and American texts. And, among other projects, he was working at that time on *The Woman Question: Society and Literature in Britain and America, 1837–1883*, a three-volume critical source book in which the authors, Elizabeth Helsinger, Robin Sheets, and Veeder, declared, 'We have also departed from prevailing practice by considering British and American discussions together as parts of a single debate.'[2]

So, when I came to write my dissertation on Henry James under Veeder's direction, I was not guided into either an Americanist reading or, for that matter, a Victorian (which at the time meant 'British') one. Writing on James and perception, I studied nineteenth-century psychological and philosophical theories of seeing, none of which proceeded according to strictly national categories. For example, in order to understand William James's work on perception, I needed to read the Scottish and English associationists. So, too, the categories of 'American' and 'British' were of little use in studying art historical theorists of perception like Rudolf Arnheim and Ernst Gombrich.[3] Later, revising my dissertation into a book, I realised that a chapter on American landscape painting was required. Here, too, the field of study turned out to be a broad one: eighteenth- and nineteenth-century American painting is unintelligible if one does not read John Ruskin or learn the history of landscape painting in France, Italy, and England.

I was lucky, too, in that, throughout my graduate school years (and to this day), I was involved in reading groups, almost always with other women, and often centred around women writers.[4] The composition of the groups shifted, but, in graduate school, included other students from English and comparative literature, as well as non-students. These gatherings not only made for a steady stream of new texts, but they also fostered the practice of reading and talking about books in groupings rarely defined by national literatures. We were focused as to genre, however, typically reading fiction, along with the occasional memoir, reading habits that, for better or worse, are with me still, both professionally and personally. (I have accepted that I am a narrative junkie.) When asked what I work on, my shorthand answer is: 'nineteenth-century novels'.

Then came the job market. Having been in on the hiring of a dozen or so assistant professors over the years, I find it amazing that I secured a tenure-track position. The English department at Chicago was still operating under the assumption that if you were good, a good job or jobs would be offered to you. There was no preparation or assistance for those entering the market. If the word 'professionalise' was ever uttered in my hearing in those days, it would have been used negatively – an attitude with which, admittedly, I still have some sympathy. Certainly, I had not chosen coursework that made me a match for the kinds of jobs that the Modern Language Association listed (perhaps because of the fact that I did not look at a MLA job list until the year I went on the market). Having written a dissertation on Henry James, I blithely sent off letters for positions in nineteenth-century British and nineteenth- and twentieth-century American literature.

Although this behaviour now looks wilfully ignorant – and was certainly not smart – it was not unheard of at the time, and I actually did get quite a few interviews and several campus visits. However, while my ability to talk intelligently across a range of literary topics stood me in good stead, the drawbacks of being neither one thing nor the other definitely emerged. Some experiences now seem straight out of a David Lodge novel. One interview for a job in nineteenth-century British literature with the chair at a small liberal arts college went very well; he asked me to meet with some other department members later that day. That second meeting scotched my chances when my lame responses to questions on Wordsworth made it clear that I was not the properly trained specialist they were looking for. At a campus visit to an Ivy League school for an American literature position, I erred in the other direction by admitting that I had not read Sacvan Bercovitch's *American Jeremiad* (1978).

In 1982, I did get a tenure-track job in nineteenth-century American literature at the University of Louisville, which meant that, among other things, I quickly taught myself how to teach the first half of the American literature survey, a class on American short fiction, and so on. When it came time to give mid-term and final exams, I realised that, since I had been teaching works one by one, I had not given the class the kinds of threads, themes, and connections that were needed in order for me to write exam questions that the students could answer. Hence my self-education in American studies: what was American about American literature? This was all very interesting, but only added to my sense that the texts I was teaching seemed remarkably similar. I thought back to a women's reading group meeting some years earlier. We had teased a member who was specialising in nineteenth-century American fiction: why would she work on literature with no women? That certainly seemed to be the case in 1982 when the first edition of the *Norton Anthology*[5] was the standard text for surveys. Teaching the first half of the American literature survey, I used volume 1, which contained all of 183 pages of work by seven women writers, out of 2,392 pages and forty-one authors.

Then I came across Nina Baym's remarkable 1981 'Melodramas of Beset Manhood: How Theories of American Fiction Exclude Women Authors'.[6] Baym's incisive analysis of the circular reasoning of American literary criticism was game-changing for my teaching, my scholarship, and my peace of mind. Looking at the history of American literary criticism, she demonstrates that the attempt to define and defend an American literature apart from that of Britain came to rest on judgements about a work's 'Americanness': 'The earliest American literary critics began to talk about the "most American" work rather than the "best" work because they knew no way to find out the best other than by comparing American to British writing.'[7] What one might expect to be a very broad, inclusive quality turned out to be, in fact, quite narrowly defined. For literature to count as 'American' it must follow a particular plot and be written by an author whose own career could be read as embodying that plot: a 'melodrama of beset manhood'. (This is also a plot that, not incidentally, the Americanist male critic saw as his own story.) In this scenario, 'the American individual, the pure American self',[8] rebels against and flees from the constraints of society, setting himself against debased, popular culture, embodied very specifically as female, for the freedom of the American wilderness, a landscape also imaged as female, although here nurturing rather than restrictive. Baym's point is that such a narrative is unlikely to find a female author. In fact, the narrative effectually divides American literary culture in two: serious male author versus popular female writer.

The essay also helped me think through something that had been puzzling me in critical constructions of Henry James.[9] Teaching and reading 'as an Americanist', I was surprised to find that Henry James was, in those contexts, exclusively located in relation to his American literary forbears, especially Hawthorne. Of course, James's writing was profoundly influenced by Hawthorne, both positively and negatively. But how could one understand James's literary genealogy without George Eliot? The Eliot example pointed up another problem for me. It was not just that Americanists read James only through American authors, it was the fact that this American literary genealogy was a male one.

I was able to work through some of these issues in a 1989 article, 'The Discourse Within: Feminism and Intradisciplinary Study'. I argued that feminist studies, which was and is by its very nature interdisciplinary, could help us overcome the Americanist dichotomy of serious male novel of rebellion versus the popular female fiction of convention. Focusing this analysis on nineteenth-century fiction called into question the disciplinary division between American and British literatures that governed matters of employment, specialisation, curricula, and publication. Simply put, 'one can define the serious nineteenth-century novel as exclusively the psychological novel of male individualism only if one does not read British novels.'[10] Mutually reinforcing gender and national distinctions had, in fact, made certain matters of influence and exchange invisible. I suggested that reading American novelists through their British literary mothers would allow us to perceive classic American texts in new ways.

The example that I used was one that I had been mulling over. I had noticed what seemed to me strikingly similar scenes in Charlotte Brontë's *Villette* (1853) and Nathaniel Hawthorne's *Marble Faun* (1860). In both novels, a lonely young Protestant woman, parentless and unmarried, is tempted to go to confession to a Roman Catholic priest. In doing so, she risks confinement in a convent, a danger that she narrowly escapes. Reading Hawthorne's version of this episode in light of, and as a revision of, Brontë's, I then turned to its rewriting in James's *The Ambassadors*. The genealogy of this scene, I demonstrated, crossed and recrossed national and gender boundaries. Warrant for this break with twentieth-century disciplinary divisions could readily be found, I pointed out, in the practices of nineteenth-century reading audiences, whose access to affordable books was profoundly influenced by the lack of international copyright law: Americans, for example, could purchase books by British writers more cheaply than those by native authors.[11] Critics and reviewers were also often transatlantic in their orientation, discussing Brontë and Hawthorne together.[12]

If reading these American and British authors together made sense, what I still did not understand was the horrified reactions of the other characters to these confessional scenes. Why, specifically, was confession – especially female confession – so scandalous? This question was the genesis of *Anti-Catholicism and Nineteenth-Century Fiction*,[13] a project that occupied some years in part because I uncovered masses of materials, most of which were unread after their time period. This considerable archive coupled with the nature of Anglo-American anti-Catholicism made it difficult to decide how best to structure the book. The evidence was a shared, transatlantic body of material that included journalism, fiction, court-reporting, sermons, tracts, political speeches, and popular religious writings, as well as serious historical and theological works. Yet, pervasive and extensive as anti-Catholic literature was, it was also remarkably repetitive. The same figures, plots, and arguments appear again and again: stock characters like the crafty Jesuit and the sadistic mother superior; standard narratives like a young woman's imprisonment in and escape from a convent; set pieces like rapes in confessionals by lascivious priests and death-bed swindles by crafty clerics. While seemingly ahistorical, these anti-Catholic tropes recur at historically and geographically specific times and places, taking on changing cultural and political functions.

Eventually I settled on chronological chapters that alternated between American and British materials and events. While this could be seen as actually perpetuating transatlantic division, the chapters built on and referred comparatively to one another. In addition, the book's introduction, final chapter, and conclusion treated both British and American texts together. I was happy to have the book published by Cambridge University Press, but its transatlantic orientation did present the publisher with some marketing problems. It was actually brought out, in fact, as part of the Cambridge Studies in American Literature and Culture series.

In 1995 I was asked to take over the editorship of the *Henry James Review* (Johns Hopkins University Press). While grateful for this opportunity, I was also afraid that editing a journal would reduce my publication rate, keeping me from 'my own work', a fear that I suspect haunts most editors. But I was also wary because the *Henry James Review* is a single-author journal, and I was not interested in the sort of coterie boosterism that can vitiate such publications. The *Review* had avoided this narrowing under my predecessor, Daniel Mark Fogel, the founding editor, but I did not see many other examples of single-author journals that published a wide range of critics across a spectrum of critical and theoretical approaches or that reached across multiple disciplines. Henry James was the saving grace here. A lot of smart, interesting people write on James, many of them not 'Jamesians'. (Not that there is anything wrong with Jamesians – I'm one.) James attracts those working in American studies, Victorian literature, Modernist studies, and literary theory, not to mention art history, philosophy, and so on. While my aims here were not solely 'transatlantic', certainly that was part of my general goal of continually broadening the journal's scope while retaining the focus on James. To that end, I instituted the Leon Edel prize, a yearly award for the best essay on Henry James by a beginning scholar. This contest brings a cross-section of new work by younger colleagues to the journal. And 'my' first issue, on James and race, began the practice of yearly special issues that, ranging from James and philosophy to global James, invite interdisciplinary contributions.

Throughout these years, I was fortunate indeed to be in a department that did not view these critical excursions negatively. On the contrary, I received support and encouragement and was also, crucially, allowed to teach courses that furthered that exploration. The fact that the English department was understaffed for a university of our size made for a range of course assignments, which actually worked to my advantage. But also important was the generosity of senior colleagues: I never encountered turf-tending. Then there is the fact that the English department at the University of Louisville has deliberately kept our numbered course designations relatively open (some might say 'vague' or 'boring'); this has made for flexibility and allows faculty to teach to their strengths and scholarly interests. I've taught a seminar on *Middlemarch* and one on Toni Morrison, as well as many nineteenth-century courses with transatlantic reading lists, including 'Sensational Fictions' and 'Fantastic Metamorphoses'.

The syllabi for such courses naturally shape student attitudes and reading practices: studying British and American texts together comes not to seem exceptional. In teaching I also stress the transnational nature of nineteenth-century publishing, marketing, reading, and criticism. For example, in a class on sensation fiction, we study how both nineteenth-century and contemporary critics define 'sensation'. Always included is Margaret Oliphant, one of the most astute nineteenth-century literary reviewers and one whose take on the sensation novel is firmly transatlantic: 'Mr. Willkie Collins is not the first man who has produced a sensation novel . . . The higher class of American fiction, as represented by Hawthorne, attempts little else.'[14] I often begin an upper-level undergraduate or graduate class by distributing a list of research web resources and assigning each student one site to describe and evaluate for the class: some of these websites are devoted to American literature and culture, some to British, and some are transatlantic.[15] Thinking across – or beyond

– national borders has actually come to my rescue in creating some syllabi. Planning a seminar on 'Hawthorne, Eliot, and James' (apparently some of my ideas die hard), I realised that it would be nearly impossible for students in a fifteen-week course to write an original essay that took into account the state of criticism on *The Scarlet Letter*, *Middlemarch*, or *The Portrait of a Lady*, the major texts for the course. My solution was to give students the option of researching and writing in three areas: world literatures (how one of these novels has appeared outside of Anglo-America), reappearance (the 'afterlife' of one of the texts in literary, popular, political, or commercial cultures), or serial publication(s).[16]

I suggested at the start of this essay that thinking about these matters might give us tools for better articulating the aims and methods of our pedagogy. As chair of the English department at the University of Louisville for ten years, I am acutely, even painfully, aware of the often redundant demands for assessment of our teaching, our graduation rates, our advising – the list goes on. My syllabi, like those of my colleagues, have grown ever longer, spelling out policies, procedures, grading rubrics. Among the additions required of us at the University of Louisville are lists of 'course objectives' as well as 'SLOs' – student learning outcomes. What will students who take this course know, and how will we assess whether or not they know it? I won't address here whether these are correct – or even useful – questions to ask. However, it is the case that many of us design syllabi based on our scholarly practices and critical instincts without fully spelling out our reasoning either to ourselves or to our students. Rather than dismissing assessment tools as challenges to our expertise and authority, perhaps we might use them as occasions to think through why it is important or useful (what kind of use?) to teach certain texts together, why one would develop a course along national or genre lines. What literary and cultural categories does this set of assignments present to our students? How should the field(s) of knowledge that they are entering be arranged and structured? For me, at least, pondering such questions has not only helped with syllabus design, it has also allowed me to be clearer with my students about what we are up to and what I expect. I may have started on this path not knowing any better, but I'd like those I teach to have a clearer sense of where we are going and why. I want to better their knowing.

NOTES

1. First published in 1950 by Scribner's. See Diane Middlebrook: 'Most of us who went to college from the fifties to the mid-sixties were taught to read by Caroline Gordon. *The House of Fiction* (1950), the anthology that Gordon edited with her husband, the poet Allen Tate, was widely

adopted in college courses because of Gordon's trenchant commentaries, which brought to bear on "masterpieces" the techniques of formal analysis ("close reading") engendered in the then-lively school of New Criticism.' Diane Middlebrook, 'The Life of a Good Old Girl', *Hudson Review*, 41: 3 (Autumn 1988), 581. My class probably used the 1960 edition, but our training was similar to Middlebrook's.

2. Elizabeth Helsinger, Robin Sheets, and William Veeder, *The Woman Question: Society and Literature in Britain and America, 1837–1883* (Chicago: University of Chicago Press, 1983), p. viii.

3. For example, Ernst Gombrich, *Art and Illusion* (Princeton: Princeton University Press, 1972); Rudolf Arnheim, *Art and Visual Perception* (Berkeley: University of California Press, 1969).

4. On women's reading groups, see Elizabeth Long, *Women and the Uses of Reading in Everyday Life* (Chicago: University of Chicago Press, 2003).

5. Ronald Gottesman, Laurence B. Holland, David Kalstone, Francis Murphy, Hershel Parker, and William H. Pritchard (eds), *Norton Anthology of American Literature*, vol. 1 (New York: Norton, 1979).

6. On the widespread influence of Baym's essay, see Margaret McFadden, 'Commentary', in Lucy Maddox (ed.), *Locating American Studies: The Evolution of a Discipline* (Baltimore: Johns Hopkins University Press, 1999), pp. 232–4.

7. Nina Baym, 'Melodramas of Beset Manhood: How Theories of American Fiction Exclude Women Authors', *American Quarterly*, 33: 2 (Summer 1981), 125.

8. Ibid., p. 131.

9. See Jane Gallop, *Around 1981: Academic Feminist Literary Theory* (London: Routledge, 1991) for an example of how Baym's critique of theories of Americanism could be used to analyse problems within feminist criticism.

10. Susan M. Griffin, 'The Discourse Within: Feminism and Intradisciplinary Study', *Arizona Quarterly*, 44: 4 (Winter 1989), 4.

11. In recent years, scholars have complicated the picture of transatlantic reading habits. See, for example, Meredith McGill, *American Literature and the Culture of Reprinting, 1834–1853* (Philadelphia: University of Pennsylvania Press, 2003).

12. For example, Margaret Oliphant, 'Modern Novelists – Great and Small', *Blackwood's Magazine*, 77 (1855), 554–68, and Leslie Stephen, 'Nathaniel Hawthorne', *Hours in a Library*, vol. 1 (London: Smith, Elder, 1874), pp. 256–98.

13. Susan M. Griffin, *Anti-Catholicism and Nineteenth-Century Fiction* (Cambridge: Cambridge University Press, 2004).

14. Margaret Oliphant, 'Modern Novelists – Great and Small', 565.

15. See Griffin, Appendix A, 'The Book', available at <http://teachingtrans-atlanticism.tcu.edu>. My main difficulty with this assignment is a happy one: more and more resources appear yearly.

16. While the latter two did not dictate transnational projects, they certainly allowed for it. For a more detailed example of transatlantic classroom practice, see the syllabus for a recent course, 'Scenes of Reading' (Griffin, Appendix B, 'The Book', available at <http://teachingtransatlanticism. tcu.edu>.

CHAPTER 3

Transatlantic Networks in the Nineteenth Century

Susan David Bernstein

From over two decades of teaching the transatlantic nineteenth century, I have gradually developed a network with four principal hubs: genre, space, time, and intertextuality. Although my pedagogical thinking about the transatlantic predates Albert-László Barabási's *Linked: The New Science of Networks* (2002), his exploration of patterns of social interconnectivity, drawing on the digital web as the chief network structure of today, provides some interesting touchstones for the transatlantic nineteenth-century syllabus. In Barabási's scheme, levels of connections across networks ascend from nodes to hubs to clusters.[1] In the transatlantic syllabus, specific texts, like *Uncle Tom's Cabin* or Elizabeth Barrett Browning's slave poems, are nodes that are linked through these hubs that then form larger clusters of print culture networks across the Atlantic and beyond. As Barabási explains, 'The truly central position in networks is reserved for those nodes that are simultaneously part of many large clusters', while hubs 'dominate the structure of all networks . . . like small worlds'.[2] The national highway and airline networks offer familiar examples of this structure of nodes (regional airports), hubs, and clusters (airlines). Let me detail the teaching route that brought me to this juncture.

A few years before the spate of books on transatlantic scholarship, such as Paul Giles's *Transatlantic Insurrections* (2001), I taught both undergraduate and graduate courses on nineteenth-century social problem fiction. What prompted me in that direction before 'transatlantic' appeared in book and syllabus titles? My PhD programme was titled 'English and American literature', and it was not unusual for courses to combine the study of texts across national lines, even if at that time 'English' subsumed Irish and other Anglophone literatures. Once I determined that the nineteenth century was my historical period, I saw no roadblocks to pairing *Moby Dick* with *Middlemarch* or *In Memoriam* with *Leaves of Grass*. What I didn't realise, however, was that transatlantic readers of the nineteenth century were reading Eliot and Melville as well as Whitman and Tennyson. The national barriers of the discipline of literary studies, and not the original publishing patterns, erected these barriers that were not evident at all for reading patterns a century earlier. My preliminary exams included literature from both sides of the North Atlantic, although when it was time to set my dissertation topic, my advisor steered me toward British literature given that tenure-track positions were either 'American' or 'British' literature but seldom both and not, in the late 1980s, 'transatlantic'.

When I arrived at Wisconsin from graduate school and was assigned an introductory literature course from 1800 to the present, I was expected to devise a syllabus that was 'transatlantic' *avant la lettre*. Only more advanced undergraduate courses tended to divide up the nineteenth century across national boundaries. I paired condition of England novels by Disraeli, Gaskell, and Dickens with social gospel fiction by Stowe and Phelps. While twentieth-century modernism and postmodernism were routinely taught as not just transatlantic but also international literary movements, the convention until quite recently has been to segregate nineteenth-century American literature from its British contemporaries. Although a cursory survey of print circulation and readerships made manifest that British readers consumed American publications, especially on the subject of slavery like *Uncle Tom's Cabin*, the all-time bestseller in Britain, and that American readers could not escape reprints of British authors such as Dickens, Eliot, and Gaskell, still the regular curricular fare continued to read through national division rather than transatlantic interconnections. In those first classes, my students were intrigued by the evident echoes between the plight of the British poor or socially disenfranchised and the horrors of American slavery. Yet I remember an Americanist colleague who balked at this curricular and scholarly union because 'that's not how the discipline works'. When Kirsten Jamsen, then a graduate student at Wisconsin who had taken my seminar, went on to write her dissertation, my colleague marvelled later that such transatlantic convergences would be a future direction in literary studies. Jamsen's 1998 dissertation, 'Voices Carry: Authorship, Community, and British and American's Women's Advocacy Fiction, 1848–1876', argued for the robust 'transatlantic conversation' between Gaskell's *Mary Barton* and Stowe's *Uncle Tom's Cabin*, and between Phelps's *The Silent Partner* and Gaskell's *North and South*, and the surprising links between Stowe's *Dred* and Eliot's *Daniel Deronda*.[3]

A decade later, when searchable databases of nineteenth-century periodicals facilitated the research of transatlantic reading, I taught another graduate course on the nineteenth-century transatlantic, this one titled 'Transatlantic Popular Literature and Print Culture in the Nineteenth Century'. Given the recent work on material culture studies and the history of the book, I was able to frame this course through scholarship that had not existed even a decade earlier on the Atlantic rim. The syllabus included the genres of fiction, poetry, and essays; we examined how the material forms of serial instalments and magazine paraliterary elements shaped the circulation and reception of these texts on either side of the ocean. The intertextuality theme emerged especially through Hannah Crafts's *The Bondwoman's Narrative* as a performative reading of *Bleak House* in particular, given the reprints of this serial in many American periodicals including *Frederick Douglass's Paper*. Genre, intertextuality, spatiality (transatlantic circulations), and temporality (the serial timetable as a guide to reading across borders) framed how the class investigated the networking of specific texts. While the transatlantic echoes between Dickens and Stowe, or Crafts and Dickens, or Gaskell and Phelps, or Barrett Browning and Stowe, are all too familiar, I posed one other networking possibility that has received scant scholarly attention: Henry Rider Haggard's *She* and Pauline Hopkins's *Of One Blood*. By researching databases of the late 1880s, we discovered that *She*, initially serialised in *The Graphic* (1886–7), was reissued widely in both regional and national American periodicals. Given the targeted circulation of *Colored American Magazine*, which Hopkins briefly edited and where her spiritualist adventure tale was published in instalments, it is not surprising that Hopkins's fiction didn't circulate in Britain. Yet the echoes between the imperial explorers' tale of a lost African kingdom (or queendom) in *She* and Hopkins's reworking of the Rider Haggardian mythology with attention to American racial politics invited us to reconsider the transatlantic as a spatial terrain that encompassed not just circulation patterns but also embedded geographical settings.

Fruits of that semester include 'Literary Graftings: Hannah Crafts's *The Bondwoman's Narrative* and the Nineteenth-Century Transatlantic Reader', Rebecca Soares's article that received the 2010 Van Arsdel Essay Prize. Soares argues that *The Bondwoman's Narrative* performs a transatlantic reading that conflates different genres that circulated between the US and the UK; like the patchworked narrative of the text itself, the reader-writer referred to as 'Hannah Crafts' cannot be narrowly or confidently classified. Using the serial forms of *Bleak House* as it appeared in *Frederick Douglass's Paper*, Soares sketches how this unpublished text emerges from a print network.[4]

I also taught two different undergraduate courses that pursued these four hubs of transatlantic literary culture. One course on transatlantic social debates updated my initial foray into this material by including Frederick Douglass's autobiographies, which enjoyed an avid reception in the UK, and Elizabeth Barrett Browning's poetry published in the abolitionist paper the *Liberty Bell*. The syllabus paired *North and South*, which was serialised in both Dickens's *Household Words* and in *Harper's Monthly Magazine*, with Rebecca Harding Davis's *Life in the Iron Mills* published in the *Atlantic Monthly* in 1861. One student in that class wrote an essay on the role of art in social reform literature by comparing Barrett Browning's 'Hiram Powers' Greek Slave' with

Life in the Iron Mills. In addition to comparing Davis and Barrett Browning on aesthetics and social protest, this paper drew some compelling parallels about how Stowe and Gaskell used the domestic sphere to enter the realm of public sphere reform.

After teaching a course in nineteenth-century Anglo-Jewish literature, I discovered a textual bridge from East End London to the Lower East Side of New York. Israel Zangwill's *Children of the Ghetto* closes with characters whose families had emigrated to London a generation earlier now aboard a 'throbbing vessel that glided with its freight of hopes and dreams across the great waters towards the New World'.[5] This passage across the Atlantic offered a fulcrum for juxtaposing Jewish immigrants in London and New York. Framing the course around Jewishness, identity, and language, the syllabus incorporated two major units on Anglo- and on American-Jewish literature. For this first unit, 'From Romance to Revolt to Revision in Victorian England', we read poetry, essays, and fiction by Grace Aguilar and Amy Levy, and concluded with *Children of the Ghetto*, which offers an embedded response to Levy's *Reuben Sachs*, about not-quite assimilated Anglo-Jewish characters in London. The second section extended the bridge Zangwill began with the transatlantic crossing at the end of *Children of the Ghetto* by turning to *The Melting Pot*, Zangwill's play about the son of Russian Jewish immigrants to New York who composes a symphonic vision of the new identity of 'melting pot' assimilation. From here we read Abraham Cahan's *Yekl: A Tale of the New York Ghetto* and paired this with a screening of Joan Micklin Silver's 1975 *Hester Street*, a creative adaptation of the story. Anzia Yezierska's *Bread Givers* complements Cahan's depictions of Jewish immigrants with a feminist critique of both Old and New World patriarchy and sexism. To recap the themes of the course on the transatlantic Jewish diaspora, we concluded with Eva Hoffman's *Lost in Translation*, a memoir about her girlhood in Poland and Vancouver, an itinerary that broadens the reach of the London to New York trajectory by following Hoffman to the edge of the Pacific. A course on transatlantic Jewish literature recasts the themes of genre, time, space, and intertextuality evident in the other syllabi that link social reform fiction and poetry on American slavery with literary accounts of British factory workers and servants. Instead, the interconnections seem more explicit between authors centred on one side of the Atlantic, such as Levy and Zangwill, or on the other, including Cahan and Yezierska. Aesthetic genres – such as the symphonic composition of 'The Melting Pot' or the autobiographical novel of *Bread Givers* – show how forms illuminate transatlantic and diasporic identities beyond national boundaries. For this course, an ungraded 'Crossings' project offered students the opportunity to write creatively about the variously networked and diasporic identities we had studied. These projects opened up possibilities through digital media or visual design or fiction or memoir to reconstruct immigrant life stories as temporal and spatial networks. Some students chose fictionalised letters or diary entries from ancestors who had emigrated to the United States. One project collated recipes for the intertextual references to food across genres to show how cuisine is a marker of dispersed migratory subjects over time. For the final graded essay of the course, students chose one or more projects to launch their reflections back through the semester's readings by focusing on a particular strand of identity networks over time (family histories, across generations) and space.

In fall 2011, my graduate seminar 'Transatlantic Networks' capitalised not only on the previous teaching and research I had accomplished, but also on the recent scholarship, including discussions about what is transatlantic literature. We read both Kate Flint's *The Transatlantic Indian* (2008) and *Victorian Studies'* book review forum on this publication. Here an Americanist in literature, Jonathan Elmer, Cecilia Morgan, a historian, and Daniel Hack, a transatlanticist-Victorianist, explore how the field has emerged through the lens of Flint's book. In different ways this forum allowed us to examine the key conceptual hubs of the course. Elmer asks how *The Transatlantic Indian* straddles lines of disciplinary genres: 'Not exactly literary history, nor precisely postcolonial cultural studies, Flint's book is, rather, "transatlantic." But does that word apply to a method as well as an archive?'[6] Like my course on Jewish transatlantic literature, it is productive to consider how 'transatlantic' as an approach or archive can assume different geographical boundaries. As Morgan notes, 'Flint's work brings to the fore questions about the conceptualisation, methodology, and practice of the transatlantic and transnational history; it also raises the question of whose transatlantic world we choose.'[7] As we explored one specific network of circulation, with the majority of our texts focused on North America (and primarily American writers) and Great Britain (and primarily English writers), we considered ways of broadening the boundaries and the implications of that widening scope, or what Elmer refers to as the inclusive drive that 'leads to ever-larger units: the hemispheric, the global, the planetary'.[8]

Fortunately we had a forum of our own for comparing the 'transatlantic' with the 'global' nineteenth century. Because my colleague Caroline Levine was also teaching that semester a seminar, 'Nineteenth-Century Literature as World Literature', we arranged to hold a one-day conference on 'The Transnational Nineteenth Century: World Literature and Transatlantic Traffic' in which students from both classes gave presentations based on their seminar papers. Julia Dauer had written her essay for my 'Transatlantic Networks' course on William Wells Brown's comments on his unstable American identity in his travel narrative, *Three Years in Europe*, as he toured national landmarks including the British Museum and the Crystal Palace. Dauer was intrigued by Brown's responses to the displays at the Crystal Palace of American goods produced by slave labour and entwined that account with Brown's treatment of British Museum artifacts as, from Brown's perspective, 'very much mutilated'.[9] She argued that Brown reclaims his identity by inscribing himself through the British Museum catalogues and its 'elite transnational context', and she presented this research later at a national conference. However, for the symposium presentation Dauer turned to the work she'd pursued for the other course, although the material was part of the syllabus in 'Transatlantic Networks'. Stretching beyond the transatlantic approach, which my seminar had taken, to Barrett Browning's anti-slavery poems in the American abolitionist annual the *Liberty Bell*, Dauer widened that attention by examining the international range of writers contributing to the journal, as she argued that rather than an American political and social problem to which British authors like EBB responded, slavery is positioned as a humanitarian travesty that required a global community to redress it. Dauer followed the editor Maria Weston Chapman's organisation of the journal's contents, which included both women and men writers from many nations, as a way to envision a better nation through international dialogue. Again fusing the print culture emphasis of my seminar with the world literature theories and practices in Levine's course, Dauer further claimed that the hybridity of the *Liberty Bell* in form and in content meshed with the transnationalist implications for a reimagined national literary tradition. Not only did this anti-slavery annual gift book emerge from the syllabus of 'Transatlantic Networks', but also one of the seminar presenters, Zachary Marshall, had brought to Dauer's attention the surprising range of contributors to the *Liberty Bell*, including some contributions in translation. These juxtapositions encouraged our explorations of networks of reading, circulation, and intertextuality including and beyond the transatlantic in scope.

Digging deep into transatlantic print culture turned up some surprising artifacts, such as a dime-store version of Gaskell's *Lois the Witch*, a story set in the seventeenth-century Massachusetts Bay Colony. In '"English No More": The American Assimilation of Elizabeth Gaskell's *Lois the Witch*', Chelsea Smith discovered the transatlantic editing of this story from its original serial publication in Dickens's *All the Year Round* to the *Harper's Weekly* version, also in 1859, and finally to a dime-novel pirated and retitled version also published in the US a few years later. Finding that this was less a matter of the reprinting of a British author in American periodicals that capitalised on the appeal of Anglophilia, Smith analysed the substantial cuts in the American versions as revisions to distance Lois Barclay from her English origins. In other words, the American copyediting repurposed the heroine into a colonial American rather than the estranged Englishwoman Gaskell's original story posits. By comparing the transatlantic print contexts of *Lois the Witch*, Smith examined the role of international copyright disputes in mediating and enabling such transatlantic editorial practices. In revising this work for publication, Smith is considering an 'authorisation' continuum from the *All the Year Round* version, to the partially authorised *Harper's* edition, to the entirely unauthorised dime-novel abridgement. Her larger argument also asks that we reconceptualise what 'authorised edition' means in the unevenly regulated production and circulation of transatlantic print. In doing further research, Smith has turned up correspondence suggesting that Dickens actually mediated Gaskell's connection to *Harper's* agent in England. While scholars like Barbara Harman have pointed to Gaskell's difficult working relationship with Dickens as her editor, Smith explores Dickens's other role in Gaskell's career as he negotiated her contact with the *Harper's* agent.

Another exciting project that emerged from 'Transatlantic Networks' is Zachary Marshall's treatment of the serialisation of *Martin Chuzzlewit* as a crucial component in how this novel has been read by scholars including Meredith McGill in *The Culture of Reprinting*. In 'Some Assembly Required: Reading *Martin Chuzzlewit* as a Transatlantic Serialised Novel', Marshall takes to task other scholars who have tended to excise the American chapters from the larger novel rather than pay attention to how the American scenes are integrated through the serial format with the English portions. What seems Dickens's wholesale dismissal of American frontier culture functions as a cultural analogy to the hypocrisy of self-interested British capitalists in much of the rest of the novel. Marshall develops a theory of reading transatlantic serials by pointing to 'discontinuous' and 'extractionary' practices in contrast to what he calls a method of 'stitching together' across the larger print divides of chapters and instalments as a corollary with the geographical boundary of the Atlantic ocean.

As this journey across my curricular changes shows, teaching transatlantic currents flows into wider transnational and global waters. All these projects that emerged from courses on transatlantic studies reveal the generative potential of this approach that traverses more traditional national boundaries of literature in the nineteenth century. To encourage students to make their own fruitful discoveries, my watchword is 'the proof is in the printing'. Exploring what and how periodicals advertised, printed, or reprinted novels and poetry across the Atlantic makes manifest the particular pathways of transatlantic literary networks. Given the searchable online databases of so many nineteenth-century periodicals including American Periodicals Series (APS) and British Periodicals, it is possible to turn up all kinds of publication details that prompt further research. For example, the first instalment of *Romola* appeared in *Harper's Monthly Magazine* in August 1862, one month later than the initial instalment issued in London in the *Cornhill*. While the novel was published in the *Cornhill* under the name 'George Eliot', *Harper's* used 'Marian C. Evans', a moniker never attached to any of Eliot's novels printed in Britain. Investigating British periodicals unearths equally suggestive leads. In December 1882 the *Nineteenth Century* published an article 'Walt Whitman' detailing the publication and reception of the poet in Britain, and even directs followers to the national library: 'The reader at the British Museum may find there a copy of *Democratic Vistas*, but he will search in vain for *Memoranda during the War*.'[10] In the same issue of the *Nineteenth Century* is a review of a book titled *Uncle Pat's Cabin; or, Life among the Agricultural Labourers of Ireland* by W. C. Upton on the 'Irish agrarian revolution', with suggestive allusions to Stowe's novel and American slavery.[11]

Examining the contents of these magazines, students glimpse surprising transatlantic connections to be pursued further. To facilitate such explorations, I assign in both undergraduate and graduate courses short reports on research into periodical print culture to demonstrate some angle of transatlantic circulation. As the example from the *Nineteenth Century* exemplifies, researching Whitman in British periodicals leads to unexpected transatlantic links between *Uncle Tom's Cabin* and Irish peasant farmers, which are fertile ground for further investigation. To share research discoveries, my courses utilise online bibliographic reference management tools like RefWorks; the university catalogue system allows direct access to RefWorks from the subscribed databases. For each class, a shared RefWorks account operates as a collaborative research site with downloaded items. Abstracts of the reports students present in class appear on the course website. Such assignments both map the pathways of transatlantic print networks and prompt unsuspected intersections. Where I have organised my courses around the four hubs of genre, space, time, and intertextuality to chart the networks of circulation and exchange in nineteenth-century literature, my future itinerary will track genres in the widening circles of the Atlantic rim and transnational passages. As one example, the serial, whether fictional instalments or periodical print and reprints, opens up multiple pathways for researching the transportability of literary forms. Beginning with the transatlantic printing of *Romola* in the same monthly instalments, with the American publications a month later than the British appearance, further work might consider how the novel was received by American and by British readers, and might even expand beyond Great Britain to research reading *Romola* in colonial India or Australia or Canada. A syllabus that captures this expanse might begin with readings and research assignments on the transatlantic circulations of American and British writers and then pursue those writers across the British Empire and the global Anglophone print world from Australia and the Indian subcontinent to Africa and South America. With online databases, browsing periodicals around the nineteenth and early twentieth-century print world might be an assignment for a class in which students work in clusters around different continents. For example, the World Newspaper Archive includes 'African Newspapers' and

'Latin American Newspapers'. The online archive indicates the language of the periodical publication, the span of its run, and the location. Students can browse through issues of, say, the *Gold Coast Times* (1874–85) or the *Sierra Leone Weekly News* (1884–1922), or a bundle of Anglophone periodicals from Cape Town issued from 1831 to 1913. By reviewing the contents of these publications, we can discover which poems and serial novels travelled not only across the Atlantic Ocean between Britain and the United States, but also across many other borders. Emphasising the way print carried and readers read voraciously across the Atlantic and around the globe likewise poses intriguing parallels with our current networks of Internet circulations.

NOTES

1. Albert-László Barabási, *Linked: The New Science of Networks* (Cambridge: Perseus Publishing, 2002).
2. Ibid., pp. 61, 64.
3. Kirsten Jamsen, 'Voices Carry: Authorship, Community, and British and American Women's Advocacy Fiction, 1848–1876', PhD dissertation, University of Wisconsin-Madison, 1999.
4. Rebecca Soares, 'Literary Graftings: *The Bondwoman's Narrative* and the Nineteenth-Century Transatlantic Reader', *Victorian Periodicals Review*, 44: 1 (Spring 2011), 1–23.
5. Israel Zangwill, *The Children of the Ghetto*, ed. Meri-Jane Rochelson (Detroit, MI: Wayne State University Press, 1998), p. 502.
6. Jonathan Elmer, 'Questions of Archive and Method in Transatlantic Studies', *Victorian Studies*, 52 (Winter 2010), 251.
7. Cecilia Morgan, 'Rethinking Nineteenth-Century Transatlantic Worlds: With and Through "Indian Eyes"', *Victorian Studies*, 52 (Winter 2010), 258.
8. Elmer, 'Questions of Archive', 252.
9. William Wells Brown, *Three Years in Europe* (London: Charles Gilpin, 1852), p. 105.
10. G. C. Macaulay, 'Walt Whitman', *Nineteenth Century*, 12 (December 1882), 903.
11. Philip H. Bagenal, 'Uncle Pat's Cabin', *Nineteenth Century*, 12 (December 1882), 925.

CHAPTER 4

Rewriting the Atlantic: *Symbiosis*, 1997–2014

Christopher Gair

> I can't look at the English–American world or feel about them, any
> more, save as a big Anglo-Saxon total, destined to so much an amount
> of melting together that an insistence on their differences becomes
> more and more idle and pedantic; and that melting together will come
> the faster the more one takes it for granted and treats the life of the two
> countries as continuous or more or less convertible, or at any rate as
> simply different chapters of the same general subject. . . . I have not
> the slightest hesitation in saying that I aspire to write in such a way that
> it would be impossible to an outsider to say whether I am at a given
> moment an American writing about England or an Englishman writing
> about America (dealing as I do with both countries), and so far from
> being ashamed of such an ambiguity I should be exceedingly proud of
> it, for it would be highly civilised.
>
> Henry James (1888)[1]

In 'The Novel and the Middle Class in America' (1986), Myra Jehlen posits
a reading of nineteenth-century American literature that characterises it
through its difference from European realism. For Jehlen, 'in quintessentially
middle-class America the major authors . . . seem not to have written novels at
all'. Rather, they 'spun tales of extravagant individuals in flight to the wilderness and beyond', in marked contrast to European counterparts that 'explored
the lives of ordinary people at home'.[2] Jehlen's summary clearly points towards
the hyper-canon of nineteenth-century literature, and to figures such as Ahab,
Hester Prynne, Natty Bumppo, and Huck Finn, but – while her account of
the division between American romance and European novel sounds familiar
– there is a note of caution that questions the celebratory readings of the first
great wave of American Studies scholarship published during the 1950s and
1960s:

However far away into the wilderness American romances take us, ultimately they find it an impossible situation and, whether out of commitment or by default, lead us back to society. For the self-reliant individuals . . . all fail in the end to create their private worlds, and their failure sounds dire warnings of the dangers of isolation and solipsism.[3]

This danger, for Jehlen, is identifiable in what may be most recognisable to literary scholars as an Emersonian belief in the ultimate unity between self and society, in which (as Jehlen summarises) apparent contradictions are 'dissolved in that single higher Reality which is already complete and will in its own time manifest itself'.[4] Accordingly, any effort to take flight from society will inevitably result in defeat, such as Ahab's silent death or Hester's return to civilisation. In practical terms, for Jehlen, such an ideology can take hold because 'America' was built by the middle class in a way that they perceived 'not only as desirable but natural', with oppositional voices either appropriated into the hegemonic narrative or dismissed as residual traces of an old (European) order with no place in the New World.[5]

In contrast, in Europe, the rise of the novel corresponds with the emergence of middle-class hegemony and challenges to what had previously been seen as a natural order (shaped by church and monarchy), with the subsequent ongoing conflicts and realignments resulting in both personal and societal histories being understood as in permanent states of flux and lacking stable moorings. By extension, 'the protagonist of the European novel is born already an existential outsider . . . No longer able to identify with their society, in short, men and women in a bourgeois society identified themselves in terms of their existential distance from it.' Thus – and drawing on critics such as Raymond Williams and J. Hillis Miller – Jehlen asserts that the 'basic factor' in the European novel 'is the absence of transcendent order or unifying purpose in the novelist's bourgeois culture' that is in marked contrast to 'a contrary sense of order so pervasive as to seem inescapable that generated the American romance'.[6]

I cite Jehlen here not to suggest that her reading of the American Renaissance is necessarily 'wrong', or that it is an example of poor scholarship. Far from it: as an American Studies graduate student at the time, I recognised her essay and, more widely, *Ideology and Classic American Literature*, which Jehlen co-edited with Sacvan Bercovitch, as cutting-edge research (also widely used in the classroom) that applied sophisticated theoretical models – often based, ironically enough, on European theory – to question the assumptions underpinning a previous generation of American Studies scholarship. Rather, I refer to this piece to indicate how, as late as the mid-1980s, the Atlantic was habitually used to identify difference rather than continuity, national coherence rather than either internal dislocation or transnational connection. For

Jehlen, following many earlier critics, this point is a question of form as well as content: the American writers she examines (in particular, Hawthorne and Melville, with the possible exception of *Pierre*) are marked not only by the ways in which their protagonists seek (unsuccessfully) to disengage from American society, but also by the sense that their literary creations do not match the definitions of 'the novel' as it was understood in Europe in the nineteenth century. What strikes me now, re-reading the essay at a distance of more than a quarter of a century, is the extent to which an argument that appeared radically different at the time has come to bear striking resemblances to earlier criticism. While Jehlen's thesis revolves around class rather than myth and symbol, in terms of genre Jehlen is happy to accept the distinction drawn up by Hawthorne in his Preface to *The House of the Seven Gables* (1851), between the (European) novel and (American) romance, which was engrained in American literary scholarship with Richard Chase's *The American Novel and Its Tradition* (1957).[7] Ideologically, too, Jehlen's essay – while offering a radically different perspective – maintains Chase's separation of old and new worlds. For Chase, implicitly, this distinction is a matter of asserting the supremacy of American individualism at the height of the Cold War; for Jehlen, writing (as it transpired) near the end of the Cold War, it relates to the respective positions of the middle class in the United States and Europe, with the former depending, as outlined above, on an Emersonian 'identity of interest' between the individual and society and the latter 'born of the recognition that the individual is inevitably separate from society'.[8]

Of course, such an argument depends on where we look for examples: while it is hard to disagree with Jehlen's claims if we focus on the hyper-canon of American literature – Ishmael going to sea and returning to report on Ahab's silent death, Huck fleeing downriver before being reunited with Tom Sawyer (even if he vows to light out again at the end of *Adventures of Huckleberry Finn*) – the distinction is less clear in, for example, other writings by Melville and Twain. 'Bartleby, the Scrivener' (1853) and *Pudd'nhead Wilson* (1893), to paraphrase Jehlen's account of European realism, feature plots about 'ordinary people' (Bartleby in the lawyer's office, Wilson rooted in his adopted home) in which the leading characters are either marked through a fatal estrangement from an economically determined social order (Bartleby), or ensure that, in opposition to their avowed ideological beliefs, an oppressive and alienating social order based upon a system they despise is reinscribed (Wilson). Likewise, in *A Connecticut Yankee in King Arthur's Court* (1889), an extraordinary protagonist settles into comfortable married life only to re-emerge as the alienated progenitor of modern, technological genocide and victim of the quintessentially European conflict between old and new 'natural' orders. In a parallel challenge to the narrative proffered by Jehlen, an equally quintessential English protagonist, Martin Chuzzlewit, can only become an 'ordinary [person] at home' after he has experienced his own 'flight to the [American] wilderness and beyond', an instance of symbiotic encounter that facilitates one form of 'national' identity through the enactment of another.

While it seems more than coincidental that the transnational turn occurred soon after the collapse of the Soviet Bloc and the end of the Cold War, it would be a mistake to think that no critics (let alone writers of fiction) had understood the symbiotic relationship between old and new worlds before then. Although much American literary scholarship tends to emphasise the manner in which American literature both depended upon and disguised its indebtedness to European ideas, constantly manifesting anxiety about perceived inferiority, there is a parallel history running from the mid-nineteenth to the mid-twentieth centuries in which the hierarchy is challenged. While this is not the place for an extended reading of this current, I would like, briefly, to note two examples central to the thinking behind the launch of *Symbiosis* and to the concurrent emergence of curricular moves to engage with the transatlantic. In 'The Philosophy of Composition' (1846), Edgar Allan Poe – in an essay that combines an awareness of the economic obstacles to becoming a professional writer in the United States with a characteristically robust attack on the notion of specifically nationalistic definitions of authorship – uses what could be mistaken for a throwaway remark about Charles Dickens as the introduction to speculations on genre in which he cites *Robinson Crusoe* (1719) as an example of an occasion when a novel can achieve the effects more commonly generated from the successful short story. Poe thus refers to an early (and pre-national in the case of the United States) example of literary transnationalism that imagines a community of writers to complement his identification with Dickens as literary doubles, rather than as transatlantic rivals.

My second example comes from the middle of the twentieth century, at the very moment when Richard Chase, R. W. B. Lewis, Henry Nash Smith, Leo Marx, and others were publishing the myth/symbol studies that effectively founded American Studies as an academic discipline. Although, at the time, he received less attention (at least within the university sector), C. L. R. James was formulating a pioneering – and I use the word advisedly, if somewhat ironically – approach to the study of literature and culture that addressed the Atlantic and the nations on either side of it as radically entwined. As a Trinidadian who had moved to England in the early 1930s and lived in the United States for fifteen years from 1938 before being deported back to England, James was uniquely placed to develop such a methodology. In *Beyond a Boundary* (1963), he reflects on what he perceives to be his younger self's colonial subjectivity:

Me and my clippings and magazines on W. G. Grace, Victor Trumper and Ranjitsinhji, and my *Vanity Fair* and my puritanical view of the world . . . A British intellectual long before I was ten, already an alien in my own environment among my own people, even my own family.[9]

While James sees himself as a 'British intellectual', the interests and names he cites hardly place him as such at a moment long before popular culture became an acceptable subject of academic interest: the list of cricketers seems designed to call into question national stereotypes; Grace subverted the notion of the 'gentleman' amateur, taking centre stage in the transformation of cricket, and sport more generally, into popular culture and making a fortune while he did so; Trumper, the dashing Australian, whose sportsmanship and panache were more akin to prevailing notions of the English gentleman; and Ranji, the Indian prince who became a sporting hero as a member of the England cricket eleven, appropriating and adapting the colonists' game to assume a place at the high table of populist acclaim at the 'heart' of empire.

While James may not fully have recognised the significance of his early interests, the introduction to *Beyond a Boundary* demonstrates that, by the 1950s, he was theorising the (trans-)Atlantic in new ways. He recalls that, in 1952, he 'planned a series of books. The first was . . . a critical study of the writings of Herman Melville as a mirror of our age, and the second is this book on cricket.'[10] The key word here is 'series': *Mariners, Renegades and Castaways: Herman Melville and the World we Live In* (1953) was written as James's attempt to avoid deportation by demonstrating that his own values were more American than those of the men who would see him deported. And yet James's appeal to the Constitution seems uncannily close to an adherence to the laws of cricket, as internalised on the playing fields of his Trinidadian high school, itself based upon the English public school. In contrast, *Beyond a Boundary*, apparently a study of the quintessentially English game of the British empire, at times rewrites Herman Melville – and, in particular, his band of transnational 'mariners, renegades and castaways' – as a way of understanding the hierarchies inherent to cricket and the English class system.[11]

Myra Jehlen's reconstruction of 'classic' American literature was part of what, with hindsight, seems like a late effort – following both the myth/symbol approaches of the 1950s and 1960s and the multiculturalism that interrogated it increasingly from the 1970s – to insist upon categorisation, whether by nation, genre, race, or other typology. As I have noted above, *Ideology and Classic American Literature* was a key classroom text for educators seeking to challenge foundational American Studies narratives that still held considerable currency in the 1980s, despite challenges from multiculturalism, women's studies, and other revisionist accounts of the United States and its literature that had proliferated in the 1970s. While lack of space prevents a full discussion of the reasons for this enduring legacy, one factor would seem to be a long-standing suspicion of 'theory' that marked American Studies as very different from, for example, English Literature departments of the time. While a full understanding of this suspicion would require an essay of its own, I suggest that the explanation may largely be seen through an extension of the Emersonian legacy of (individual and national) self-reliance from nineteenth-century literature into the Cold War era studies of that literature. My own interests at the time (determined, perhaps, by a first degree in English Literature and graduate work in American Studies) were persuading me to question and challenge these structures in ways that led directly to an investigation of 'the transatlantic' and ultimately to *Symbiosis*. A Master's dissertation on Jack Kerouac was the first stage in what has become a lengthy (if occasional) engagement with the paradoxical question of how a writer so quintessentially 'American' – in terms, for example, of myth/symbol focus on landscape, the individual, and the quest – could simultaneously articulate ideas that not only stemmed, for him, from his French-Canadian heritage (and a concomitant sense of alienation from United States culture), but also resonated so closely when adapted to other cultural and historical circumstances, for example by Lefteris Poulios and other Greek poets writing during the dictatorship of 1967–74. In some ways, such questions mirror the work of Amy Kaplan in *The Anarchy of Empire in the Making of U.S. Culture* (2002) and Paul Giles in *Virtual Americas* (2002). For Kaplan, 'domestic metaphors of national identity are intimately intertwined with renderings of the foreign and the alien'. Thus Kaplan is more concerned with the relationships between nation and empire: for example, her analysis of W. E. B. Du Bois's account of the 1917 East St Louis race riots examines the 'shared racial identity' that took shape through 'the parallel experience of violent dislocations and exploited labor' at home and abroad and demonstrates how the riots are manifestations not only of Southern history, but also 'as part of the world history of a global economic system'.[12]

Applying a more specifically transatlantic gaze, Giles, following Jean Baudrillard, argues that 'American studies should be seen as involving not just domestic agendas, but also the points of intersection and crossover where the United States interfaces with the wider world'.[13] Although Giles does not discuss him, Kerouac serves as a perfect example of such crossover: while early Kerouac scholars tended to emphasise the significance of the American genealogies of Thomas Wolfe, Walt Whitman, and Herman Melville, or of bebop and Charlie Parker, Kerouac did nothing to disguise the fact that Proust and Joyce were of equal importance in the development of his spontaneous prose. Indeed, Kerouac's writings seem, in many ways, to exemplify Giles's claim that 'a virtual American studies should be organised around a more general idiom of dislocation and estrangement, serving to interrogate not only the boundaries of the nation-state, but also the particular values associated explicitly or implicitly with it'.[14]

Likewise, my doctoral thesis on naturalism and Jack London led me to question both the manner in which genre was theorised and, via London, how national literary genealogies were imagined. Examinations of naturalism in the 1980s typified the efforts to categorise or catalogue that I highlighted above, as well as the problems inherent to such efforts: among others, June Howard, Walter Benn Michaels, and Lee Clark Mitchell produced important studies that read the genre through market relations and the culture of consumption, through class, and through its stress on determinism.[15] While it is unsurprising that naturalism should have received such attention at a time when Thatcherism and Reaganomics were fostering displays of extreme wealth and forms of class conflict and inequality reminiscent of naturalism's zenith in the 1890s, the fact that none of the studies could construct models where discontinuity and disjunction did not seep through the cracks seemed to highlight the need to look at these instances of dislocation rather than insist upon coherence.

Jack London became, for me, the pivotal figure in this investigation: like Kerouac, London has been slotted neatly into myth/symbol accounts of American literary history, with his tales of men (and dogs) in the Klondike or at sea being used to exemplify the ongoing relevance of the frontier in American history, after Frederick Jackson Turner had famously declared it 'closed'. In such readings, new frontiers continue to serve as spaces where a particular form of individualistic American masculinity can be constructed. Equally, however, London sought an ideology drawn from Friedrich Nietzsche and Herbert Spencer on the one hand, and Karl Marx on the other, a fusion of superman and international socialism that used European theory to imagine a new world (rather than national) order. While London's proclivity for self-contradiction could be seen as the legacy of Emerson and Whitman, it also positioned London as a writer with a disdain for the regional or the national, a descendant of Poe who challenged political, generic, and spatial boundaries determined by Atlantic division.[16] London's moments of radical dislocation of plot, such as the apparently arbitrary loss of a sledge and its men or an encounter with a lifeboat in the middle of the ocean, seem, in this regard, to be entirely logical instances of the sorts of rupture and discontinuity that were frequently overlooked by critics and may help to explain why, despite the 'American-ness' of much of his writing, he was so often written out of literary histories and anthologies attempting to instil what Giles concisely summarises as the 'mythic integrity and interdisciplinary coherence that gave [American Studies] its methodological rationale during its nationalist heyday of the 1950s and 1960s'.[17]

THE LAUNCH OF *SYMBIOSIS*

The concerns surveyed above were very much in my mind when, in 1995, Richard Gravil and I were preparing the first (1997) volume of *Symbiosis*.

Despite our backgrounds in very different areas and periods, we agreed upon the need to insist on certain key issues. First, while the title referred to 'Anglo-American Literary Relations', the journal was designed to serve a doubly symbiotic purpose, also challenging the separation of research and teaching. The publication of the journal's first issue took place in the same year as the launch of a Master's in Anglo-American Literary Relations at the College of St Mark and St John, Plymouth, UK, where we both then worked. The two were conceived as interconnected in that the former was intended to publish innovative and theoretically informed essays that, while delivering complex and often challenging and unfamiliar readings of (generally) much-studied texts, were written in accessible fashion and free from what we perceived to be the jargon-laden material that formed much of what was then being published in other journals. This was not because we were 'anti-theory' in the manner of much of the history of American Studies scholarship. Far from it: we sought essays that were informed by theory, but which articulated ideas in a way that encouraged students to explore new alignments that challenged not only preconceptions about literary nationalism, but also the relationship between this and how literature was defined and understood within different cultures, moments, and spaces.

One consequence of the creation of the journal – and one that seemed particularly apt, given the ideological imperative that underpinned the project – was that we quickly 'discovered', or helped to define, a transatlantic community that had not previously been widely recognised as anything more than a group of like-minded individuals. As we approached potential contributors to the first volume, we realised that, far from being isolated voices striving to be heard in academic cultures still dominated by narratives framed around national tropes, Susan Manning, Robert Weisbuch, Ian F. A. Bell, Robert D. Richardson, David Murray, Fiona Green, and others were already producing a sizeable canon of transatlantic research, and that they were also considering how best to adapt teaching to accommodate their ideas. The first volume also demonstrated that interest in Anglo-American literary relations was not confined to a particular period: while my expectation had been that the overwhelming majority of submissions would be addressing Romanticism and Transcendentalism, or the long nineteenth century, it quickly became apparent that both earlier and later periods (alongside many studies of writing by women, members of ethnic minorities, and other frequently marginalised groups) were generating substantial research and teaching interests and that, while a trans-historical narrative would miss the significance of cultural realignment, attempts to posit or define a historically limited account of literary connections would be equally unsuccessful.

In the editorial to the first issue, we suggested that *Symbiosis* should be a 'forum in which specialists in Anglophone literature can explore the links and associations and influences and collaborations and competition between writers in English on both sides of the Atlantic', making the claim that 'Few writers in the Americas or the British Isles have worked without an alert awareness of what was being done and written on the other side of the water.' We felt, however, that these connections had too often been overlooked because the 'system of academic disciplines has resulted in the training of professional readers whose literary horizons frequently coincide with national boundaries'.[18] Again, this claim was also based upon experience in the classroom, where American and English literatures, for example, were traditionally taught separately.

While I would not go so far as Henry James, who in the epigraph to this essay writes to his brother William that he would treat the 'life of the two countries as continuous or more or less convertible, or at any rate as simply different chapters of the same general subject', the notion that 'national' literature has been problematised through the study of transatlantic relations would now be taken as self-evident by most scholars. James's assertion that 'I have not the slightest hesitation in saying that I aspire to write in such a way that it would be impossible to an outsider to say whether I am at a given moment an American writing about England or an Englishman writing about America' is both hyperbolic and inconsistent with his approach to the majority of his fiction, yet it is also suggestive of more recent questions of literary voice. Jhumpa Lahiri's first novel, *The Namesake* (2003), has an American protagonist of Indian parents, who is named after a Russian novelist. Lahiri herself is of Bengali descent, but was born in London and lives in the United States. While Lahiri may be an unusual example, she is far from alone in drawing upon a range of ethnic, geographic, and cultural experiences in her writing, which challenges notions of what constitutes a national literature, or whether such a thing can be said to exist. More broadly, a case is often made for Canadian literature being significantly shaped by immigrant writers, and recent anthologies of Canadian literature generally stress the high percentage of material by non-native-born Canadians within their pages. Native-born American novelists now also routinely draw upon and re-imagine English literature, in ways that seem to follow the trajectory initiated by Poe in 'The Philosophy of Composition': Jonathan Franzen's *Freedom*, for example, utilises a quintessentially Dickensian structure of split narratives, disruption, character flaw and redemption, and structural resolution to represent contemporary American life without feeling any need to signpost what seems taken for granted as a transatlantic genealogy. While both *The Namesake* and *Freedom* may be relatively 'obvious' examples of (different kinds of) literary exchange, the degree to which each text manifests a 'surface' transnationalism allows them to serve as ideal introductions to classes where students can probe the more deeply embodied relations and dislocations identifiable in works that have previously been catalogued within this or that national canon, especially where – as with Dickens or Hawthorne, for example – an identification of author and nation has become so deeply engrained. These challenges to the notion of what constitutes national literature have certainly been foregrounded in the pages of *Symbiosis*, not only in individual essays, but also through the exponential increase in proposals for special issues. It now seems self-evident that we should be talking in terms of transatlantic literatures (for *Symbiosis*, those written in English), rather than of a homogeneous transatlantic literature, and of the ways in which the transatlantic is as much of a contested space – culturally, generically, theoretically, etc. – as is the ground of any national literature.

Counter-intuitively, I now introduce students to discussion of Anglo-American literary relations with two studies that helped codify the national literary genealogies that became institutional orthodoxies for around half a century. F. R. Leavis commences *The Great Tradition* (1948) with the assertion that 'The great English novelists are Jane Austen, George Eliot, Henry James and Joseph Conrad', a list that, as students are quick to spot, contains two women, one American and one Russian-born Pole.[19] What may take slightly longer to answer is why James, who only became a British subject in 1915 (the year before his death), should be embraced by the creators of the English literary canon when he has habitually been seen as problematic, or excluded altogether, from the American counterpart. Likewise, the absence of any 'genuine' white English males from Leavis's list, alongside the presence of Austen and Eliot, leads to discussion of the ways in which early canon-construction in the United States focused almost entirely around white males and more or less systematically devised criteria for determining literary value that would exclude other groups.[20] In *American Renaissance* (1941), F. O. Matthiessen is primarily concerned with literary value, and his understanding of what this entails is at the heart of his construction of American literature through a study of 'our past masterpieces'. Matthiessen makes clear from the outset that his study is of the 'best books . . . in accordance with the enduring requirements for great art'.[21] Again, most classes will quickly pick up on the presumptions that Matthiessen brings to his work and the tensions that emerge. It is apparent that Matthiessen is at one with Hawthorne's well known condemnation of the 'damned mob of scribbling women', and he observes that 'Such material still offers a fertile field for the sociologist and for the historian of our taste' – but not for the student of great art.[22] Yet what is also apparent is the tension between an insistence on 'our' literature (that is American literature) and the prevailing belief in a universal understanding of what constitutes 'great' art and what is beneath the gaze of the true literary critic. As with my introductory comments on Myra Jehlen's reconceptualisation of American literature in the 1980s, I cite Leavis and Matthiessen not because their works are 'wrong', but because they are masterpieces of their time. Scholars should continue to learn from each, even while we question some of their central premises. What is more important, however – at least, if we want our students to think beyond national paradigms – is the degree to which establishing a dialogue between two foundational constructs of national literary genealogy can facilitate our own understanding of the transnational circulation of 'British' and 'American' literature.

NOTES

1. Henry James to William James, 29 October 1888, in Percy Lubbock (ed.), *The Letters of Henry James*, 2 vols (London: Macmillan, 1913), vol. 1, p. 143.
2. Myra Jehlen, 'The Novel and the Middle Class in America', in Sacvan Bercovitch and Myra Jehlen (eds), *Ideology and Classic American Literature* (Cambridge: Cambridge University Press, 1986), p. 125.
3. Ibid., p. 125.
4. Ibid., p. 131.
5. Ibid., p. 127.
6. Ibid., pp. 128–9.
7. Hawthorne, in his preface to *The House of the Seven Gables* (1851), seems to anticipate much of the American studies scholarship of a century later in explaining the reasons for calling his longer works 'romances' rather than 'novels'. In drawing the distinction, Hawthorne argues that the dominant European form of storytelling – the realist novel – is unsuitable to American needs. While Dickensian realism, for example, depended upon the complex and multi-layered class relations, urban geography, and political and legal intrigue stemming from hundreds of years of history, the relatively new and egalitarian nation, which lacked such self-evident complexities, demanded a different form. Hawthorne explains that the writer of a romance should 'claim a certain latitude, both as to its fashion and material' not available to the novelist. To discover the truths of the 'new' nation, Hawthorne felt it necessary to look beneath the surface, and to apply the powers of the imagination to the bare bones of historical detail. Unlike in the old world, where exteriors presented the realities of individual and social identity, Hawthorne argued that in the United States the potential of the nation – the self-reliance that he called the 'truth of the human heart' – could only be presented 'under circumstances . . . of the writer's own choosing or creation', through the use of symbolism and allegory. Nathaniel Hawthorne, *The House of the Seven Gables*, ed. Fredson Bowers (Columbus, OH: Ohio State University Press, 1965), p. 1.
8. Jehlen, 'The Novel and the Middle Class in America', pp. 130–1.

9. C. L. R. James, *Beyond a Boundary* (London: Serpent's Tail, 1994), p. 18.
10. Ibid., p. 19.
11. For a detailed examination of James as proto-transnational subject, see Christopher Gair, 'Beyond Boundaries: Cricket, Herman Melville, and C. L. R. James's Cold War', *Symbiosis*, 6: 2 (October 2002), 159–77.
12. Amy Kaplan, *The Anarchy of Empire in the Making of U.S. Culture* (Cambridge, MA: Harvard University Press, 2002), pp. 4, 202.
13. Paul Giles, *Virtual Americas: Transnational Fictions and the Transatlantic Imaginary* (Durham, NC: Duke University Press, 2002), p. 283. *Virtual Americas* is the second of Giles's three interconnected studies of transatlantic literary relations, which remain the most sustained single-author attempt to theorise the literary Atlantic. Also see *Transatlantic Insurrections: British Culture and the Formation of American Literature, 1730–1860* (Philadelphia: University of Pennsylvania Press, 2001) and *Atlantic Republic: The American Tradition in English Literature* (Oxford: Oxford University Press, 2006).
14. Giles, *Virtual Americas*, p. 284.
15. See June Howard, *Form and History in American Literary Naturalism* (Chapel Hill, NC: University of North Carolina Press, 1985); Walter Benn Michaels, *The Gold Standard and the Logic of Naturalism* (Berkeley: University of California Press, 1987); and Lee Clark Mitchell, *Determined Fictions: American Literary Naturalism* (New York: Columbia University Press, 1989).
16. Of course, I do not wish to suggest that London always sought to dissolve such boundaries. At times, his fictions insist upon Anglo-Saxon supremacy, or undermine it; they contain moments of chest-thumping American nationalism and instances of collective, working-class resistance to national typing.
17. Giles, *Virtual Americas*, p. 7.
18. Chris Gair and Richard Gravil, 'From the Editors', *Symbiosis*, 1: 1 (April 1997), 2.
19. F. R. Leavis, *The Great Tradition: George Eliot, Henry James, Joseph Conrad* (Harmondsworth: Penguin, 1986), p. 9.
20. See the chapters by Susan Griffin and Sandra Zagarell in this collection for related comments.
21. F. O. Matthiessen, *American Renaissance: Art and Expression in the Age of Emerson and Whitman* (Oxford: Oxford University Press, 1941), pp. vii, xi.
22. Ibid., pp. x–xi.

PART II

Organising Curriculum Through Transatlantic Lenses

CHAPTER 5

Anthologising and Teaching Transatlantic Romanticism[1]

Chris Koenig-Woodyard

> Anthologies are shaped by pedagogies, and pedagogies are shaped by anthologies.
>
> Jeffrey Di Leo[2]

The chiastic phrasing of Jeffrey Di Leo's comment in the introduction to the 2004 collection *On Anthologies: Politics and Pedagogy* captures the choreography of literary canonisation. Do readers or anthologists lead in the cultural and intellectual dance that sees literary works selected for inclusion in an anthology? Lisa Berglund imagines one version of this scenario when she pictures the optimistic course instructor who aspires to be an anthologist; she imagines that John Mullan and Christopher Reid, the editors of *Eighteenth-Century Popular Culture: A Selection*, 'collected [and taught] these materials over a number of years' until 'they had gathered enough supplemental material to fill a book – and lo! achieving the fantasy of English instructors the world over, their combined course supplements became a handsomely printed volume from a renowned academic press'.[3] George P. Landow, on the other hand, elegises this proto-anthology, culturally censuring the course pack as it agglomerates selections from other sources:

> Since the invention of xerography, instructors . . . have increasingly cobbled together their own anthologies of reading material . . . These cobbled-together non-books assemble collections of texts in different typefaces, design, reference conventions, and even page orientation. Such on-demand compilations play an increasing role in the reading experiences of many young adults today, and to them the book has lost both most of its aesthetic stature and its sense of solidity and permanence.[4]

I disagree. Following the discussion of his undergraduate books in a wider conversation on the role of hypermedia in literary studies, Landow's comments are informed by a biblio-nostalgia that minimises the value of course packs. A synecdoche for an anthology, the course pack has the potential to serve as the site for the critical investigation of a range of canonical and pedagogical issues: the course pack and anthology are both lenses through which to consider the history and sociology of anthologisation and, ultimately, the institutionalisation of literary studies.

More than an expedient pedagogical tool that facilitates course instruction, a course pack is the front line for canon challenge and transformation. Writing in 1996, Landow's course pack with its Frankenstein-like typography simply does not apply in 2014. In a post-PDF age (Adobe widely released its Portable Document Format in 2008) the photocopied monstrosity of aggregated grainy and mismatched pages is itself a relic. Rather, the bibliographical and intellectual conversation that a course pack – whether print, digital, or a mix – inserts itself into necessarily calls for an examination of canonical paradigms, curricular conventions, and the editorial philosophies and practices of the anthologisation of English-language literary history. Compiling a course pack is a metonymic critical performance that interrogates and transmogrifies the canon as a constituent part of a larger historical and cultural dialogue about literary studies and the university.

As the subject of literary analysis, the anthology allows for the grammatological cartography of all literary studies from the Middle Ages to the present day. My essay, however, focuses on Romanticism and in particular on my experiences teaching a senior undergraduate seminar on Transatlantic Romanticism in 2004–5. In the seminar, the twenty-five students and I explored 'Romanticism' as a cognitive literary and cultural field that is constructed in a wide range of literary collections, anthologies, and miscellanies from the 1790s to the present day. We deconstructed the course anthologies that I had assigned to represent American, British, and Canadian literature from the late eighteenth to the nineteenth century in order to postulate a Transatlantic Romantic period; this, in turn, framed our discussions of the historical anthologisation of Romanticism. Our work in the seminar ran in parallel to my work with Joel Pace and Lance Newman as the three of us compiled *Transatlantic Romanticism: An Anthology of American, British and Canadian Literature, 1767–1867* for publication in December 2006.[5] These parallel yet interwoven editorial and pedagogical projects situate Robert Scholes's 'canon of methods' as a grammatology for the transatlanticisation of British Romanticism.[6]

The healthy professional fantasy of transforming a course pack into a well-received anthology is partially fuelled by Sarah Lawall's suggestion that the anthology is 'a theoretically interesting form whose potential for opening up discourse has yet to be sufficiently explored'.[7] In a discussion of the challenges of editing an anthology of critical theory, David Downing expresses this tension between the traditional and the pioneering – the friction between idea and praxis that Lawall has in mind:

> Every contemporary anthology of theory confronts an institutional double bind: they must inevitably do two things at once, both of which are mutually contradictory. On the one hand, many of the *theoretical* essays included in the *anthology* tend to challenge, cross or disrupt disciplinary borders; on the other, *anthologizing* itself cannot avoid its essentially disciplinary function. Much of what counts for *theoretical* discourse implicitly, if not explicitly, offers a critique of traditional academic disciplines.[8]

Downing's chiastic phrasing expands Di Leo's waltzing 'anthologies and pedagogies/pedagogies and anthologies'. Indeed, the critical trivium of anthologies, pedagogy, and theory conveys a historical sense of the emergence of the shared cultural, social, and aesthetic values that superintend literary studies throughout the nineteenth and twentieth centuries. To teach and anthologise transnationally, however, is to transgress the thresholds of the disciplinary, curricular, and employment confines that have governed literary studies, English departments, and the academic job market since World War II. The anthology is a transformative tool for canon expansion, and I would argue that a historical understanding of the anthology as an object of literary study instructively guides our understanding of the pedagogical and intellectual forces that shape 'university studies' and the sub-genre 'anthology studies': the rise of theory since World War II, the canon wars of the 1980s, and the rise of the computer and digital humanities.[9] The course pack (and its matriculated sibling the anthology) puts into practice the 'grammatological pedagogy' that Gregory L. Ulmer argues for in *Applied Grammatology: Post(e)-Pedagogy from Jacques Derrida to Joseph Beuys*.[10]

A grammatological pedagogy explores the educative as textual as it probes the logo-centric strictures that shape surrounding intellectual, historical, and cultural contexts. If the pedagogical is textual, as Ulmer argues,

> the assumption guiding a semiotic pedagogy is that a 'professor is the faithful transmitter of a tradition and the worker of a philosophy in the process of formation' [*La carte postale: De Socrate à Freud et au-delà* (76)], with the latter notion – *the classroom as a place of invention rather than of reproduction* – being the attitude of grammatology.[11]

Such a transformative pedagogy centres on 'change rather than . . . reproduction [and] would seize upon the irreducibility of the medium to the message (apropos of education as a form of communication) as the point of departure for its program'.[12] A grammatological pedagogy drives centrifugally against the centripetal forces of patriarchal aesthetics and traditions – the Althusserian Ideological State Apparatuses (educational, political, cultural, and theological) that socialise and homogenise an intellectual and cultural civility under the guise of consensus.[13] It engages in the procedural shift required for the revitalised understanding of literary studies that Robert Scholes calls for in *The Rise and Fall of English: Reconstructing English as a Discipline*, where he urges literary scholars

> to replace the canon of texts with a canon of methods – to put a modern equivalent of the medieval trivium at the center of English education . . . I mean a canon of methods to be used in studying three aspects of textuality: how to situate a text (history), how to compose one (production) and how to read (consumption).[14]

The anthology offers a compelling framework in which, as Ulmer describes it, to 'take up the implications of deconstruction for an institutional critique'.[15] Anthologies merit study in their own right as grammatological artifacts freighted with multiple cultural discourses – discourses that can be approached along the multi-lane hermeneutic avenue of pedagogy, cultural studies, postcolonial studies, comparative literature, Marxism, feminism, and bibliography and the sociology of text.

My own commitment to helping create such an anthology arose from a highly specific transatlantic textual exchange. My formative transatlantic spot of time occurred while, in the late 1990s, I wrote a Doctor of Philosophy thesis at Oxford on the nineteenth-century transmission and reception of Samuel Taylor Coleridge's 'Christabel' (1816). Following the poem's May 1816 publication in London, *Christabel: Kubla Khan, a Vision; The Pains of Sleep* was printed that summer in Boston. This speedy American pirated publication wove a transatlantic thread into the already intricate tapestry of the British transmission and reception history of the poem, in which the poem was twice orphaned from anthologies: Wordsworth removed it from the 1800 *Lyrical Ballads* for reasons of aesthetic friction because Coleridge's gothic histrionics abraded his rustic pastoralism; and in late 1799, Coleridge demurred publication in Robert Southey's 1800 *Annual Anthology*, fearing that readers would dismiss it as 'extravagant ravings'.[16] 'Christabel' is a compelling case of the Romantic attitudes about organicism that Neil Fraistat discusses in *The Poem and the Book: Interpreting Collections of Romantic Poetry*. He argues that individual texts and the volumes they appear in participate in a delicate bibliographical, thematic, and ideological dance of (dis)organisation.[17] 'Christabel', then, first framed my current interests in the aesthetics, politics, and economics of literary collections, on the one hand, and Transatlantic Romanticism on the other.

As my research perspective on Romanticism widened from the British to the transatlantic following completion of the Doctor of Philosophy in 2001, I was eager to teach a course in transatlantic literature. In a senior undergraduate seminar on Transatlantic Romanticism in 2004–5, twenty-five students and I explored intersections of Romanticism and anthologies as we studied thematic clusters of American, British, and Canadian authors and texts. The syllabus was gestural. It functioned diachronically and synchronically with initial readings arranged historically by authors' birth dates (then by composition and publication dates) that morphed, in the second term, into thematic clusters. It was as much a course in 'syllabus studies' as it was in 'anthology studies' (and by extension 'university studies').[18] Any course that posits the transatlantic or transnational as a field of study must imbricate into the fabric of the syllabus, lectures, class discussions, and student assignments an awareness of the intellectually fluid centre and circumference of such an endeavour.

Two anthologies formed the core of the seminar – the second edition of the *Longman Anthology of British Literature* (*The Romantics and Their Contemporaries*) edited by Peter Manning and Susan Wolfson (2002) and the fourth edition of *The Heath Anthology of American Literature* with an editorial team led by Paul Lauter (2002).[19] I also included a paper-based course pack of nineteenth- and twentieth-century articles from the mid-1990s to 2004 that examined Romanticism and the anthology as a genre. Accompanying these were general introductions, tables of contents, and individual author and text selections from many nineteenth- and twentieth-century anthologies. (For a list of these anthologies updated to 2014, see Appendix A on the Teaching Transatlanticism website).

While this time period, roughly the mid-1990s to 2004, was personally formative for me, it was during this decade that British Romanticists inaugurated a public and critical conversation about anthologies of their period. At the 1996 Modern Language Association convention, for instance, one session considered 'Anthologizing Romantic-Era Writing: Shaping the Canon for the Commercial Marketplace'. Led by Susan Wolfson, the round table discussed technology, multiculturalism, pedagogical practices, and marketplace issues, and consisted of a number of prominent editors of Romantic anthologies: Wolfson with Peter J. Manning – the Longman *Romantics*; Jerome J. McGann – *The New Oxford Book of Romantic Period Verse*; Jack Stillinger – *John Keats: Complete Poems* and several editions of *The Norton Anthology of English Literature*; Anne K. Mellor and Richard Matlak – the Harcourt Brace *British Literature 1780–1830*; and Duncan Wu – the Blackwell *Romanticism: An Anthology*. A special issue of *Romanticism on the Net* in 1997, edited by

Laura Mandell, entitled 'Canons Die Hard: A Review of the New Romantic Anthologies', continued the MLA conversation.[20]

These conversations about Romantic anthologisation in 1996–7 were part of a larger discussion in the late 1990s and early 2000s. The canon wars of the 1980s shaped the publication of anthologies that deployed culturally informed editorial models designed to challenge existing disciplinary consensus. The publication of the *Heath Anthology of American Literature* in 1990 and the *Norton Anthology of Theory and Criticism* in 2001, in particular, alongside a wave of 'World Literature' anthologies, informed the educative and editorial environment of my Transatlantic Romanticism seminar.[21] Our discussions in the seminar were informed by a series of journal issues devoted to the anthology, Romanticism and the Transatlantic:

- a 1997 issue (7) of *Romanticism on the Net* [later *Romanticism and Victorianism on the Net*] on 'Canons Die Hard: A Review of the New Romantic Anthologies';
- a 1998 issue (48–9) of *The Minnesota Review* on 'The Academics of Publishing';
- a 2000 issue (11.1) of the *European Romantic Review* on 'The Romantic Century';
- a 2000 issue (8.1–2) of *Symplokē* on 'Anthologies';
- a 2003 issue (66.2) of *College English*, with a 'Symposium: Editing a Norton Anthology';
- a 2003 issue (3.3) of *Pedagogy* on 'the construction and use of the literary anthology'; and
- a 2003 issue (11.1–2) of *Symplokē*, with a forum on the *Norton Anthology of Theory and Criticism*.

We also read from Di Leo's collection of essays *On Anthologies: Politics and Pedagogy*, which reprints many of the essays from *Symplokē* and *College English*.

These course readings offered a framework in which to think historically, pedagogically, and anthologically about British and transatlantic Romanticism, and the arc of the seminar was shaped by ongoing conversations about periodisation and national canonisation. Our point of departure was William Keach's call for a radically expanded Romantic period in a 2000 article entitled 'A Transatlantic Romantic Century':

> The grounds on which we claim the continuing relevance and coherence of a 'romantic century' need to be transatlantic . . . If thinking transatlantically about romanticism consolidates by expanding the contours and content of the 'romantic century,' it also raises new questions about when we understand this century to begin and end.

1750–1850, or more flexibly the 1750s to the 1850s, makes sense within an exclusively British literary frame of reference . . . When we take in American developments, however, we should want to extend into the 1860s to connect Blake on the American Revolution . . .[22]

Keach's transatlantic romantic century, from 1750 to 1865 (the date of the thirteenth amendment to the US constitution), is provocative, but the students and I decided that Keach's temporalisation of the period along transatlantic lines is framed by a restrictive bi-national model. Where did we fit? Where did Canadian literature fit in? We were, after all, Canadians studying at a Canadian university. We argued that a truly transatlantic Romantic period would include Britain, and North and South America, even Africa, and decided that if Keach's century extended from 1750 to 1865, it could inch forward two years in order to cover a decisive moment in British and North American political history: the confederation of Canada in 1867.[23]

With 1867 in mind, we turned to the politician, poet and journalist Thomas D'arcy McGee (1825–68) and his address that year to the Montreal Literary Club entitled 'The Mental Outfit of the New Dominion' for an assessment of the state of Canadian literature. As McGee notes 'Our reading supplies are . . . drawn chiefly from two sources; first, books, which are imported from the United States, England and France'.[24] But as he argues for the origins of a national corpus of Canadian literature in periodicals, he rendered our 117-year Romantic period problematic: 'Thirty years ago a *British Quarterly Review* asked: "Who reads an American book?" . . . Those Americans might, in turn, taunt us to-day with "Who reads a Canadian book?" I should answer frankly, very few, for Canadian books are exceedingly scarce'.[25] This highlights the difficulty of expanding Keach's bi-national 115-year century to include Canada – or for that matter to include French and Hispanic literature in Quebec, Mexico, and South America. As an aesthetic movement of shared literary, cultural and political sensibilities (interests in nature, the self, the creative process and imagination, human and gender rights, and political and literary revolutions), Romanticism necessarily periodises differently according to the three countries' radically different histories. In defining the temporal boundaries of Romanticism, then, the students and I were experiencing an orismological and epistemological problem with the fundamental practices of literary scholarship: what is Romanticism? How do we define Romanticism in each of these nations? And, moreover, how do we define nationality – when 'nation' is a fluid construct and many of our authors were residents of all three countries at various points in their lives?

To periodise Romanticism along a transatlantic tri-national model would call for an expansion of the 117-year century framed by 1750 to 1867. A vast majority of Canadian writers that display a Romantic sensibility were born in the 1860s and did not publish until the 1880s.[26] Dubbed the 'Poets of Confederation' by Malcolm Ross in his 1960 anthology *Poets of the Confederation*, Charles G. D. Roberts (1860–1943), Bliss Carman (1861–1929), Archibald Lampman (1861–99), and Duncan Campbell Scott (1862–1947) extended our Transatlantic Romantic period well into the twentieth century.[27]

This longer Transatlantic Romantic period allowed us to accommodate what we came to think of as the echoic structure of Romanticism: the literary, cultural and political sensibilities of British Romanticism (1789–1832) reflected in the American Romantic period (1830s–60s) and, with a slightly longer delay, in the literature of the Confederation in Canada (1867–1900). Given the passing of Roberts and Lampman in the 1940s, our Transatlantic Romantic period would have to extend from 1750 to the mid-twentieth century. For instance, in order to capture the sound of Canadian frogs responding to British birds, we spanned from Keats' 'Ode to a Nightingale' (1819) and Shelley's 'To a Skylark' (1820) to Lampman's sonnet sequence 'The Frogs' (1888) and continued further to an encomium like Duncan Campbell Scott's 'Ode for the Keats Centenary', 'Where the loon laughs and diving takes' and should with the

> Spirit of Keats, unfurl thy wings,
> Far from the toil and press,
> [And] Teach us by these pure-hearted things,
> Beauty in loneliness.[28]

Published in 1921 for the centenary of Keats' death, Scott's poem framed a 171-year transatlantic Romantic period (1750–1921). The issue of periodisation, however, did not end in the seminar: as Joel, Lance, and I were compiling *Transatlantic Romanticism: An Anthology of American, British and Canadian Literature, 1767–1867* for publication with Longman in 2006, our Romantic century expanded to 186 years (framed by the 1757 publication of Edmund Burke's *A Philosophical Enquiry into the Origin of Our Ideas of the Sublime and Beautiful* and the 1943 publication of Lampman's sonnet 'Temagami').

In this critical framework in which the students and I had reconfigured the relationship of three national literatures through the lens of our historical understanding of Romantic anthologisation and current debates about anthologies, Romanticism, and the transatlantic, we discussed whether a logical pedagogical component of our seminar was our co-production of an anthology. Based on my experience in two previous courses in which I did not set any or all of the texts and the students and I collaboratively compiled course readers, I argued that we could do the work of anthologists without producing an anthology. I described two experiences to students in which the time-consuming efforts to anthologise in other courses threatened to submerge the educational

goals of the courses: the overwhelming amount of logistical time spent format-
ting and editing a glossary of 120 literary and rhetorical terms for a course on
rhetoric and the essay, and the building and coding of a wiki site for a course on
the 'Age of Sensibility'. Instead, with the paratextual machinery of the twenty-
first-century anthology and our deep historical reading of nineteenth- and
twentieth-century anthologies of Romanticism in mind, I devised a series of
assignments that considered the intersections of the anthology, the Romantic,
and the transatlantic – assignments that capture the work of an anthologist.

For both terms of the seminar, students were responsible for writing one
long essay (fifteen to thirty pages) or two short essays (ten to fifteen pages) on
topics that engaged transatlantic Romanticism and anthologisation. Students
wrote on matters such as the table of contents, the anthology introduction, and
footnotes (assignment descriptions for which can be found on the Teaching
Transatlanticism website), and on the headnote.

The headnote assignment yielded fascinating results, providing a keyhole
through which to consider all of the editorial and pedagogical issues that the
seminar was focused on. Most students used the 'Protocols for Anthology
Headnotes' that Vincent B. Leitch devised for the *Norton Anthology* of theory
in his 'Ideology of Headnotes' as a methodological staring point, often setting
them in comparison with Barbara Johnson's eight axioms.[29] In their comparison of headnote entries from the early to mid-twentieth century to the present
day, students argued for explicit and implicit patriarchal attitudes in the spirit
and letter of the headnotes. In hindsight, we were identifying the situation
with the 'bouncing wife' that Johnson writes of. In her fifth axiom, 'follow
the bouncing wife', Johnson discusses the difficulty of dividing 'sexuality and
intellectual work'.[30] Students observed how the biographies of male writers in
the early anthologies focused on their intellectual, political, and cultural work
and roles, with some mention of family and personal relationships. In contrast,
the order of details in the biography of female authors was often reversed, and,
if not, there was, generally, an emphasis on sexual relationships not seen in the
headnotes of male writers (with the exception of Byron). Even late twentieth-
century feminist anthologies showed the signs of the inertia of patriarchal
pressures on anthologisation – women were often presented in headnotes as
wives, mothers, and lovers before they were presented as writers and thinkers, thus rarely escaping the separate spheres ideology of the eighteenth and
nineteenth centuries.

In addition to Leitch's protocols and Johnson's axioms, students also
employed Laurie Finke's 'Observable features of the headnote' as a methodological framework in which to compare a number of different headnotes
on the same authors.[31] Drawing on all or any three theories of headnotes, students also explored the challenges that the transatlantic scope of our seminar
posed for the basic details of headnote writing. The students and I argued

Assignment 1: Headnotes. Long Essay – 15–30 pages.

A neighbor of the character sketch and the case study as well as
the short essay, the headnote aims to set up for the uninformed
student reader a reading experience to come. In seeking to direct
the reader, it typically links the text(s)-to-come with the author (a
biography), her or his other work (an oeuvre), and a tradition or set
of texts and topics defining a field of inquiry (a canon). The headnote
tends to foreground what is common knowledge to the specialist,
using a normative prose marked by accessibility, relative simplicity,
impartiality, that is, a certain kind of invisible ventriloquized
style. It is part of a project of enlightenment, clarification, and
demystification. Leitch, 'Ideology of Headnotes' (*Symplokē*, 178)[32]

Write an essay on the headnote as a genre. Headnotes, as we have discussed,
comprise an aggregate critical conversation in an anthology: are they
informational and historical, or interpretive? In addition to the biographical details of individual authors' lives, the combined headnotes (often in
conjunction with an anthology's other editorial paratexts – general introduction, thematic introductions, and text headnotes) argue for an editorial,
cultural, and historical position for an author or text. For this essay, in addition to discussing and comparing headnotes from our course anthologies, I
would like you to wade into the recent historiography on headnotes:

From Di Leo, *On Anthologies: Politics and Pedagogy*:
  (a) 'Headnote Disdain' (22–4)
  (b) Part 5 – Notes on Headnotes (373–410):
      (i)   Leitch, 'Ideology of Headnotes' (373–83)
      (ii)   Johnson, 'Headnotes' (384–94)
      (iii) Finke, 'The Hidden Curriculum' (395–404)
      (iv) McGowan, 'Headnotes, Headmasters, and the Pedagogical
           Imaginary' (405–9)

Three authors in Di Leo who discuss the headnote in the course of larger
discussions of the anthology are:
  (c) Damrosch, 'From the Old World to the New World' (31–46)
  (d) Lawall, 'Anthologizing "World Literature"' (47–89)
  (e) Z. Bloom, 'Once More to the Essay Canon' (90–111)

From *Symplokē*
  (f) Gerald Graff and Di Leo, 'Anthologies, Literary Theory and the
      Teaching of Literature: An Exchange' (113–28)[33]
  (g) Leitch, 'Ideology of Headnotes' (177–9)

for and against models in which an author's nationality was fixed or fluid, for instance. Simply, is nationality determined by one's country of birth or death, or by the length of residency in each of a number of countries? The answers to these questions had implications for other aspects of anthologisation: if a fixed, determinate mode of national identification was used, should this be systemised throughout the anthology on an organisational level? We collectively joked about whether or not a series of editorial emoticons or symbols could indicate nationality in the table of contents: an eagle for an American author, a beaver or maple leaf for a Canadian, and a Union Jack for a Brit.

Other assignments underscored similarly complex issues. For example, when students worked to produce a table of contents, they confronted key political and aesthetic questions highlighted by the shift from a single to a multinational model of Romanticism. The students came to see the value of a hybrid diachronic and synchronic table of contents, one that was organised temporally, following authors' birth and death dates, and within this structure, by date of publication. A linear diachronic structure was challenged by issues of transatlantic publication: that is, how could pirated editions of British works in North America be handled? Indeed, how could the cross-Atlantic appearance of all or portions of a text (in a review with lengthy extracts) be handled? Are such works to be given equal aesthetic and historical weight to the words penned by the composing authors?

Such questions had two theoretical consequences for the seminar: first, we had to confront basic orismological issues – those raised by postmodern theory – about the fundamental terminology of literary study. If early in the seminar we were asking ourselves what is 'Romanticism'? we were now asking what is a text? what is a work? – and is it comprised of all texts (or written and oral versions) composed by the originating or a pirating author? Students often argued for answers to these questions by forwarding a mixed diachronic and synchronic anthology organisation. The clusters of readings that highlighted a particular political or cultural issue (such as slavery and abolition, or gender, to name only two) that became increasingly common in anthologies from the late 1980s onward, as they employed a cultural studies methodology, were well suited to the representation of transatlantic issues – from the aesthetic to the political. Students argued for a wide range of synchronic sections: for instance, in transatlantic landscapes, from England, France, and Greece to Niagara Falls, the Grand Canyon, or sublime mountains (from the Alps to the Rockies).

The Transatlantic Romanticism seminar and the anthology assignments fashioned a concrete grammatological pedagogy that explored how anthology studies allowed us to recast (even historically recuperate) Romanticism as transatlantic. By pursuing our theoretical discussions of the anthology as a genre, and the effect this had on our understanding of institutional, political, and historical canons, we deconstructed our course anthologies as pedagogical, ideological, and bibliographic artifacts.[34] Our critical engagement with the machinery of anthologies naturally extended through a grammatological pedagogy that helped me to fashion assignments that performed Scholes' 'canon of methods'. Students composed portions of anthologies that, potentially, stand as preludes to future anthologies of literature of their own composition.

NOTES

1. An earlier version of this essay was presented in March 2010 at 'Anthologies: A Conference' (Trinity College, Hartford, Connecticut). I am indebted to Susan Belasco, Barbara Benedict, Paula Bennett, Lynn Bloom, Thora Brylowe, David Damrosch, Michael Gamer, Linck Johnson, Karen Kilcup, Paul Lauter, Robert Levine, Tom Mole, Cary Nelson and Jeff Williams for many stimulating conversations and presentations about anthologies and editing.

2. Jeffrey Di Leo, 'Analyzing Anthologies', in Jeffrey Di Leo (ed.), *On Anthologies: Politics and Pedagogy* (Lincoln, NE: University of Nebraska Press, 2004), pp. 1–2.

3. John Mullan and Christopher Reid (eds), *Eighteenth-Century Popular Culture: A Selection* (Oxford: Oxford University Press, 2000); Lisa Bergland, ' "Like the Pedant of Hierocles": Thoughts on the Present and Future of the Eighteenth-Century Studies Anthology', *Age of Johnson: A Scholarly Annual*, 15 (2004), 331–65.

4. George P. Landow, 'Twenty Minutes into the Future', in Geoffrey Nunberg (ed.), *The Future of the Book* (Berkeley: University of California Press, 1996), p. 211.

5. Lance Newman, Joel Pace, and Chris Koenig-Woodyard (eds), *Transatlantic Romanticism: An Anthology of American, British, and Canadian Literature 1767–1867* (New York: Longman, 2006).

6. See Paul Lauter, 'Teaching with Anthologies', *Pedagogy*, 3 (Fall 2003), 331.

7. Sarah Lawall, 'Anthologizing "World Literature" ', in Jeffrey R. Di Leo (ed.), *On Anthologies: Politics and Pedagogy* (Lincoln, NE: University of Nebraska Press, 2004), p. 47.

8. David B. Downing, 'The "Mop-up" Work of Theory Anthologies: Theorizing the Discipline and the Disciplining of Theory', *Symplokē: A Journal for the Intermingling of Theoretical, Literary, Cultural Scholarship*, 8: 1–2 (2000), 129 (emphasis added). See Barbara Benedict for a compelling argument about the eighteenth-century origins of theories and practices of anthologisation that touch on Downing's argument; Benedict,

'The Paradox on the Anthology: Collecting and Différence in Eighteenth-Century Britain', *New Literary History*, 43: 2 (2003), 231–56.

9. See Jeffrey Williams, 'Teach the University', *Pedagogy*, 8: 1 (Winter 2008), 25–42.

10. Gregory Ulmer, *Applied Grammatology: Post(e)-Pedagogy from Jacques Derrida to Joseph Beuys* (Baltimore: Johns Hopkins University Press, 1985), pp. 157–88.

11. Ibid., p. 163.

12. Ibid., p. 162.

13. See James Sosnoski, *Token Professionals and Master Critics: A Critique of Orthodoxy in Literary Studies* (Albany, NY: SUNY Press, 1994), pp. 3–30.

14. Robert Scholes, *The Rise and Fall of English: Reconstructing English as a Discipline* (New Haven, CT: Yale University Press, 1998), pp. 145–7.

15. Ulmer, *Applied Grammatology*, p. 159.

16. Samuel Taylor Coleridge, *Collected Letters of Samuel Taylor Coleridge*, ed. Earl Leslie Griggs, 6 vols (Oxford: Clarendon Press, 1956–71), vol. 1, p. 545.

17. Neil Fraistat, *The Poem and the Book: Interpreting Collections of Romantic Poetry* (Chapel Hill, NC: University of North Carolina Press, 1985), pp. 23–45.

18. John Guillory's 'pedagogic imagination' in *Cultural Capital* captures this claim succinctly: 'The literary syllabus is the institutional form by means of which this knowledge [of cultural capital] is disseminated.' See Guillory, *Cultural Capital: The Problem of Literary Canon Formation* (Chicago: University of Chicago Press, 1993), p. ix; see also pp. 28–38. A number of instructors put into practice Guillory's claim. See Beverley Peterson, 'Inviting Students to Challenge the American Literature Syllabus', *Teaching English in the Two Year College*, 28: 4 (May 2001), 379–82; Karen M. Cardozo, 'At the Museum of Natural Theory: The Experiential Syllabus (or, What Happens When Students Act Like Professors)', *Pedagogy*, 6: 3 (Fall 2006), 405–33; Lucy E. Bailey, 'The "Other" Syllabus: Rendering Teaching Politics Visible in the Graduate Pedagogy Seminar', *Feminist Teacher*, 20: 2 (2010), 139–56; and Stefanie Stiles, 'From "Representative" to Relatable: Constructing Pedagogical Canons Based on Student Ethical Engagement', *Pedagogy*, 13: 3 (Fall 2013), 487–503.

19. Peter Manning and Susan Wolfson (eds), *Longman Anthology of British Literature (The Romantics and Their Contemporaries)*, 2nd edn (New York: Longman, 2002); Paul Lauter et al., *The Heath Anthology of American Literature*, 4th edn (New York: Heath, 2002).

20. Laura Mandell (ed.), 'Canons Die Hard: A Review of the New Romantic Anthologies', *Romanticism on the Net*, 7 (August 1997), online at: <http://

www.erudit.org/revue/ron/1997/v/n7/index.html > (last accessed 14 February 2014).

21. Vincent B. Leitch et al. (eds), *Norton Anthology of Theory and Criticism* (New York: W. W. Norton, 2001). A more complete discussion of world literature anthologies is beyond the scope of my discussion in this essay. But one example is David Damrosch et al. (eds), *Longman Anthology of World Literature*, 6 vols (New York: Longman, 2004).

22. William Keach, 'A Transatlantic Romantic Century', *European Romantic Review*, 11: 1 (2000), 31, 33–4.

23. In this spirit of critical and cultural expansion of 'Romanticism', see Robert W. Rix's excellent anthology *Norse Romanticism: Themes in British Literature, 1760–1830. A Romantic Circles Electronic Edition*, online at: <http://www.rc.umd.edu/editions/norse/> (last accessed 20 May 2014).

24. Thomas D'arcy McGee, 'The Mental Outfit of the New Dominion', *Montreal Gazette*, 5 November 1867, n.p.

25. Ibid.

26. As Robert Lecker argues in *Keepers of the Code: English-Canadian Literary Anthologies and the Representation of Nation* (Toronto: University of Toronto Press, 2013), the 1880s saw the rise of the Canadian Literature anthology – in which many of the Poets of Confederation began to appear. See Chapter 1 (pp. 22–60) and the list of anthologies of Canadian literature in the Works Cited (pp. 343–51).

27. Malcom Ross (ed.), *Poets of the Confederation* (Toronto: McClelland & Stewart, 1960), reprinted in Tracy Ware (ed.), *A Northern Romanticism: Poets of the Confederation* (Ottawa: Tecumseh, 2000), pp. 423–9.

28. Archibald Lampman, 'The Frogs', lines 63, 77–80, *Among the Millet and Other Poems* (Ottawa: Durie, 1888), pp. 6–9.

29. Leitch, 'Ideology of Headnotes', in Di Leo (ed.), *On Anthologies*, pp. 373–83; Barbara Johnson, 'Headnotes', in Di Leo (ed.), *On Anthologies*, pp. 387–94.

30. Johnson, 'Headnotes', pp. 391–2.

31. Laurie Finke, 'The Hidden Curriculum', in Di Leo (ed.), *On Anthologies*, p. 399.

32. Vincent B. Leitch, 'On Anthology Headnotes', *Symlokē: A Journal for the Intermingling of Theoretical Literary, Cultural Scholarship*, 8: 1–2 (2000), 177–9.

33. Gerald Graff and Jeffrey R. Di Leo, 'Anthologies, Literary Theory and the Teaching of Literature: An Exchange', *Symlokē: A Journal for the Intermingling of Theoretical, Literary, Cultural Scholarship*, 8: 1–2 (2000), 113–28.

34. Our survey of anthologies extended Christoph Bode's survey of eighteen

published 1970–98 in 'Re-Definitions of the Canon of English Romantic Poetry in Recent Anthologies', in Barbara Schneider, Ralf Lethbridge, and Stefanie Korte (eds), *Anthologies of British Poetry Critical Perspectives from Literary and Cultural Studies* (Amsterdam: Rodopi, 2000), pp. 268 n. 10, 275–88. See too Jim Egan, 'Analyzing the Apparatus: Teaching American Literature Anthologies as Texts', *Early American Literature*, 32: 1 (1997), 102–8; Kenneth Roemer, 'The Tales Tables (of Contents) Tell', *Heath Anthology Newsletter*, 20 (1999) online at: <http://college.cengage.com/english/lauter/heath/5e/ins_resources/newsletter/fall99/roemer.html> (last accessed 12 May 2014); Tim Murnen, 'Making Literature with the Anthology', in Anne Ruggles Gere and Peter Shaheen (eds), *Making American Literatures in High School and College* (Urbana, IL: National Council of Teachers of English, 2001), pp. 22–33; and Joe Lockard and Jillian Sandell, 'National Narratives and the Politics of Inclusion: Historicizing American Literature Anthologies', *Pedagogy*, 8: 2 (2008), 227–54.

CHAPTER 6

'Flat Burglary'? A Course on Race, Appropriation, and Transatlantic Print Culture

Daniel Hack

How does attention to the transnational circulation, reception, and after-lives of literary texts alter our understanding of those texts themselves, of literary history, of the nature of creativity and authorship, and of the cultural work of literature? This set of questions motivates 'Race and Nineteenth-Century Transatlantic Print Culture', a graduate seminar I have been teaching regularly since 2006. Drawing on a growing body of research, this course explores the traffic in texts and tropes between Britain and the United States from the antebellum period to the turn of the twentieth century, with a particular emphasis on African American writings and periodicals.

Thus far I have taught this course only as a graduate seminar (thanks to departmental exigencies). In this essay I will discuss the undergraduate version of the course I am preparing to teach. Besides carrying a substantially lighter reading load than the graduate course, this version will have a slightly narrower focus and place a somewhat greater emphasis on the interpretive and literary-historical, as opposed to methodological and theoretical, stakes and rewards of our investigations. For this reason – and because the term 'print culture' will mean nothing to most students – a better title for the undergraduate course might be 'Nineteenth-Century African American and British Literature: Transatlantic Connections'. Both versions of the course, however, are premised on the belief that our understanding of nineteenth-century African American and British literature alike is enriched not only by reading them together, but also by attending to the ways they were brought together in the nineteenth century itself.

The course asks students to approach texts in ways to which they are typically unaccustomed: namely, to think about texts as both situated and mobile, and to attend to the interpretive implications of different frames and contexts – that is, to the ways different frames and contexts make more or less salient various aspects of a text and shape understanding of its meaning and import.

Further, it asks students to think about texts not only as open historically to recontextualisation and repurposing but also as engaging in such acts with other texts. In the pursuit of these goals, we practise bringing both book history and formalist methods of analysis to bear on materials drawn from a broad range of genres and forms, including the novel, the short story, the slave narrative, the newspaper column, the newspaper itself, and poetry. Students may find this range dizzying as they try to make sense of how such disparate materials fit together. On the one hand, a certain degree of disorientation can be pedagogically productive; on the other, the making of connections and sorting out of relationships is precisely the work of the course – and often, as I emphasise, the work of these texts themselves.

Accordingly, I begin the course by starting to develop with the class a vocabulary with which to describe relationships between texts, including relatively specific formal devices and practices from allusion and quotation to parody and pastiche, and on to less well-defined relationships such as borrowing, sampling, adapting, rewriting, reworking, repurposing, and plagiarism. I also introduce students to nineteenth-century transatlantic publishing practices, in particular what Meredith McGill has dubbed the US 'culture of reprinting'.[1] From the outset, I emphasise that the stakes of these relationships and practices are not only aesthetic and hermeneutical but also political. This is especially true in the cases at hand, I explain, because of the long-standing Western belief that Africans as a race were only capable of producing imitative, derivative, cultural artifacts – and the associated view that this creative incapacity was a sign and product of their less-than-full humanity. I think it is important to acknowledge that this historical prejudice renders somewhat fraught the course's very interest in – indeed, its structuring assertion of – the importance of British literature for the development of African American literature. I address this concern in several ways: I make clear my belief that what makes these relationships worth studying is precisely the extent to which they are creative, unpredictable, transformative, and by turns enigmatic and illuminating; and I make these relationships the occasion to consider historical notions (and our own) of creativity and authorship. In addition, as we proceed, we consider the possibility that the vectors of engagement run in both directions – the possibility, that is, that Victorian authors were themselves responding to or drawing on writings by (as well as about) African Americans. Even as we do so, however, we keep in view the massive asymmetries of power and cultural capital that structure this encounter.

Nineteenth-century stereotypes about the imitativeness of the 'African race' combine with these asymmetries to render all the more fraught a choice that is tricky for any course focusing on intertextual connections: namely, the choice of a starting point. Because whichever work one begins with can easily take on a privileged status as uniquely original and originating, it is tempting to challenge expectations by beginning with an African American work. However, I have not taken this route, precisely because I do not want to obscure those historical asymmetries; moreover, rather than have texts or traditions swap places in a hierarchy of originality and indebtedness, I want the course to deconstruct – or simply defang – this binary itself. I begin therefore with a text that not only participates in the tradition the course traces but also allegorises some of its key mechanisms, as it represents creativity as the revivifying, transformative combination of existing materials while also providing an enduring metaphor for the tendency of works thus created to take on a life of their own. I refer, of course, to *Frankenstein*.

Whether or not they have previously read Mary Shelley's novel, virtually all students have an understanding of what they take to be its basic story and some degree of familiarity with works in various media that adapt or riff on it. As a result, they are very attuned to – and typically fascinated by – the differences between Mary Shelley's novel and the Frankenstein myth. (The creature is not named 'Frankenstein'! He's articulate! There's no Igor!) This makes *Frankenstein* an exemplary text with which to introduce the notion of cultural afterlives. Drawing on the work of H. L. Malchow, William St Clair, and Elizabeth Young, I give an overview of the novel's nineteenth-century history of adaptation and deployment, emphasising in particular this history's transatlantic and racial aspects, while also indicating the ways in which the novel itself reflects contemporary racial discourse.[2] When considering the novel's own treatment of creativity and authorship, we pay special attention to the work's rich paratexts – in particular, the title pages and prefatory material in both the 1818 and 1831 editions. Such attention is valuable not only for what it can teach us about *Frankenstein* but also as a model for our approach to the later works we read, especially the next one: *Narrative of the Life of Frederick Douglass, an American Slave, Written by Himself.*

The first, most obvious reason I follow *Frankenstein* with Frederick Douglass's *Narrative* is so that the class can explore the intriguing resonances between these two works.[3] Strikingly, these resonances are strongest with the very elements of the novel that tend to drop out of later adaptations: the creature's command of language and, more specifically, his moving autobiographical narrative, with its focus on his entrance into literacy and the prejudice and mistreatment he encounters. Yet the later text's echoes of the earlier one are distant enough that it is not absolutely clear that Douglass was in fact taking Shelley's novel as his model, or was even familiar with it. This ambiguity provides the class not only with the opportunity to form and defend their own opinions but also to think about whether and how an answer to this question matters to our understanding of Douglass as an author or of his *Narrative* – or *Frankenstein* – as a text.

I also like to begin with these two iconic works precisely because of their hypercanonicity: both are viewed today as absolutely essential to their respective literary traditions, and to read them together, therefore, is to locate the kind of interpenetration and dialogue between traditions highlighted by the course at the heart of both the African American and nineteenth-century British canons – and not just, say, in the obscure reaches of print culture (although we will spend some quality time there too). But the course's consideration of Douglass in relation to transatlanticism goes beyond the connection to *Frankenstein*, however that is construed. I supplement the *Narrative* with the chapter of Douglass's second autobiography, *My Bondage and My Freedom*, which recounts his trip to Ireland and Britain, as well as with the alternative paratexts – both frontispiece and preface – of the *Narrative*'s Irish edition. These texts also serve as the occasion to introduce Elisa Tamarkin's notion of 'black anglophilia', one important theory for explaining why African Americans drew on British literature as they did.[4]

After studying Douglass as author, we turn to his role as newspaper editor and publisher to explore the ways he incorporated Victorian literature in *Frederick Douglass' Paper* (*FDP*). Working primarily with online, digitised reproductions of *FDP* (which crucially include scanned images of the pages themselves, not just transcriptions of the articles), we look at Douglass's reprinting of contemporary British literature and at the discussions of and references to those reprinted works (along with other British literature) by Douglass and his contributors, whether in the form of explicit commentary, allusion, or parody. More material forms of engagement – especially the act of reprinting itself – can seem rather distinct from the literary practices highlighted earlier, but Douglass's participation in both modes helps smooth this transition and show just how imbricated the material and the literary were (and remain).

After surveying *FDP*'s reprinting practices, we focus in particular on its treatment of two texts: 'The Charge of the Light Brigade' and *Bleak House*. Here I draw extensively on my own research to lead the class in thinking about why these texts get reprinted in *Douglass' Paper* and what uses are made of them.[5] The piece we examine at greatest length is a column that appeared in the same issue of *Douglass' Paper* in which Tennyson's 'Charge of the Light Brigade' was reprinted. In this column, which takes the form of a dialogue, regular contributor James McCune Smith argues that the Poet Laureate's celebrated new poem is based on an African war chant that had been used in Haiti to help start the Haitian Revolution. Indeed, he declares the poem 'Flat burglary!', 'a translation from the Congo, feebler than the original'.[6] This is a wonderful text to teach, first, because it so baldly challenges the dominant understanding of the relationship between British or Western and African/African American art and artistry, and second, because its tone is so elusive.[7] Questions we discuss therefore include: is Smith's claim sincere or tongue in cheek? How can we tell? Were the types of specific formal similarities he goes on to identify widely considered 'burglary' or plagiarism at the time? Samples from Edgar Allan Poe's articles accusing Longfellow of plagiarism are helpful in providing a sense of what the discourse of plagiarism looked like in the period.[8]

We return later in the semester to the question of plagiarism, but more immediately we move from the uses made of British literature in *Douglass' Paper* to consideration of the difference these uses – including the act of reprinting itself – make to our understanding of the reprinted works. Taking seriously McCune Smith's reframing of 'The Charge of the Light Brigade', we read that poem in relation to poems by Tennyson that are set in the tropics, including both Africa and Haiti. In particular, we read it in relation to two poems that (also) make use of transatlantic source material: one of Tennyson's most famous poems, 'The Lotos-Eaters', and one of his more obscure ones (which the poet suppressed in his lifetime), 'Anacaona', both of which draw from Washington Irving's *Life of Columbus* (relevant passages of which we also read). These juxtapositions open up various interpretive avenues to explore, including the paradoxical possibility that the self-discipline of the soldiers of the Light Brigade allows them to achieve the very end sought by Odysseus' drugged, exhausted mariners: death. We also compare these poems (including the multiple published forms of 'The Light Brigade') for the extent to which they locate themselves in a specific time and place or instead enact a departicularisation – and even, whether by the former means or the latter, seem to invite their transposition to a new context. This is also an occasion to note that a broader understanding of 'the transatlantic' comes into play here, one that includes the Caribbean. Finally, we read poems that transpose, reference, or otherwise make use of 'The Charge of the Light Brigade' to describe the actions of African American soldiers in the Civil War, such as (the white author) George Henry Boker's 'The Second Louisiana' (1863), which goes so far as to borrow the dactylic dimeter of 'The Light Brigade', and Paul Laurence Dunbar's 'The Colored Soldiers' (1895), which echoes Tennyson's poem in more subtle ways.

From Tennyson we turn to Dickens, and specifically *Bleak House*. It is with hesitation that I include this massive and difficult novel on an undergraduate syllabus, as one must devote several weeks to it (that is, if one really expects students to read it). Moreover, the novel does not, in any obvious or sustained way, seem to engage with the central concerns of *Douglass' Paper*, where it was reprinted in its entirety in weekly instalments from April 1852 to December 1853, hard on the heels of its initial publication. But then again this seeming mismatch is what makes its presence in *Douglass' Paper* so intriguing and revealing: aspects of the novel that do seem relevant – like the satiric treatment of the 'telescopic philanthropist' Mrs Jellyby, who organises missions to Africa while neglecting her own family, or Harold Skimpole's rarely noted reference to 'the Slaves on American plantations' (the contemplation of whose 'enterprise and effort' gives him pleasure) – take on heightened saliency.[9] Some of these elements, such as the racially inflected valorisation of the local and proximate to which the criticism of Mrs Jellyby contributes, raise questions about seeming ideological tensions between novel and newspaper. At the same time, even as class discussion strays from the most obviously relevant aspects of the novel we continually ask how other aspects, from its attack on Chancery to its blackmail plot, might be relevant in non-obvious ways. This line of inquiry culminates in a creative assignment, as I ask students to sketch a version of the novel that 'African-Americanises' it – that is, that transposes (some components of) the novel into a story about African Americans, just as Douglass arguably transposes Frankenstein's creature's narrative and as various writers transpose 'The Charge of the Light Brigade' into a poem about the heroic sacrifices of African American troops in the Civil War.

I have students complete this assignment before we turn to our next text, *The Bondwoman's Narrative*, by Hannah Crafts.[10] Written, it seems, in the 1850s but first published in 2002, this fictionalised slave narrative enacts its own African Americanising transposition of Dickens's novel, which Crafts notoriously mines for scene-setting and descriptive passages, plot elements, characters, and dialogue.[11] Students who have just read *Bleak House* will have no trouble recognising its presence in *The Bondwoman's Narrative*, and comparison of the two texts – and of Crafts's reimagining of *Bleak House* with their own projected versions – illuminates the complexities of both novels as well as the relationship between them.

For example, Crafts incorporates versions of *Bleak House*'s blackmail and mother/daughter plots, both of which she transforms into stories about race and slavery. Thus, whereas Lady Dedlock's secret is the scandalous liaison with Captain Hawdon that produced Esther, the secret of the woman similarly blackmailed in *The Bondwoman's Narrative*, Hannah's mistress, is that she was removed from her slave mother as a baby to take the place of her owner's dead child. Similarly, Hannah, like Esther Summerson, is separated from her mother as a baby, but unlike Esther this is not because of any sexual transgression but simply because Hannah and her mother are slaves. Even as Crafts models her story on Dickens's, then, she presents her characters as victims of their society's defining injustice; by contrast, *Bleak House*'s treatment of illicit sexuality and illegitimacy seems separate from its attack on Britain's legal system and ruling class. This restructuring thus demonstrates Crafts's creative agency while also illuminating the structure of Dickens's novel.

Besides asking what Crafts's use of *Bleak House* can teach us about both novels, I also encourage my students to think about what *Bleak House* might have to say about the kind of use Crafts makes of it. Dickens himself, I suggest, was well aware of his work's appropriability, and I ask how this awareness is inscribed in his novel. Here I call on James Buzard's argument concerning the novel's interest in the refunctioning of cultural artifacts, and I point out that *Bleak House* allegorises its own reproduction, as the novel ends with Esther living in a second house modelled on (and also named) Bleak House.[12] Crafts's authorial practice itself thus becomes visible as a form of engagement with the concerns of Dickens's novel. Further scrambling relations of priority and causality, we consider the possibility that Esther's autobiographical narrative, transformed into a slave narrative by Crafts, already bears traces of that genre; Dickens, I note, owned a copy of Douglass's *Narrative*.

Questions of appropriation and repurposing remain central when the class turns next to William Wells Brown's novel *Clotel* (1853), which borrows extensively and at times verbatim from a range of sources. Bringing in the example of Alexandre Dumas, whose controversial views of authorship were as widely publicised as his part-African ancestry, I have my class read a contemporary defence of the prolific Dumas in the *Anglo-African Magazine* which exclaims, 'Take from Shakespeare, all his borrowed stories, and what of invention have we left?'[13] Yet rather than claiming that the nature and circumstances of these examples are identical, I encourage students to think (or write) about the differences among them. For instance, Brown does not rely as heavily on any single work as does Crafts, he acknowledges his indebtedness in his novel's final chapter, and he borrows mainly from American texts explicitly concerned with slavery.

This last feature might suggest that *Clotel* is less transatlantic in origin or orientation than the works by Crafts or Douglass, but in fact its transatlanticism takes a different form: this first published novel by an African American was originally published in Britain (as it happens, in the same year *Bleak House* completed its serialisation and appeared in book form). This bibliographical history prompts us to ask: is *Clotel* therefore a Victorian novel? What does it mean to assign or deny Brown's work this status? What frame of reference does the novel itself seem to assume or provide, and what readership does it address? A discussion of these matters might well begin with the first edition's title page, which features an epigraph attributed to what it calls the 'Declaration of American Independence'.

One of Brown's sources is Lydia Maria Child's short story 'The Quadroon', which serves as a hinge connecting this unit of the course to the next. 'The Quadroon' provides one of the earliest examples of what has come to be called the tragic mulatto/a plot: a character who has been raised as white gets reclassified as (that is, revealed as always already) black based on his or her newly discovered black ancestry; this revelation results in the character's enslavement and/or madness and/or death. Brown lifts this story virtually wholesale; when reading it in relation to *Clotel*, then, questions of appropriation and authorship are paramount. Next, though, we trace the transatlantic career of the tragic mulatto/a plot itself – or rather, of a particular, revisionary permutation of it. In this version of the plot, the individual who discovers he or she is descended from a stigmatised minority is not doomed by this discovery but instead is able to choose between group-identities – and chooses the newly revealed one, which serves now not as a death-sentence but as a vocation.

I devote part of the course to this plot because it held particular appeal to one major figure in both the Victorian and nineteenth-century African American literary traditions – George Eliot and Frances Ellen Watkins Harper, respectively, both of whom used it more than once in their careers. Crucially, moreover, this genealogical plot's own genealogy is transatlantic, for while Eliot seems inspired by American writings about African Americans (by Harriet Beecher Stowe as well as Child), she in turn serves as a resource for Harper. Although Eliot's novel *Daniel Deronda* provides the best-known nineteenth-century British version of this plot of unwitting passing and voluntary racial re-identification (with the 'race' in question here the Jews), I assign an earlier work of Eliot's in which she first introduced this plot: her long dramatic poem *The Spanish Gypsy*, in which a young woman who was raised as Spanish learns that she is a gypsy by descent. This young woman, Fedalma, eventually accedes to the demand of her rediscovered father, who is the king of the gypsies, that she take her place as a leader of her people and help establish a homeland for them in Africa. Although students can find the length, structure, and style of the poem challenging, by this point in the semester they are steeped in the themes and readerly protocols of the course and can approach the poem accordingly.

I assign *The Spanish Gypsy* rather than *Daniel Deronda* because the poem has a much longer and richer afterlife in African American literature and print culture.[14] It is cited on occasion in periodicals and books of non-fiction and is explicitly echoed in several works of fiction, including two of Frances Harper's novels, both of which employ the plot in question: her most famous work, *Iola Leroy* (1892), and her earliest known novel, *Minnie's Sacrifice*, which was published serially in 1869 in the African Methodist Episcopal Church's newspaper, *The Christian Recorder* and only recently rediscovered. Harper also quotes extensively from *The Spanish Gypsy* in her published lecture 'A Factor in Human Progress' (1885), which the class also reads.

One might assign either of Harper's novels – while the later one is more canonical, more influential, and undoubtedly more accomplished, the earlier one is not only closer in time to *The Spanish Gypsy* but also opens a window onto post-bellum African American periodical writing. Moreover, the fact that some chapters of *Minnie's Sacrifice* are still missing, while potentially frustrating for students, serves as a rather dramatic lesson about the transmission and preservation of texts and also empowers students to fill in the literal blanks themselves.

Whichever Harper novel one teaches, one might share with the class the passages from both novels that recall a statement by Fedalma's father, Zarca, in which he identifies a group's dispossession and stigmatisation as a basis for solidarity: agreeing with Fedalma's characterisation of the gypsies as 'despised', the king of the gypsies explains,

> So abject are the men whose blood we share;
> Untutored, unbefriended, unendowed;
> No favorites of heaven or of men,
> Therefore I cling to them![15]

'The lesson of Minnie's sacrifice is this', writes Harper in the 'Conclusion' to the novel of that name: 'that it is braver to suffer with one's own branch of the human race, – to feel, that the weaker and the more despised they are, the closer we will cling to them, for the sake of helping them . . .'; similarly, Iola Leroy declares of the man she marries that 'I cannot help admiring one who acts as if he felt that the weaker the race is the closer he would cling to it.'[16] Taking this point of convergence between Harper and Eliot as a starting point, the class can discuss the appeal of Eliot's text for Harper as well as the ways the latter departs from the former, and the reasons for and implications of these departures. Two differences that make for especially lively discussion are those between a mixed-race protagonist and one who has no genealogical connection to the racial or national identity she grows up with, and between a text authored by a member of the stigmatised people it portrays and a text that is not so authored.

I envision two different ways to conclude the course, depending on whether one wants to extend the exploration of the thematically rich but formally conventional modes of intertextuality on display in the Eliot/Harper pairing, on the one hand, or to return to the more radical, transgressive kinds of appropriation highlighted earlier in the semester. Taking the latter course, I would jump ahead several decades into the twentieth century for a late, notorious example of an African-Americanising reworking/plagiarism of a British text: Nella Larsen's 1930 short story 'Sanctuary', which undeniably borrows from Sheila Kaye-Smith's story 'Mrs. Adis', published eight years earlier – undeniably, that is, except that Larsen did deny it, in a statement that should also be read and discussed. While I would draw on (or assign) Hildegard Hoeller's forceful defence of Larsen's actions in terms of the aesthetic practices and racial politics of modernism, by now the class will be well equipped to consider this case in relation to various nineteenth-century precedents – and to think about what difference, if any, is made by the existence of these precedents, as well as by the time elapsed between those instances and 'Sanctuary'.[17]

Alternatively, one might bring into sharper focus the preceding unit's imbrication of racial and literary kinship by concluding with a different pair of short stories: Charles Chesnutt's 'The Wife of His Youth', which was first published in the *Atlantic Monthly* in 1898, and Marie Louise Burgess-Ware's 'Bernice, the Octoroon', a 1903 story from the *Colored American Magazine*. Published at virtually the same time and in the same place (Boston) – but with Chesnutt's story appearing in a magazine with a primarily white reader-ship and Burgess-Ware's in a magazine intended to speak to and for African Americans – both stories use a courtship plot to explore questions of racial identity and solidarity, and in both works Victorian literature figures impor-tantly if ambiguously. A story of unwitting passing, 'Bernice, the Octoroon' gives its protagonist the same surname as that of Fedalma's fiancé in *The Spanish Gypsy* (Silva) and thereby asserts a relationship to Eliot's poem while leaving the nature of this relationship open to interpretation. Like Fedalma, when Bernice learns of her ancestry she refuses to continue living as a member of the dominant race, even though (like Fedalma) she believes this will separate her from her beloved. However, Burgess-Ware replaces the tragic denouement of the poem's courtship plot with a happy ending: whereas Eliot's Silva tries and fails to become a gypsy, and the two lovers separate forever after he kills Fedalma's father, Bernice's fiancé learns that he too is in fact a mulatto, making possible their marriage (as is allusively foreshadowed by the fact that Bernice already has the last name of 'the fiancé', albeit Fedalma's rather than her own). In comparing this story to both Eliot's poem and one of Harper's novels, the class might also ponder why, even after the publication of *Iola Leroy*, Burgess-Ware still chose to return to *The Spanish Gypsy* as an intertext.

Given its direct connection to *The Spanish Gypsy*, I would teach 'Bernice, the Octoroon' before 'The Wife of His Youth', chronology notwithstanding. 'The Wife of His Youth' is not a story of unwitting passing or even racial passing per se, but it resonates with the preceding texts because it too fea-tures a protagonist forced to choose between social identities: Mr Ryder, an upwardly mobile mulatto who is not light enough to pass as white but who conflates class and racial aspirations, must decide whether to acknowledge the dark-skinned, illiterate titular character whom he had married before escap-ing from slavery and who appears at his doorstep the day he is planning to propose to a well-educated, light-skinned mulatta. 'The Wife of His Youth' makes a particularly appropriate capstone for this course because Mr Ryder is perhaps the first African American fictional character ever portrayed as a reader of Victorian literature: he is browsing in 'a volume of Tennyson – his favorite poet'[18] – for an apt quotation with which to toast the woman he hopes to marry when his wife, 'Liza Jane, shows up. Just as the quotations Chesnutt provides from several Tennyson poems invite intertextual analysis, the story's insistent attention to the actual book in Ryder's hands invites a more book-historical analysis: armed with Google Books, students can discover which contemporary US editions of Tennyson seem to match the story's references to the volume Ryder is holding and reading – and, at a key moment, writing in – and consider what insights and ironies such research might yield. This approach can be folded into a larger consideration of the relationship the story represents and enacts with Victorian literature, whether through its explicit use of Tennyson, its style, or its plot, which concludes with Ryder publicly acknowledging 'Liza Jane as his wife.

The Larsen/Kaye-Smith and Burgess-Ware/Chesnutt readings suggest different conclusions to the historical narrative of literary relations the course implicitly constructs, with the former representing an ongoing scandalousness, the latter a turn to more conventional forms (with this normalisation itself construable as either maturation or retreat). However one chooses to end the course, I recommend making that choice's implications explicit and acknowledging the ongoing and contested state of scholarship in this area. After a semester's worth of attention to textual afterlives, it should come as no surprise that the story of the relationship between British and African American literary traditions remains subject to revision.

NOTES

1. Meredith McGill, *American Literature and the Culture of Reprinting, 1834–1853* (Philadelphia: University of Pennsylvania Press, 2003).
2. Howard L. Malchow, *Gothic Images of Race in Nineteenth Century Britain* (Stanford: Stanford University Press, 1996); William St Clair, *The Reading Nation in the Romantic Period* (Cambridge: Cambridge University Press, 2004); Elizabeth Young, *Black Frankenstein: The Making of an American Metaphor* (New York: New York University Press, 2008).
3. See Eduardo Cadava, 'The Monstrosity of Human Rights', *PMLA*, 121: 5 (2006), 1558–65, for the fullest discussion of these resonances.
4. Elisa Tamarkin, 'Black Anglophilia; or, The Sociability of Antislavery', *American Literary History*, 14: 3 (2002), 444–78.
5. Daniel Hack, 'Close Reading at a Distance: The African-Americanization of *Bleak House*', *Critical Inquiry*, 34: 4 (2008), 729–53; Hack, 'The Canon in Front of Them: African American Deployments of "The Charge of the Light Brigade"', in Lara Cohen and Jordan Stein (eds), *Early African American Print Culture* (Philadelphia: University of Pennsylvania Press, 2012), pp. 178–91; Hack, 'Wild Charges: The Afro-Haitian "Charge of the Light Brigade"', *Victorian Studies*, 54: 2 (2012): 199–226.
6. James McCune Smith, *The Works of James McCune Smith, Black Intellectual and Abolitionist* (New York: Oxford University Press, 2006), p. 110.

7. Smith's text is so striking, and raises some of the semester's key questions so forcefully, that on occasion I have used it to begin the semester. While effective, the danger of starting with Smith is that he offers a misleading precedent insofar as he primes students to expect a subversive, adversarial relationship between African Americans and Victorian literature, and to make the charged concept of plagiarism more central to the course than I like, as it tends to obscure more nuanced and subtle relationships of indebtedness and intertextuality.

8. Poe's series of articles appear in 1845, with a final return to the topic in 1850. See <http://www.eapoe.org/people/longfehw.htm#criticism> (last accessed 1 May 2014) for a bibliography of these articles and links to most of them. For a helpful discussion of this episode, known as 'the little Longfellow war', see McGill, *American Literature*, pp. 204–17.

9. Charles Dickens, *Bleak House* (New York: Norton, 1977 [1853]), p. 227.

10. The following three paragraphs draw on Hack, 'Transatlantic Transformations: Teaching Bleak House and The Bondwoman's Narrative', in Gordon Bigelow and John O. Jordan (eds), *Approaches to Teaching Charles Dickens's* Bleak House (New York: MLA, 2009), pp. 126–31.

11. The real identity of the apparently pseudonymous Crafts remains uncertain. For a recent claim to have solved this mystery, see Julie Bosman, 'Professor Says He Has Solved a Mystery Over a Slave's Novel', *New York Times*, 18 September 2013, p. A1.

12. James Buzard, *Disorienting Fiction: The Autoethnographic Work of Nineteenth-Century British Novels* (Princeton: Princeton University Press, 2005), pp. 105–56.

13. 'Alexandre Dumas', *Anglo-African Magazine*, 1(January 1859), 4–5.

14. See Hack, 'Transatlantic Eliot: African American Connections', in Amanda Anderson and Harry E. Shaw (eds), *A Companion to George Eliot* (Hoboken, NJ: Wiley-Blackwell, 2013), pp. 262–75.

15. George Eliot, *The Spanish Gypsy* (London: Pickering and Chatto, 2008 [1868]), p. 103.

16. Frances Ellen Watkins Harper, *Minnie's Sacrifice, Sowing and Reaping, Trial and Triumph: Three Rediscovered Novels* (Boston: Beacon Press, 1994), p. 90; Harper, *Iola Leroy, or Shadows Uplifted* (New York: Oxford University Press, 1988 [1892]), p. 263.

17. Hildegard Hoeller, 'Race, Modernism, and Plagiarism: The Case of Nella Larsen's "Sanctuary"', *African American Review*, 40: 3 (2006), 421–37.

18. Charles W. Chesnutt, *Charles W. Chesnutt: Stories, Novels, and Essays*, ed. Werner Sollors (New York: Library of America, 2002), p. 104.

CHAPTER 7

Dramatising the Black Atlantic: Live Action Projects in Classrooms

Alan Rice

The rupture of the slave trade, then the experience of slavery, introduces between blind belief and clear consciousness a gap that we have never finished filling. The absence of representation, of echo, of any sign, makes this emptiness forever yawn under our feet.

Édouard Glissant[1]

Texts obscure what performance tends to reveal; memory challenges history in the construction of circum-Atlantic cultures, and it revises the yet unwritten epic of their fabulous co-creation.

Joseph Roach[2]

How to fill the emptiness left by the destructive force of the impact of the transatlantic slave trade on our knowledge of African Atlantic lives in a classroom context so reliant on documentation and literary texts? As academics we try to find methodologies that seek to rescue these lives from the amnesia of a written record that far too often silences them; in pondering over these problematics and also being charged with trying to explain to local people here in North West England the ramifications of a transatlantic slave trade in which their forebears were responsible for the enslavement and transportation of a significant proportion of those Africans from slave ports ranging from the infamous Liverpool to the more marginal but still significant Lancaster and Whitehaven, and with finance and markets coming from places beyond the ports in manufacturing cities such as Manchester, I was determined to develop new methods of explanation and pedagogy. I needed a methodology/pedagogy which could work for a variety of ages and constituencies, from schoolchildren through undergraduates to adult learners and from museum visitors through community groups to young offenders. I wanted my students and these differ- ent publics to learn basic facts about the slave trade and its historical relevance and importance, but also to ponder its ramifications in the here and now. A brief synopsis of this context is relevant before I discuss the pedagogical method I developed.

Robin Blackburn has discussed how 'the pace of capitalist advance in Britain was decisively advanced by its success in creating a regime of extended private accumulation battening upon the super-exploitation of slaves in the Americas'.[3] Significantly, by the mid-seventeenth century the British, French, and Dutch had begun to develop slave trades of their own in competition with the Portuguese and in opposition to the Spanish dreams of monopoly, and between 1500 and 1860 around twelve million enslaved Africans were traded to the Americas (three and a quarter million in British ships). Profits to be made on these voyages were often very large as, for instance, in the seventeenth century the Royal African Company could buy a slave in Africa with trade goods worth £3 and have them sold for £20 in the Americas. The sweet tooth developed in Britain and other European populations meant the demand for sugar could only be met by the expansion of the slave trade to feed the voracious plantations where at its worst (in Brazil for instance) slave mortality was so extreme that whole populations needed to be replaced each decade.

Slavery was the essential lubricant to the development of these transatlantic economies so that by the 1760s annual exports from the West Indies alone to Britain were worth over £3 million (equivalent to around £250 million today). Individuals made large profits: for instance, the merchant Thomas Leyland, thrice Mayor of Liverpool, made a profit of £12,000 (approximately £1 million today) on the 1798 voyage of his ship *Lottery*. Slavery was integral to British industrialisation and the super-profits made on the backs of enslaved Africans provided the capital for the rapid industrial expansion in Britain. In the North West, even more important than sugar was the development of slave-labour cotton plantations in the American South that enabled the development of a new industrial economy throughout the region. The growth in the slave population in the United States from less than half a million in 1789 to nearly four million in 1860 attests to the importance of the transatlantic cotton trade to the solidifying of a slave culture in the South; as primary international consumers of that cotton, industrialists in Manchester must bear significant responsibility for the longevity of the system of slavery in the Americas. As Robin Blackburn has said, '[c]aptive Africans and their descendants paid with their blood and sweat for the phenomenal expansion of human possibilities in the Atlantic world'.[4]

Like most interpreters of the black Atlantic I struggled with communicating the geographic reach and scale of the transatlantic slave trade, but it was the geometric shape of the trade explicated in numerous diagrams that I decided to exploit as central to my teaching methodology. This triangular shape could illustrate the movement (and occasional stasis) of ships, goods, and people (both enslaved and free) around the nodal points of the circum-Atlantic and help to illustrate the complex and multi-faceted nature of slavery. In doing this, though, I was determined to move beyond the dry statistics that sometimes occlude the narratives of the people involved: in a trade dominated by numbers, I wanted to put faces to some of the statistics and to introduce characters elided by traditional histories, both to show the way slavery touched the lives of people far beyond its main players through the profits it engendered and to illustrate the humanity of its victims who, in the words of the writer SuAndi, we need to 'Remember . . . were People Before [they] were slaves'.[5] Overall, I wanted to emphasise ten key aspects of the transatlantic slave trade: movement, complexity, scale, silence, collusion (both conscious and unconscious), survival, agency, revolt, trauma, and remembrance.

The triangle provides the backdrop, and in a large space I set up (usually using chairs with different coloured muslin sheets covering them) the three continents of Africa, Europe, and the Americas. I usually do this without telling the audience what is represented, and the first part of the task is to discuss the triangle and what it represents. What follows is an interactive dramatic tableau which is a unique way to teach the history and cultures of the black Atlantic. Using around twenty character cards for a variety of historical participants in the triangular slave trade and its aftermath, and moving these characters around an imagined Atlantic space, I make real an interwoven history. I tell the stories of the characters and their interactions. The cards are representative of a full range of character types in the trade and the subsequent story of abolition, from investors in Britain, slave ship captains on their long triangular voyage, slave traders on the African coast, enslaved Africans held in forts and then transported to the Americas and beyond, slaves born in the Americas and their masters and mistresses, those who rebelled and escaped, those who lived their whole lives in slavery, and finally those who re-crossed the Atlantic to Europe both as enslaved men and as abolitionists to fight (as Frederick Douglass put it) against 'Republican Slavery' in 'Monarchical England'.[6] This helps explain complex issues such as the depopulation of Africa, the agency of African slaves even when most degraded, the responsibility of both European and African merchants for the trade, and the way in which a small minority of enslaved Africans shook free of their chains and emancipated themselves in the black Atlantic space. Some students who have taken part are so enthusiastic that they have researched and created their own characters to add to the tableau. Teachers of students from eight years to eighteen who have taken part in the tableau to increase their knowledge of the slave trade have praised it as a truly original and fun way to learn a troubling subject, and I have delivered it in various ways in my own and other universities, to school groups, and with museum visitors, prisoners, and community groups.

The methodology I use is important to the learning process as it is based on improvisatorial and interactive learning to encourage participation and showcase the dynamic and often life-changing interactions created by economic systems and decisions taken in Western metropoles that have profound effects in locations thousands of miles away from there. The tableau encourages an active learning among participants that means it often has a profound effect on them too. They take part in the activity in ways that most pedagogic practice is unable to replicate. They literally embody the movement and stasis of their characters and learn through this spatial awareness the workings of a horrific system that has helped to create the inequalities and racism of the world we inhabit now.

Having established that we have modelled a crude three-dimensional map of the Atlantic and the land masses it washes and having labelled each continent, I ask all to look at their character cards and to move to their birthplaces. Usually, only around two-thirds of the participants find this an easy task as the information given on the cards is representative of the gaps and elisions in the history of slavery and its aftermath. Several characters have birthplace 'unknown' so that early on participants learn the challenging task historians have of writing accurate histories of the topic. With each of these characters, standing mid-ocean, I talk through, for the whole group, the specific problematics of locating their origins. So, for instance, the female enslaved African, Dolly (circa 1712–74), only comes to our attention when she is bought by Elias 'Red Cap' Ball (1676–1751), a plantation owner in Comingtee, South Carolina, and we have no idea whether she was born in Africa or the Americas. Ball, along with many planters from the region, often bought Africans fresh off the boat as their skills in rice cultivation were crucial to the development of this lucrative crop, so for the purposes of telling this narrative of African agricultural legacy for American development, which only happened because of the slave trade, I place Dolly in Africa to be transported by British slave traders in the early eighteenth century. Later in the tableau I describe how Dolly had an exalted status on the plantation such that she was the only slave who had shoes ordered specially for her. This and other clues lead Edward Ball, who has extensively researched his family history, to uncover the importance of Dolly for Elias, who has ongoing sexual relations with her and eventually fathers two of her children. I tell this narrative later using the historical clue of the shoes to highlight the importance of archival research for uncovering the nuances of relationships in slavery.[7] For another character, Ignatius Sancho (1729–80), there is a different issue. His card describes him as being born 'aboard a slave ship'. I indicate that for the moment the character needs to be located midocean awaiting birth later as we move characters around the virtual map. Sancho's case also gives me the opportunity to talk about his luck in surviving murder by a slave captain or infanticide by his African mother. Many slave ship captains did not appreciate nursing mothers as it could undermine their value as field hands, while the enslaved African mother, already living through the horrors of slavery, sometimes saw death for her child as being preferable to enslavement. Having distributed my characters to the continents of their birth, I ask participants to comment on the numbers in each continent. As the exercise begins, Africa and Europe both have relatively large populations while the Americas seems scarcely inhabited; participants are invited to think about the situation now and compare it with that at the end of the tableau when the consequences of the slave trade have played out with over twelve million enslaved Africans transported away from their home place to the Americas and beyond.

I begin the tableau with a British family, the Irvings, whose patriarch James (1759–91) moves from Langholm in Scotland to Liverpool in search of work; in common with Elias Ball, he is not a first son and must move from home to seek his fortune. The dynamics of economic need have profound effects on their choices and then of those whose lives they affect later. Ball heads to America to become a landowner and eventually a slave-owning planter, and Irving learns the trade of a surgeon and joins a merchant vessel engaged in the slave trade. His biography allows me to talk about the way Liverpool develops into a magnet for fortune hunters of all kinds as it becomes the premier European port of the slave trade in the second half of the eighteenth century. The narrative of such lives is important as the reality of the black Atlantic is that most European narratives begin not with black voices, but with 'enlightened' white men engaged in a trade known as 'respectable', exchanging finished goods for what they choose to call 'black cattle'.[8] Howsoever hard these slavers try to nullify the voices of the enslaved Africans, though, through 'significant and underscored omissions'[9] which deny their humanity, their journals and letters home reveal the African captives as people of active intelligence long before the boon of literacy allows them to record their own feelings for posterity. These everyday European and American documents are, in effect, in Marc Bloch's apposite phrase, 'witnesses in spite of themselves'.[10] Moreover, these slavers' relations with African traders on the coast undermine traditional over-simplistic narratives of wicked Europeans and exploited indigenous inhabit-ants as their journals and letters exemplify how 'Africa was a full partner in the development of the Atlantic world'.[11] The African elites' and mulatto traders' willingness to trade, albeit on their own terms, is attested to by the tortured meanderings of John Newton and James Irving and other slave ship captains and crew up and down the coast in search of slaves and provisions for their transatlantic journey. Writing to his wife, when a surgeon on the *Jane* in 1786, Irving laments, 'In my last I hinted that our stay would be short, but I am now sorry to say that most probably we shall be here two months hence. Trade is dull and . . . exorbitant price.'[12] These African elites desired luxury goods so much they would exchange war captives and domestic slaves to an unknown fate across the ocean for them. I move James Irving (having signed him up for a ship) south to Africa and have him participate in the trade as surgeon, checking the 'stock' for illness or injuries that would undermine their value. Irving is a particularly interesting example as, in common with many surgeons, he is able to make profits over a few voyages (in his case at least five) and become a slave ship captain, ultimately negotiating directly in old Calabar with African traders such as Antera Duke (circa 1760–1800), who is a key character in the tableau. Duke, unlike most of the African-born participants, stays in Africa throughout his life trading enslaved Africans for goods that make his fortune. Irving's wife Mary is also key – she never moves from Liverpool – and is able on the basis of her husband's profession to have a comfortable life. She sits drinking sugared tea, representative of the British at home living off the riches of the barbaric trade. As Robin Blackburn, describing women in Britain notes, by buying goods like sugar, 'her action not only expresses but makes possible a global structure of imperialist politics and labour relations which racialize consumption as well as production'.[13] Her privileged whiteness is confirmed by her consumption of goods traded for black bodies, a status the tableau dramatically confirms. For the participants in the tableau, embodied movement and stasis are key, and this is reflected by the characters they play. Antera Duke and Mary Irving are in stasis, and that is crucial to their privilege, meanwhile in movement to and from them are goods and enslaved Africans from whose profits come their wealth and comfort. The action learning of the exercise means that such lessons are easily understood.

For the tableau, the Irving family's story is important to convey the everyday nature of the contemporary belief in the efficacy of enslaving Africans to create profits. Far from seeing it as abhorrent, many white Europeans both in Europe and the Americas saw it as everyday and normal. This is often the hardest aspect of the triangular slave trade to communicate to a post-human rights twenty-first-century audience. The story of the Irving family helps to bridge this chronological gap to the trauma of slavery and its effects throughout the circum-Atlantic region as embodied by the participants in the tableau. It is also important because it exemplifies a key aspect of the historiography of the transatlantic slave trade, that the history of enslaved Africans that we describe has to be reconstructed from the documents of their oppressors. Irving refers to his captives as 'black cattle';[14] the tableau reveals them as fully human actors in making their own history despite their horrific circumstances.

Not only the goods from the transatlantic slave trade came to Europe; sometimes Africans themselves were brought to Europe to work as servants for the rising classes whose wealth was dependant on the plantation economy. In the 'old country' these slave/servants' presence displayed a form of conspicuous wealth made abroad to aggrandise the family at home. The tableau tells the story of the voyages of some of these figures and the multiplicity of their experiences – from Ignatius Sancho through Sambo (1720–36) (whose grave is still extant and a site of pilgrimage near Lancaster) to Pompey (1856–84), bought for four shillings from his impoverished mother in Cape Verde in 1866 but an eventual major-domo to the Victorian writer and *bon vivant*, Wilfred Scawen Blunt. These lives lived on European shores, far from their birthplaces, illustrate the way the transatlantic slave trade and the colonialism that followed were responsible for the movement of Africans beyond the plantation econo- mies and back to the metropoles that funded the trade. Despite the paucity of records, the tableau reconstructions allow participants to link local geographies and even buildings to the trade that provided much of the wealth that can be seen exhibited even today. For instance, the Georgian splendour of Lancaster was created during the heyday of its short-lived slave trade between the 1740s and 1770s. As historians we can trace family links to the slave trade and to the plantation economy in the Americas; however, the presence of enslaved Africans (even if designated servants for the sake of appearances) enables us to detail the human cost of mercantile trade. Sometimes these biographies resemble ghost stories rather than dry historic narratives, and their retelling in the tableau makes compelling and dramatic exemplars of lives on the margins of society which nevertheless expose that society's true nature and deficiencies.

As we have seen, black hands were mostly not writing hands; they were for labour, and the catalyst for one particular character is a black female hand that is a remnant from the eighteenth century. As Eliza Dear explains in her autobiographical pamphlet:

> My story starts in the 1940s, in the Gloucestershire countryside where my parents had settled after coming South from Lancashire. The three of us lived in a rambling Elizabethan house, its walls covered with antlers, heads of animals and pictures of horses. In between these in prize position over the fireplace, was a black hand. It was dried, the bones were cut neatly and I was told it had belonged to someone's favourite slave. My mother was very proud of this hand. I used to play with it and, as I was often lonely, I used to wish the owner of the hand was there with me.[15]

The hand had almost certainly belonged to Frances Elizabeth Johnson (Fanny), born in St Kitts in the West Indies in 1751 and brought to Lancaster by her owner John Satterthwaite in 1778. He had just married Mary Rawlins, and this marriage had combined two significant Lancaster families who made their money in the slave and West Indian trades as many other families did in the period when the city was the fourth largest slave port in Britain. After making this money they were able to invest in a fine Georgian house on Castle

Hill in Lancaster which still stands today.[16] Johnson would not have been the only black person in Lancaster, but there was no nascent community as there was in London or Liverpool at this time. The only words we have describing her life come from her baptismal record at the Lancaster Priory church from April 1778. 'Frances Elizabeth Johnson, a black woman servt. to Mr John Satterthwaite, an adult aged 27y.' The mummified hand has to speak for her presence beyond the parish register. We can conjecture that her hand had been kept in a sentimental act of appropriation by the Satterthwaite family to remember a 'cherished' slave/servant; in effect their ownership of her body was not even interrupted by her death. Fanny's mummified hand can stand as a material spectre to remember black lives that made little or no mark on the written record, and the tableau foregrounds such hitherto marginalised biographies. Sadiya Hartman articulates this persuasive idea when she thinks of these bodies ravaged by slavery:

> The recognition of loss is a crucial element in redressing the breach introduced by slavery. This recognition entails a remembering of the pained body, not by way of a simulated wholeness but precisely through the recognition of the amputated body in its amputatedness . . . in other words it is the ravished [ghostly] body that holds out the possibility of restitution, not the invocation of an illusory wholeness.[17]

The mummified black hand is a powerful symbol of such amputated bodies which refuse over-easy closure. Here we can see the body acting as Hershini Bhana Young contends, 'as a form of memory . . . non-linear, heterogeneous, resistant and, above all, lived'.[18] Hartman and Young's powerful arguments cut across glib redemptory readings of slavery and abolition that either glory in the triumph of emancipation and gloss over the horrors that went before or wallow in sentiment, showing how slave bodies anonymised and broken can intervene as spectres to perform their narrative work of radical revisionism and to complicate such shallow, self-serving readings. The ghostly human presences revealed by a thoroughgoing historical praxis can undermine such amnesiacal praxis. It is these ghostly presences that I hope to bring forth in the tableau to exemplify lives forgotten and disremembered in more conventional histories of slavery.

Celebrating African Atlantic agency is also crucial to the making of a comprehensive narrative in the tableau, and this is achieved through narrated biographies of the leader of the *Amistad* revolt, Joseph Cinque (1814–79), and slave narrators Mary Prince (1788–18?), Harriet Jacobs (1813–97), and Henry Box Brown (1815–?), all of whom traversed the Atlantic on their various liberating sojourns. Box Brown's biography provides one of the most dynamic narratives of transatlantic abolition, showcasing drama both in the initial escape and then in its recapitulation in meetings in towns and cities in America and even more extensively in Britain after his arrival here in 1850. Henry Box Brown, like Frederick Douglass before him, spoke at abolitionist meetings throughout the country. Box Brown, in a dramatic escape in 1849, had been transported in a crate measuring three feet long by two and a half feet deep and two feet wide labelled 'this side up with care' by post from Richmond in the slave South to Philadelphia in the free North, and he now retold this story in meetings all over North Britain. It was in Manchester that Brown made the contacts that enabled him to publish the second, definitive edition of his book, *Narrative of the Life of Henry Box Brown*, in 1851 through the good offices of Thomas G. Lee, Minister of the New Windsor Chapel in Salford. The successful publication of this work in Salford attested to the widespread support for abolition in Manchester and the surrounding cotton towns in Lancashire and Yorkshire. Brown, like many other abolitionist visitors, tapped into this nascent transatlantic radicalism.

However, he was an abolitionist unlike the strait-laced, temperate norm. In West Yorkshire, he had determined to make the emergence from the box even more spectacular by having himself mailed and conveyed on the train from Bradford to Leeds. In May 1851, 'he was packed up . . . at Bradford' and forwarded to Leeds on the 6 p.m. train. 'On arriving . . . the box was placed in a coach and, preceded by a band . . . and banners representing the stars and stripes . . . paraded through the . . . town . . . attended by an immense concourse of spectators'. James C. A. Smith, who had packaged Brown for his original escape, 'rode with the box and afterwards opened it at the musical hall'. In all Brown was confined for two and three-quarter hours, a mere bagatelle in comparison with the occasion of his escape, when he had been in the box for twenty-seven hours. The carnivalesque atmosphere of such events upset many of the more po-faced abolitionists but was undoubtedly important in publicising the cause to the widest possible audience. Tickets for the show in Leeds cost from one to two shillings, and Brown's transmogrification from abolitionist orator to performing showman was sealed by such successful *coups de théâtre*.[19]

Box Brown's re-enactment at Leeds is an example of a kinetic or 'guerrilla memorialisation' that brought home to a population thousands of miles from the American plantation economy the horrors of a system that would force a man to risk death by suffocation in order to escape. By 'guerrilla memorialisation' here I mean to describe the way memorialising sometimes takes on an overtly political character in order to challenge dominating historical narratives.[20] Brown's escape symbolises much for him too, however: on leaping from the box and delivering his speech, he transformed himself into a radical transatlantic figure, transcending his slave status and becoming a free agent. The scope of his maverick performative act, performed often and over many years, can be shown by a recently discovered playbill for a Mr Henry Box Brown event at the Music Hall in Shrewsbury. This bill was found in the Shropshire archives by my student Shukar Bibi doing research into the characters in the tableau and shows Brown extending into areas of Britain where hitherto academics had not located his presence. Bibi's discovery highlights another important aspect of the tableau, as she along with other students either did research projects on extant characters or developed new ones. The bill Bibi found promotes 'For Five Days Only' in December 1859 Brown's 'Grand Moving Mirror of Africa and America! Followed by the Diorama of the Holy Land!' Central to the former was his escape in the box, which also provides the major visual image on the bill. By 1859, Brown's unconventional escape had become the visual signifier that framed his other performative activities.

Casting political action as dramatic art, the bill promises that 'Mr. H Box Brown will appear in his Dress as a Native Prince' in a performance highlighting the 'nobility of the African' before the advent of the transatlantic slave trade. 'APPROPRIATE MUSIC WILL BE IN ATTENDANCE' to provide a soundscape to the chronologies and geographies presented.[21] These details underline the importance of visual iconography and the performative in fully understanding not just Brown but also the wider culture of abolition. Brown uses his black bodily presence as a weapon against slavery, but with an eye to entertainment value that establishes him as the showman par excellence. Playbills posted throughout a town or city invited the non-literate or those unable to access slave narratives into the exotic, counter-cultural world of African American abolitionism. They advertise the presence of radical black transatlantic figures, transmitting information about the institution of chattel slavery beyond the sphere of the chattering classes, making inroads into popular culture at the same time as helping to define the political arena. Box Brown then is not only a wonderful character for the tableau allowing the *coup de théâtre* of his resurrection from slavery to freedom in the prop of a box whose exact measurements we know and can reproduce, but also his use of historical tableaux in his own practice as pedagogical tools against the horrors of the still extant institution illuminates the legitimacy of such praxis as a political weapon against reactionary forces then and now. I see my tableau as performing a similar role, enabling both the remembrance of the horrors of slavery that we should never forget, but also the determined political actions that helped to overthrow it.

Note: The tableau has been developed over fifteen years and is a wholly owned idea of Alan Rice. If you wish to have access to the materials and further methodology please contact the author at: <arice@uclan.ac.uk>.

NOTES

1. Édouard Glissant, *Caribbean Discourse: Selected Essays*, trans. Michael Dash (Charlottesville, VA: University of Virginia Press, 1989), p. 201.
2. Joseph Roach, *Cities of the Dead: Circum-Atlantic Performance* (New York: Columbia University Press, 1996), p. 286.
3. Robin Blackburn, *The Making of New World Slavery: From the Baroque to the Modern, 1492–1800* (London: Verso, 1998), p. 572.
4. Ibid., p. 23.
5. SuAndi, 'What a Celebration: When One is Too Many', in *Trade and Empire: Remembering Slavery* (Exhibition Catalogue) (Manchester: Whitworth Art Gallery & University of Central Lancashire, 2011).
6. Frederick Douglass, *The Life and Times of Frederick Douglass, Written By Himself*, new revised edn (Boston: De Wolfe & Fiske, 1892), p. 303.
7. Edward Ball, *Slaves in the Family* (New York: Viking, 1998).
8. James Irving, *Journals and Letters. Slave Captain: The Career of James Irving in the Liverpool Slave Trade*, ed. Suzanne Schwartz (Wrexham: Bridge Books, 1995), p. 113.
9. Toni Morrison, *Playing in the Dark* (London: Picador, 1993), p. 5.
10. Quoted in Gerald W. Mullin, *Flight and Rebellion: Slave Resistance in Eighteenth-Century Virginia* (Oxford: Oxford University Press, 1975), p. 10.
11. John K. Thornton, *Africa and Africans in the Making of the Atlantic World, 1400–1680* (Cambridge: Cambridge University Press, 1992), p. 129.
12. Irving, p. 110.
13. Blackburn, p. 16.
14. Irving, p. 113.
15. Eliza Dear, *In Celebration of the Human Spirit: A Look at the Slave Trade* (Settle: Lambert's Print and Design, 2007), p. 3.
16. Ibid., pp. 10–13.
17. Saidiya Hartman, *Scenes of Subjection: Terror, Slavery and Self-Making in Nineteenth Century America* (Oxford: Oxford University Press, 1997), p. 74.
18. Hershini Bhana Young, *Haunting Capital: Memory, Text and the Black Diasporic Body* (Lebanon, NH: Dartmouth College Press, 2006), p. 5.
19. Jeffrey Ruggles, *The Unboxing of Henry Brown* (Richmond, VA: Library of Virginia, 2003), pp. 127–8.
20. Alan Rice, *Creating Memorials, Building Identities: The Politics of Memory in the Black Atlantic* (Liverpool: Liverpool University Press, 2010), pp. 11, 64.
21. Ibid., Figure 11.

PART III

Teaching Transatlantic Figures

CHAPTER 8

The Canadian Transatlantic: Susanna Moodie and Pauline Johnson

Kate Flint

Canada often receives rather short shrift within transatlantic studies – except, of course, within Canada itself. Yet it occupies a distinct place within transatlantic history and within the transatlantic imaginary. To travel to Canada was not to arrive in a former colony, but in a country that was still bound to Britain. Similarly, visitors to England from Canada were – sometimes enthusiastically, sometimes critically – coming 'home'.

Any course on the nineteenth-century transatlantic needs to grapple head-on with different understandings of 'the transatlantic' and its various geographies. Very many such courses tend to concentrate on the United States and reflect the status of that country; its economic and imperialist growth; its ascent as a cultural power – one that in turn drew substantially from a range of British and European models – and its own flamboyant sense of identity. We can see this reflected in, for example, the self-presentation of its raw materials, manufactured goods, inventions, and geographical diversity in international exhibitions from the 1851 London Great Exhibition onwards. In these, the message of the dominance of the United States was frequently and increasingly reinforced through a popularised version of scientific racism and anthropological theory that set out to rank the world's peoples in terms of development, placing the United States at the apex.[1] Indeed, a comparative study of the displays of the United States and Canada at World Fairs, and the rhetoric surrounding them, would be an excellent topic to pursue.

Canada's own cartographic growth in the latter part of the nineteenth century, following its federation as the Dominion of Canada in 1867, was considerable. This included the incorporation of Rupertsland in 1869, previously the vast northern domain of the Hudson's Bay Company, of British Columbia in 1871, and of Prince Edward Island in 1873. But as John Darwin has explained, notwithstanding its huge amount of territory, 'in wealth and population it was puny. There was the rub. A *second* transcontinental state in

North America flew in the face of commercial and geographical logic. Along its whole length, the new dominion was bound to feel the immense gravitational pull of American enterprise.'[2] Combating this 'immense gravitational pull' has long been at the centre of Canadian literary and cultural studies – in Canada, of course, but also within the UK.[3] However, in the desire to establish a specifically *Canadian* tradition, and to claim and explore the distinctive qualities of Canadian writers and artists, there has been, understandably, a tendency to devalue the importance of transatlantic connections, as well as to gloss over the constant to and fro between cities on the Eastern seaboard.

Borders have a particular resonance in the consideration of Canadian transatlanticism. As Paul Giles shows in *Atlantic Republic* (2007), stressing the literary hostilities between the United States and Britain between 1776 and the present, back in the 1840s the Oregon boundary dispute between the US and the British was a bitter one, construed by the Washington politician Stephen Douglas as 'the unscrupulous attempts of Great Britain at universal dominion'.[4] The existence of these international borders is further troubled by the fact that ancestral tribal lands of First Nations/Native American people frequently span the border lines drawn across settler-nation-based maps. This provides one fundamental reason why American and Canadian treatments of Native peoples were continually contrasted throughout the nineteenth century. British administrators, in particular, were quick to condemn their counterparts south of the border. Ged Martin has plausibly argued that in many ways, British North America was especially important to the British not because of trade or investment, but because of the ideological challenge that it threw down to its southern neighbour, the United States. The responsibilities of empire, he claims, were seen as including benevolence, obligation, and duty towards colonised people – qualities that were remarkably hard to find within the United States.[5] First Nations spokespeople were, nonetheless, divided on this issue. Although the Ojibwa William Wilson could write in his 1838 poem 'England and British America', 'Hail to thee, Canada! The brightest gem / That decks Victoria's brilliant diadem',[6] plenty of other voices resented the presence and impact of settler culture and missionary interventions.

Furthermore, any broad consideration of Canadian transatlanticism should take into consideration French as well as British Canada (that is, the southern area of modern Quebec, that has been successively named the Province of Quebec (1763), Lower Canada (1791), Canada East (1840), and finally the Province of Quebec (1867) again), as well as other predominantly Francophone areas. This factor introduces linguistic, religious, and affiliative difference into the internal composition of the geographical area. Although our focus is Anglophone, to ignore the presence of people of French origins – and the ambivalent attitude of French Canadians towards the British Empire[7] – would be to ignore nineteenth-century conversations about the potential for multiculturalism that took place within Canada. We would be in danger, too, of glossing over the presence of *Métis* – people of mixed-race origins, who were mostly the product of British (especially) Scottish and French fur-traders marrying First Nations women. Scottish – and Welsh, and Irish – emigrants made up a substantial proportion of the English-speaking people who took up a new life in Canada. In practice, if not in administrative rhetoric, these internal ethnic divisions further fractured claims for a cohesive Canadian identity in the nineteenth century.

Examining Franco-American transatlanticism is, of course, crucial to an understanding of the slave trade within the United States, and to the distinctive cultural history of Louisiana in particular. Transatlantic literary studies often – once they pass beyond the literary and political milieus of the northeast – tend to adopt a southern-looking aspect, because of the triangulation of the Middle Passage, British slavery routes (including the Caribbean) and their legacy, and the southern United States. The unstable borderline between the US and Mexico, especially in the first half of the nineteenth century, and the opportunity to consider its further form of triangulation, between indigenous peoples, white settlers, and Latinos, has further distanced the cultural complexities of Canada. Yet issues of displaced and ethnically denigrated peoples are powerfully present, too, when we consider Canada's position within the nineteenth-century transatlantic. These issues play a central part in the suggestions that follow.

CLASS FORMAT

So how can one successfully integrate the Canadian transatlantic into a more geographically far-flung course? I'm envisioning here a standard fourteen- or fifteen-week semester, pitched at students who may be on a PhD track, but knowing that the class roster may also include those studying for an MA. Most probably, students will largely come from literature and history departments, and are likely to be primarily interested in the nineteenth century. I'm familiar, however, with graduate seminars in which a certain number of students have very little background in the period, and I've been mindful to suggest reading materials allowing them to situate the new material. This material would constitute a two-week unit (assuming one meeting a week), with each week introduced, ideally, by one or two students.

I organise these weeks around two central figures, Susanna Moodie (1803–85) and Pauline Johnson (1861–1913). Moodie was born in Suffolk, England. Two of her sisters were also writers: Agnes Strickland – a prolific biographer of queens and princesses – and Catharine Parr Traill, who, like Moodie, emigrated to Canada in 1832. Moodie was already a writer when she arrived:

she had published works for children in London, and, as part of her involvement in the Anti-Slavery Society, took down the story of the forty-year-old Bermudan and former slave, Mary Prince, as dictated to her. Once in Canada, in the backwoods of Ontario, she wrote letters and journals that proved invaluable sources for her 1852 account of her experiences in the 1830s, *Roughing It in the Bush*. In 1840, she, John Moodie and their five children moved to the relatively large and flourishing town of Belleville, where, in 1853, she published *Life in the Clearings Versus the Bush*, contrasting the two Canadian locations in which she had lived.

Moodie was among very many British emigrants to Canada. Numbers grew from 1817 onwards, after the first Passenger Act increased the number of passengers that ships could carry on Atlantic crossings. From 1853 – the year after she published *Roughing It* – to 1920, 9.7 million people migrated from Britain. While the majority sailed to the United States, 2.3 million went to Canada during this period, 1.7 million to Australia and New Zealand (especially after the former country's reputation as a penal colony started to wane), and 671,500 to South Africa. *Roughing it in the Bush*, if not a guide for new immigrants in a conventional sense, was nonetheless written to help prepare new settlers for the trials that might lie in front of them. It's a book written from experience, and from the heart. 'Nor is it until adversity has pressed sorely upon the proud and wounded spirit of the well-educated sons and daughters of old but impoverished families, that they gird up the loins of the mind, and arm themselves with fortitude to meet and dare the heartbreaking conflict', she wrote in her Introduction.[8] *Roughing It* looks to pre-empt the onset of adversity, but makes no attempt to gloss over the material hardships, the challenges of dealing both with the climate and with one's neighbours, and the homesickness that lie in front of the new Canadian. This is not, she stresses, 'a work of amusement' – although it does indeed contain a number of entertaining as well as hair-raising anecdotes – 'but one of practical experience, written for the benefit of others'.[9]

Pauline Johnson, by contrast to Moodie, was Canadian by birth. Her father was a Mohawk chief; her mother, born in Bristol, was an English immigrant. Johnson identified as a First Nations woman. She grew up on the Six Nations Indian Reserve outside Brantford, Ontario, in a home that brought her into contact with distinguished guests – including painters, anthropologists, and the inventor Alexander Graham Bell – and members of the Canadian government. She began to write seriously in 1884, after her father's death; her early poetic productions experimented with a variety of genres and voices. These include lyrics in praise of nature, First Nations topics, and works celebrating the Empire itself. 'To-day her reign seems to have been / A benediction of vast liberties', she gushed on the occasion of Queen Victoria's birthday in 1890.[10]

Johnson developed her career as a performer of her own poetry, as a journalist, fiction writer, and transmitter of First Nations legends. From the visit that she made to England in 1894 onwards – during which she fore-grounded her Indian inheritance and lineage by taking the stage name of Tekahionwake, her paternal grandfather's name – she became increasingly interrogative around issues of national identity. She came to figure herself as a member of an imaginary, pan-Indian nation that afforded her a vantage point from which to address both Canada and Britain. But she also became engaged with specific interventions on matters of policy and politics, notably on the occasion of her second British visit in 1906, which coincided with the visit of three chiefs from British Columbia to London, who had come to petition the King on land rights issues. Her friendship with these men, especially Joe Capilano (Squamish) led to her move to Vancouver, and her agency in putting legends from the Pacific Northwest in front of a wider public. Throughout her writing, she uses her familiarity with both Anglo and First Nations cultures to draw parallels between the two forms of society, sometimes directly claim-ing superiority for Native viewpoints, and sometimes simply highlighting the coexistence of completely different world-views.

Reading suggestions are offered in Appendix A on the Teaching Transatlanticism website (<teachingtransatlanticism.tcu.edu>).

PRESENTATION, DISCUSSION, AND POINTS TO BE CONSIDERED IN CLASS

I anticipate that students will, by this stage in the semester, have been aided in developing certain crucial skills, including:

- an ability to isolate the most important pieces of information that form the basis for subsequent points of information and argument;
- the production of a short annotated bibliography, directing the rest of the class to useful works and sites that have been consulted;
- the capacity to talk and explain clearly and to convey enthusiasm not just for the subject matter but also for ideas. These presentational skills should include the ability to use visual materials, and to think critically about *why* and *how* they are being deployed – not merely as illustration, but as texts in their own right, with their own conventions, their own contexts and modes of dissemination, and their own problems of interpretation;
- perhaps most importantly, the student should have the ability to formulate interpretive questions that will open up discussion. I'd ask presenters to devise *three* such questions to conclude their segments of the class, and to explain *why* these are important questions. I'd suggest basing each one on a short passage, or on a poem or a section of a poem – practising and

modelling skills of close reading, while also focusing the class on specific textual points.

While the primary aim of these presentations is to allow students to take temporary ownership of both text and classroom and to stimulate class discussion, they also provide an opportunity to try out pedagogical strategies. For example, they might:

- Ask the other students to free-write on a particular topic – or simply about an issue that they found especially interesting – for two minutes, and then share this with neighbours.
- Play the 60-second game. In this, each student gets to talk about what struck them most about the text/author under discussion, while the presenter writes up their points on a board – and then uses these, and the links between them, as a starting point for discussion. This both develops the skill sets of all class members (they have to select quickly and clearly) and of the presenter – mapping the points on the board is an excellent exercise in making rapid but coherent connections.

So what topics would I look to see covered? It might be helpful for the professor to give a heads-up to students at the end of the preceding week, and this would offer guidance to the presenter as well.

WEEK 1: SUSANNA MOODIE, *ROUGHING IT IN THE BUSH*

In the case of Moodie, I would expect the class to consider the role that England plays in the text as a place of origin, a stimulus to nostalgia, a site for comparison. What kinds of consolations are on offer for its remembered pleasures? I'm thinking of instances like Moodie and her family canoeing home by moonlight, with the air full of the scent of pine trees, causing her to remark 'In moments like these, I ceased to regret my separation from my native land; and, filled with the love of Nature, my heart forgot for the time the love of home.'[11] What part, indeed, is played by Nature? – and here students might also examine Moodie's and – especially – Traill's drawings and careful flower pressings (selections are readily accessible online). How does the concept of 'nature' overlap with the topics of subsistence farming and craft work? How far does the Canadian landscape force Moodie to see the natural world freshly, and how far does she assimilate it through pre-existing conventions? One introductory strategy might be to remind students of the end of Elizabeth Gaskell's *Mary Barton* (1848), or to introduce them to it, since the briefest plot summary will suffice to set the scene. Here is a working-class family from

Manchester, England, who have emigrated to Canada to start a new life, far from the crowded industrial city with its industrial unrest and the tension between masters and men. In what ways does Moodie's book – published four years later – compromise or qualify this idealism?

I'm sure that students will already have looked at one other account, at least, of settler life in the United States – such as Frances Trollope's *Domestic Manners of the Americans* (1832) – and there's scope of course for other memoirs, as well as guides for immigrants, to be considered here. What kind of comparisons would students make with these other accounts of anticipations, expectations, and challenges? Are there particular points of contrast that make one alert to the fact that Moodie is writing about Canada, not the United States? A familiar trope in accounts of travel in the United States is the rudeness of Americans (Dickens's 1842 *American Notes* is full of it). Moodie's account is strongly aware of class difference, and in places she's shocked to encounter uncouthness, lack of deference, and the inability of some settlers 'who considered themselves gentlemen, and would have been very much affronted to have been called otherwise' to behave in a seemly manner.[12] Again, how far does she impose expectations from 'home' upon her new neighbours, and in what ways do her complaints differ from those of – say – Dickens or Trollope? At the same time, she hypothesises that the 'labouring class come to this country, too often with the idea that the higher class are their tyrants and oppressors; and, with a feeling akin to revenge, they are often inclined to make their employers in Canada suffer in their turn'.[13]

Students might consider which social characteristics Moodie most comes to value in her new life, how she sees community as being built, and where power resides. How does she respond to those settlers who have arrived not from Britain, but from the United States, 'who composed a considerable part of the population, regarded British settlers with an intense feeling of dislike, and found a pleasure in annoying and insulting them when any occasion offered'[14] – and how does acknowledging the existence of these settlers complicate our sense of the transatlantic? Underlying all of these issues is the question of Moodie's own voice and her presence within the text. How does she present emotion, and what kind of response does she solicit from her readers? How are these readers directly incorporated into her work? In what ways, and for what reasons, does she deploy the voices of others? How does she structure her micro-narratives, and what ends do they serve? How does she construct a sense of selfhood on the page, and what role does this self play in giving coherence to the volume?

Finally, the class should analyse how Moodie presents her 'Indian Friends', about whom she writes at length in Chapter 15. How does she use them to make comments about human character in general, and about 'civilisation' – under which heading she clearly lumps settlers who are far from 'civilised', as well as those responsible for government policies in both the United States and Canada? How does she position their ways of living off the land in relation to the type of agriculture practised by settlers – and how do these compare in terms of environmental stewardship? Again, students might be assigned other texts, or parts of texts, for comparison, such as Anna Jameson's *Winter Studies and Summer Rambles in Canada* (1838), or Traill's *The Backwoods of Canada* (1836), or her children's novel *Canadian Crusoes: A Tale of the Rice Lake Plains* (1852). In particular, extending the reading to other texts focusing on Canadian experience will better allow students to assess the implications of First Nations people supposedly owing allegiance to the British crown – something that would help set up many of the issues to be talked about in the following week.

WEEK 2: PAULINE JOHNSON, *COLLECTED POEMS AND SELECTED PROSE*

This class could usefully begin with a discussion of literary and personal identity. Pauline Johnson poses particular challenges here, since she was a deliberate experimentalist when it came to changing voices, and, as a performer – or as the subject of photographs – donned many different costumes and poses. Even her 'Indian' stage outfit was a collage of items from different tribes. Asked a question about consistency by a reporter, she reportedly replied 'Oh *consistency*! . . . How can one be consistent until the world ceases to change with the changing days?'[15] What, one might ask, did Johnson have to gain from taking this position? What issues does it raise for the reader?

At the very least, Johnson's remark puts us on our guard against expecting coherent, sustained positions in her writing. Students should consider her *as* a performer, and as someone who wrote for dramatic recitation. A couple of class members could read aloud several different works such as the lyric, lulling 'In the Shadows', the politically charged 'A Cry from an Indian Wife', full of anger against settler appropriation of Indian lands, the meditative lament 'Silhouette', and the rollicking modern ballad (yet also a protest poem), 'The Cattle Thief'. Taken together with poems as different as 'A Request', directly addressed to the Woman's Auxiliary of Missions of the Church of England in Canada, 'The Art of Alma-Tadema' and 'Your Mirror Frame', we can see Johnson's poetry as posing a question about what it means to write for money and to fulfil the demands of particular genres. How might one assess, in this context, her vehement chastisement of those who belittle, persecute, or underestimate First Nations people? Do we find ourselves attributing more sincerity to one voice than to another, and why? For whom, and to whom, does Johnson speak and write? One topic that leads out from Johnson's own career as a performer is the consideration of her alongside other Indians who provided spectacle, entertainment, and to some extent education for British audiences, from Catlin's Indian shows in the 1840s to Buffalo Bill's Wild West, appearing regularly in Britain between 1887 and the World War I.

Students will need to think about how British readers are directly addressed in both the poetry and the journalism, and how First Nations perspectives are employed to suggest not just that these are people who should be differently understood and treated, but that British people might have important things to learn from them (see, especially, 'The Lodge of the Law-makers. Contrasts Between the Parliaments of the White Man and the Red'.)[16] What further lessons are implicit in the First Nations perspectives that Johnson conveys? What are the techniques that she employs to suggest that multiple perspectives can, in fact, exist simultaneously? It might be very useful to look at the final volume of her writings, *Legends of Vancouver* (available online), in this respect, since she here draws deliberate comparisons between London (and the London experiences of Capilano and his companions) and First Nations life in the Pacific North-West. Rather than suggest that sooner or later, 'primitive' people will catch up with the 'civilised' – a developmental model that underpins a good deal of nineteenth-century discussion of the transatlantic, and not just in relation to Indians – Johnson allows for the simultaneous existence of quite different ways of looking at the world. In effect, she's practising a form of comparative ethnography.

FINAL QUESTIONS FOR THE WHOLE CLASS TO CONSIDER

- What difference does it make that both the subjects we've been discussing are women? What differences are further created by the fact that one of these women was married with a family and the other single?
- How does travel and mobility – across the Atlantic, internally within Canada – feature in Moodie and Johnson's writing? How are the actual circumstances of travel treated, and how are travel and distance deployed to discuss the transmission of ideas? In these writings, how are familiarity and the strange treated?
- In what ways might one use the experiences of these two women to explore the concept of 'modernity'?
- What might one learn by considering the 'afterlives' of these women, especially as Canadian icons?

In the case of Susannah Moodie, this last question could be addressed through looking at Margaret Atwood's 1970 book of poems, *The Journals of Susanna*

Moodie.[17] Students might also consider the fact that the central character of Carol Shields's first novel *Small Ceremonies* (1976) is writing a biography of Moodie. This is a novel that has a great deal to say about the 'ownership' of scholarly material – rather like A. S. Byatt's *Possession* (1990): for students interested in a neo-Victorian approach to Canadian transatlanticism, Moodie and Traill offer a good starting point.

Pauline Johnson's claim to iconicity can be approached in a different way: through a study of celebrity culture. I would recommend using the chapter on Johnson in Lorraine York's *Literary Celebrity in Canada* (2007), which emphasises that there is no one specific Canadian response to fame, no monolinear version of literary celebrity. Johnson has certainly been commemorated visually as a part of national culture – like Moodie and Traill, her face appeared on a postage stamp – and Donald Sutherland read from her poem 'Autumn's Orchestra' at the opening of the 2010 Vancouver Winter Olympics. In 2014, the opera *Pauline* – with libretto by Margaret Atwood – will premiere in Vancouver. What does it mean for a country, or a city, to claim a writer as one of its own? Google search engines allow students to explore a different type of afterlife through seeing how Johnson's works have been successively packaged, emphasising the writer as a young, sensitive-looking First Nations woman, for example, or drawing on the signifying power of particular landscapes, or borrowing from traditional motifs and patterns of the Pacific North-West. The class might be asked – if you were designing a cover *either* for *Roughing It in the Bush or* for a selection of Johnson's works, what image would you choose, and why?

To conclude the second class, I'd ask everyone what is *distinctive* about the Canadian transatlantic. Yes, there's the obvious geographical (and in some cases topographical) specificity. Yes, there's the given of the particular political relationship with Britain. But how are these features made manifest in writing? What kinds of shifts and variations do we find, both between the genres that we've been considering (memoir, poetry, journalism, myth and/ or adventure-based narrative), and also between the mid-century and the later periods? What kind of investments, if any, do the writers make in the notion of 'Canadianness', and what kind of conclusions might we draw from these about the ways in which national identity becomes constituted through different cultural forms?[18] Finally – how do we *know*? Is the evidence internal to the texts, or external? What, in other words, is our evidence?

By the end of the two classes, the overall point should be well taken that although the concept of 'Canadianness' may frequently be invoked, it's not only a hard one to pin down beyond cultural stereotypes (both historical and current), but it is continually inflected, indeed, by pressures that are put on the very notion from outside, as well as from within, the country's borders. All the same, writers and performers in the nineteenth century had a vested interest in writing about a distinctive national identity. It was one that was continually posited in a triangulated way, looking southwards to the dominance of the United States within the Americas, and back across the sea to what remained, for very many, the motherland – however uneasy that family bond might be.

NOTES

1. See, in particular, Paul Greenhalgh, *Ephemeral Vistas: The Expositions Universelles, Great Exhibitions and World's Fairs, 1851–1939* (Manchester: Manchester University Press, 1988), p. 2; Robert W. Rydell, *All the World's a Fair: Visions of Empire at American International Expositions, 1876–1916* (Chicago: University of Chicago Press, 1987), pp. 1–8.

2. John Darwin, *The Empire Project. The Rise and Fall of the British World System* (Cambridge: Cambridge University Press, 2009), p. 148.

3. Canadian studies in the UK have a distinct set of emphases. Supported by the work of the British Association for Canadian Studies (founded 1975) and the Canadian High Commission, around 90 university courses focus in whole or in part on Canada, including some who emphasise Québecois studies. In terms of historical study, a good deal of comparative work is done involving other settler colonies and members of the British Commonwealth. When it comes to contemporary topics, Canada is frequently discussed in the context of tolerance and diversity, human rights, language rights, minority rights, environmental protection and what it means to have federal and provincial modes of government coexisting.

4. Paul Giles, *Atlantic Republic: The American Tradition in English Literature* (Oxford and New York: Oxford University Press, 2007), p. 73.

5. Ged Martin, 'Canada from 1815', in Andrew Porter (ed.), *The Oxford History of the British Empire*, vol. 3 (Oxford: Oxford University Press, 1999), pp. 522–45, especially 530–2.

6. Quoted in Peter Jones, *History of the Ojebway Indians* (London: A. W. Bennett, 1861), pp. 192–7.

7. See Colin M. Coates, 'French Canadians' Ambivalence to the British Empire', in Phillip Buckner (ed.), *Canada and the British Empire* (Oxford: Oxford University Press, 2010), pp. 181–99.

8. Susanna Moodie, 'Introduction', *Roughing It in the Bush*, in Michael A. Peterman (ed.), (New York: Norton, 2007), p. 9.

9. Moodie, *Roughing It*, p. 300.

10. Carole Gerson and Veronica Strong-Boag (eds), *E. Pauline Johnson, Tekahionwake: Collected Poems and Selected Prose* (Toronto: University of Toronto Press, 2002), p. 58.

11. Moodie, *Roughing It*, p. 229.

12. Ibid., p. 216.
13. Ibid., p. 167. An alternative set of perspectives may be found, incidentally, in Wendy Cameron, Shelia Haines, and Mary McDougall Maude (eds), *English Immigrant Voices: Labourers' Letters from Upper Canada in the 1830s* (Montreal: McGill Queens University Press, 2000).
14. Moodie, *Roughing It*, p. 167.
15. Quoted in Carole Gerson and Veronica Strong-Boag, *Paddling Her Own Canoe: The Times and Texts of E. Pauline Johnson (Tekahionawake)* (Toronto: University of Toronto Press, 2001), p. 258.
16. Gerson and Strong-Boag, *E. Pauline Johnson*, pp. 215–18.
17. One might note, too, that Atwood's *Alias Grace* (1996) was based on a notorious double murder that took place in 1843, and about which Moodie writes in *Life in the Clearings Versus the Bush* (1853). Atwood had already treated the murder, from a somewhat different angle, in the 1974 CBC TV film, *The Servant Girl*.
18. The question of Canadian identity might usefully be approached through studies of the topic that take a long view, including Eva Mackey, *The House of Difference: Cultural Politics and National Identity in Canada* (Toronto: University of Toronto Press, 2001), esp. pp. 36–62 and 84–103, and Erin Manning, *Ephemeral Territories: Representing Nation, Home, and Identity in Canada* (Minneapolis: University of Minnesota Press, 2003), esp. pp. xv–xxxi.

CHAPTER 9

Frederick Douglass, Maria Weston Chapman, and Harriet Martineau: Atlantic Abolitionist Networks and Transatlanticism's Binaries

Marjorie Stone

Letters to Maria Weston Chapman detailing Frederick Douglass's speaking tour of Ireland, Scotland, and England in 1845–7 read like bulletins to Boston from the Eastern front of the transatlantic abolitionist movement. 'There never was a person who made a greater sensation in Cork amongst all the religious bodies', Isabel Jennings remarked of Douglass's visit in the fall of 1845; 'the Methodists . . . are still as angry about his statements as they were during his stay here . . . he has gained friends everywhere he has been – he is indeed a wonderful man'. 'An intense interest has been excited by the oratory of Frederick Douglass during his late visit to this town and in consequence a female Anti-Slavery Society is about to be formed', Mary Ireland wrote from Belfast on 24 January 1846, likewise noting those 'offended' by Douglass's criticisms of religious complicity in slavery. 'We hope to have Frederick Douglass in Scotland shortly', Jane Wigham wrote from Edinburgh on 24 November 1845.[1] Douglass's fame preceded him within the British network Chapman had developed as Foreign Corresponding Secretary of the Boston Female Anti-Slavery Society (BFASS), an organisation she helped found in 1833,[2] months after the American Anti-Slavery Society (AASS) was formed in Philadelphia by the white printer William Lloyd Garrison, the African-American journalist Samuel Cornish, and other civil rights activists. In all three letters to Chapman, comments on Douglass arise in conjunction with discussion of contributions for the annual BFASS anti-slavery bazaar, a major fundraiser for the cause. Mary Ireland noted that a 'few lines' from Chapman 'mentioning . . . articles suitable for your Boston fair' would induce many to act.[3] '[E]ven your *name* will do much', she added, reporting rumors about Douglass and his fellow-lecturer Charles Remond:

It was first whispered, but *dare not now be repeated*, that Frederick Douglass was an imposter – it has also been insinuated that C. L. Remond was a white man who had assumed the Ethiop tinge to suit a purpose, but, every heart is filled with admiration of Mrs. Chapman. There is a feminine pride associated with the accounts we hear of your untiring efforts which make anyone here feel gratified in following any suggestion that comes from your pen. [4]

If such comments reveal the gender and race politics shaping Douglass's British reception, they also underscore the profile Chapman had acquired by the 1840s through a stream of letters and reports crossing the Atlantic. This profile was enhanced by Harriet Martineau's 1839 essay, 'The Martyr Age of the United States', a compelling account of the American abolitionist movement including a vignette of Chapman confronting a Boston mob out to lynch Garrison at an 1835 BFASS meeting.

As Martineau's essay and the earlier bulletins by British anti-slavery women to Chapman suggest, mid-nineteenth-century abolitionist writings furnish rich materials for courses in transatlanticism, especially in conjunction with the 1845 *Narrative of Frederick Douglass, An American Slave* and transcriptions of Douglass's British speeches.[5] A 'hard-hitting, lyrical, and ironic page-turner', the *Narrative* 'went through 11,000' US copies and 'nine editions in Britain'; 'by 1850 30,000 copies had been sold'.[6] The success was not fortuitous: Douglass's *Narrative* was an orchestrated transatlantic print phenomenon. First published by the Boston Anti-Slavery Society in May 1845, it was re-published 'shortly thereafter in Ireland', William Andrews and William McFeely note in their Norton Critical Edition.[7] Like most Douglass scholars, they identify the Dublin Quaker Richard D. Webb as Douglass's 'Irish publisher',[8] but the first and second Dublin editions in fact were issued by 'Webb & Chapman'. This suggests that Chapman partnered with Webb, possibly to help underwrite publication costs as she had also done at times with Garrison's *The Liberator* and the New York *National Anti-Slavery Standard*, both of which she regularly contributed to and sometimes edited.[9] Douglass's second Irish edition, dated '*Glasgow*, Feb. 6th, 1846', signalled his growing independence from his Boston mentors through the 'Preface' he inserted before the testimonials by Garrison and fellow Boston abolitionist Wendell Phillips. While there is not yet an edition of the *Narrative* geared to transatlanticism courses, the Norton includes Douglass's preface and an excerpt from his speech in Cork on 14 October 1845.

This essay surveys resources for teaching Douglass's *Narrative* within transatlantic contexts, analyses approaches that have obscured networks linking him to Chapman and Martineau, and suggests strategies for investigating these networks in the classroom. It draws on the experience of teaching

Douglass's *Narrative* in a graduate seminar on 'Nineteenth-Century Literary Transnationalism' at Dalhousie University in Halifax, Nova Scotia, Canada: a port city Douglass passed through on returning from his British tour. The seminar explores rhizomic networks connecting nineteenth-century movements within the contact zone Bill Ashcroft terms the 'transnation'; the rhizome as Deleuze and Guattari conceptualise it differs from the root's 'binary logic' by branching out in multiple directions and 'ceaselessly establish[ing] connections' to 'anything other'.[10] Criss-crossing the Atlantic, the students and I examine generically mixed texts manifesting interconnections among abolitionism, women's rights, Chartism, the Italian liberation movement, and the Zionist movement that displaces the *Risorgimento* in George Eliot's *Daniel Deronda*. In the anti-slavery unit, Douglass's *Narrative* is preceded by Martineau's 'The Martyr Age' and excerpts from the BFASS 'reports' Chapman began publishing in 1836, initially titled *Right and Wrong in Boston*. We follow Douglass with Elizabeth Barrett Browning's 'The Runaway Slave at Pilgrim's Point', first published in the transatlantic anti-slavery annual edited by Chapman, *The Liberty Bell*, and influenced, I argue elsewhere, by the 1844 and 1845 issues of the annual and by Douglass's *Narrative*; Douglass's impact is especially suggested by the poem's initial opening in manuscript, featuring a male speaker.[11] More recently, I have added EBB's newly published 'The African' (*c.*1821–2) set in Jamaica to bring in Caribbean contexts complicating the Anglo-American binary in transatlantic studies.[12] Although I have not yet incorporated my own Canadian contexts, Nova Scotia has a deeply rooted African Canadian population composed of descendants of Black Loyalists from the American Revolutionary War, Jamaican Maroons, and African Americans who sided with Britain in the War of 1812. At the undergraduate level, I mobilise these contexts by pairing Douglass's *Narrative* with Lawrence Hill's *The Book of Negroes*, awarded the 2008 Commonwealth Writers' Prize. Retitled *Someone Knows My Name* in the US, Hill's historical novel follows a strong female protagonist from West Africa to the Carolinas, New York, Nova Scotia, back to Africa in the migration of Black Loyalists to Sierra Leone, and finally to London in the period leading up to the abolition of the British slave trade in 1807.[13] Hill's text thus works to reframe the *Narrative* within a larger circum-Atlantic world, to balance its masculinist perspective, and also, through its 'Nova Scarcity' section (as the disillusioned Black Loyalists rechristened the province), to foreground a history of racism elided in representations of Canada as the 'North Star'.

In the graduate seminar, the transnational framing of Douglass's *Narrative* with prose and poetry by English and American white women writers departs more widely from customary approaches to this now canonical text. Through such conjunctions, I seek to stimulate interrogation of the deep structures of race, gender, genre, and nation that impede appreciation of the multi-directional currents of circum-Atlantic abolitionism. Rarely mentioned in Douglass studies, Martineau's essay first interested many British readers in American radical abolitionism, 'one of the first U.S. countercultures' in Michael Bennett's terms.[14] Chapman, a central agent in this counterculture, advanced the antislavery cause in America, Haiti, England, and France through her often anonymous pen and the 'creative executive' skills that made her, in Garrison's words, 'the real soul of the BFASS'.[15] Chapman also had close connections with Douglass. After speaking to BFASS members in January 1842, he 'of course came home with Maria', her sister Anne Weston reported,[16] while his first published essay, 'The Folly of Our Opponents', appeared after Chapman invited him to contribute in the 1845 issue of *The Liberty Bell*. Yet in criticism on the *Narrative* Chapman often appears only as a figure with whom Douglass clashed during his British tour, as he began to break away from Garrisonian affiliations. While I later return to this conflict as a focus for classroom debate, my emphasis here and in the seminar falls on the transatlantic networks Chapman shared with Douglass, their parallel deployments of print culture, and the very different construction of her in studies of feminist abolitionism. Like the neglect of Martineau in Douglass scholarship, the representation of Chapman speaks to the binaries that inform approaches to transatlantic abolitionism.

SCHOLARSHIP ON DOUGLASS'S *NARRATIVE* AND TRANSATLANTICISM'S BINARIES

A transatlantic approach to teaching Douglass's *Narrative* is facilitated by the burgeoning body of scholarship on Douglass's transnational contexts, including Ireland, Haiti, Europe, and Egypt.[17] Nevertheless, in the twenty-first-century curriculum Douglass is still primarily approached as a heroic 'self-made' American man, much as he is framed in James C. Hall's essential *Approaches to Teaching* Narrative of the Life of Frederick Douglass.[18] Even Fionnghuala Sweeney, in exploring Douglass's 'Atlantic world', repeatedly refers to his 'project of American self-fashioning' or his 'self-creation'.[19] In John Stauffer's words in Maurice Lee's 2009 *The Cambridge Companion to Frederick Douglass*, Douglass is the 'preeminent self-made man in American history': a designation in keeping with an orator who presented 'one of his signature speeches called "Self-Made Men" . . . over fifty times'.[20] Such overdetermined terms reflect the burden of representation Douglass carries as an iconic African American man and the extent to which studies of his transnationalism remain informed by a paradigm of American individualism and self-making that he himself internalised.

If nationalist literary formations shape approaches to Douglass's *Narrative*, so do the binary logics of black/white and male/female in anti-slavery studies, along with the privileging of novels and slave narratives over other print genres central to abolitionism such as essays, pamphlets, and reports; poetry, songs, and hymns (as in the transatlantic collection *Songs for the Free* edited by Chapman in 1836); and generic miscellanies like the BFASS *Liberty Bell* or the parallel *Autographs for Freedom* (1853) – the gift-book edited by Douglass's British editorial partner, Julia Griffiths. Race and gender binaries explain why, when Douglass is not situated within a male abolitionist tradition or a black American literary tradition still identified by Paul Giles in 2009 in the *Cambridge Companion* in exclusively male terms, he is incorporated within a white male canon of American 'Renaissance' authors, as in Ed Folsom's study of author portraits in *Approaches*.[21] Giles notes how the *Narrative* was rapidly institutionalised, supplying 'the missing racial element' within 'heroic Transcendentalism', although he does not query the gender politics of this canonical re-formation.[22] When Douglass is discussed in conjunction with women writers, genre and race categories understandably result in pairings of his *Narrative* with slave narratives by Harriet Jacobs and/or Ellen Craft.[23] I first taught Douglass's *Narrative* juxtaposed with Jacobs's *Incidents* in the mid-1990s in a graduate seminar on 'Representations of Slavery' shaped by African-American feminist theories of black women subjects as the 'other of the other'.[24] These theories are employed with particular force by Deborah McDowell in her influential 1991 analysis of Douglass's 'mythologisation' as the representative black 'racial subject'.[25] Yet the 'mythologisation' of Douglass that McDowell acutely critiqued has intensified, not diminished, much as gender and race binaries continue to inflect studies of transatlantic abolitionism.[26] Teaching Douglass in the context of black women writers thus remains vital, just as the 'minefield' of unexamined privilege in teaching a 'slave narrative that confronts instructors with the occasion and image of their own power' remains a continuing pedagogical challenge.[27]

Meeting such challenges is not necessarily aided, however, by skirting Douglass's historical connections with white women abolitionists on both sides of the Atlantic. With the exception of Douglass's relationship with Harriet Beecher Stowe, these connections are typically addressed mono-lithically under 'sentimentalism'.[28] Douglass biographers also note the role of Griffiths and transatlantic funding in establishing *The North Star* as an independent black newspaper.[29] In contrast, the large body of work on the 'abolitionist sisterhood' is seldom cited in treatments of Douglass's 1845 *Narrative*.[30] Reading Kathryn Kish Sklar and James Brewer Stewart's 2007 collection *Women's Rights and Transatlantic Slavery* in tandem with studies of transatlantic Douglass – especially the *Cambridge Companion* – thus creates a sensation of entering parallel universes. Whereas Douglass scholars fore-ground his masculine self-fashioning and relations with black or white men,

Sklar and Stewart's contributors explore nurturing and/or fraught networks among black, white, and mixed-race women participating in Atlantic abolitionism from diverse national and regional locations.

Ironically, the persisting gender binaries in Douglass scholarship and abolitionist studies embody patterns of segregation that he himself actively contested. They also replicate divisions over women's roles that split the AASS in 1838–40, when the 'old organization' headed by Garrison supported women's rights and a 'comeouter' stance towards churches complicit in slavery. The repudiation of these positions by the 'new organization' American and Foreign Anti-Slavery Society (AFASS) split the AASS and BFASS; the conflict then crossed the Atlantic with the American delegates to the world's first Anti-Slavery Convention in London in 1840. In 1845–7, Douglass was still negotiating these transatlantic divides in reaching out to British supporters of the AFASS. On women's rights and slave-holding religion, however, he never wavered from radical Garrisonian views, defending mixed-gender conventions at Seneca Falls in 1848 and in his newspaper *The North Star*.[31] Nevertheless, even treatments of Douglass on women's rights say little about Chapman, Martineau, and BFASS transatlantic networks.

TEACHING DOUGLASS WITH MARTINEAU AND CHAPMAN: CHALLENGES, RESOURCES, STRATEGIES

Studying Douglass's *Narrative* with Chapman's BFASS reports and Martineau's 'The Martyr Age' poses challenges because both women are affiliated with Garrisonian networks that Douglass scholars de-emphasise in narrating his 'self-fashioning', thus compounding differences in race, gender, and genre. This de-emphasis helps to explain why Douglass teaching resources like the Norton Critical Edition do not include excerpts or analyses of Garrison's writing from *The Liberator*, even though Douglass ranked the *Liberator* 'second only to the Bible'.[32] Since Douglass scholars have also worked to rectify historically inaccurate constructions of abolitionist leadership as predominantly white, Martineau's portrait of Garrison as the movement's leading 'martyr' similarly does not figure in criticism on the *Narrative*.[33] The national underpinnings of literary histories further contribute to this absence in Martineau's case, since her international profile has only recently been recovered by scholars working primarily within the British tradition. As Deborah Logan observes, during her 1834–6 American tour Martineau was hosted by social elites and, in Ellis Gray Loring's words, '"contemplated with great interest"' by those divided over slavery – more especially because at the tour's outset she assumed a 'noninterventionist' stance and, as Chapman noted, '"No English traveller had before visited the country with so brilliant a prestige."'[34]

Chapman's report for 1835 chronicles the English celebrity's momentous affirmation of abolitionist '*principles*' at a November 1835 BFASS meeting.[35] The ensuing lifelong friendship between the two women would contribute to Martineau's review of Chapman's first three *Right and Wrong in Boston* reports in 'The Martyr Age', Martineau's regular contributions to *The Liberty Bell*, and Chapman's editing of Martineau's autobiography.[36]

'The Martyr Age' complements a transatlantic approach to Douglass's *Narrative* for several reasons. First, Martineau's account of American abolitionism in the prestigious *London and Westminster Review* had a direct impact on Irish editions of the *Narrative*. Webb's interest in American abolitionism was first aroused by Martineau's essay, and George Thompson, in 1839, agreed with Webb that it be reprinted and 'widely circulated on both sides of the pond'.[37] Martineau's essay similarly influenced the Cork abolitionist Isabel Jennings, later among Douglass's 'most avid supporters'. As Isabel Jennings's 1843 comment to Chapman indicates:

> America was never a 'new world' to us until we knew of Garrison
> and Mrs. Chapman and N. P. Rogers and Mrs. Child and Wendell
> Phillips and Henry C. Wright – and Mr. Remond who first (after Miss
> Martineau's book) introduced them to us personally and interested us
> in them.[38]

For readers today, too, when Underground Railroad tourism implies that northern Americans were 'virtually all abolitionists', as David Blight observes, Martineau's essay remains an illuminating exposé of the 1830s 'American reign of terror' in northern states against 'people of color' and abolitionists.[39] She includes the untimely death (or assassination) of the black activist David Walker, the '[slaughter], with every refinement of cruelty' of 'many Negroes' after the Nat Turner uprising, the murder of the white printer Elijah Lovejoy, the vigilante mobs that greeted Garrison and Thompson during the British abolitionist's 1834–5 American tour, and the backlash from conservative clericals to women's increasingly prominent roles in anti-slavery organisations. Since Martineau associates the spectre of revolution with Walker and Turner and heroicises white martyrs like Garrison, the 'Moses' and 'master-mind of this great revolution',[40] her essay furthermore highlights the importance of African Americans bearing witness, as Douglass does in his *Narrative*. These historical biases in 'The Martyr Age' can be contextualised for students through Bennett's reframing of Garrisonianism as a radical biracial countercul-ture,[41] and through studies of black abolitionists who converted Garrison from colonisation to immediatism, supported the *Liberator*, or otherwise influenced him, such as Walker, James Forten, Maria Stewart, and Susan Paul of the BFASS.[42] Despite emphasising white 'martyrs', however, Martineau rightly identifies nineteenth-century American radical abolitionism as originating with 'free colored people' in 'all the principal towns north of the Carolinas' and growing to encompass 'men and women of every shade of colour, of every degree of education, of every variety of religious opinion, of every gradation of rank'.[43] Since Martineau's 'Martyr Age' draws extensively on Chapman's reports for 1835, 1836, and 1837, especially in accounts of the BFASS and Boston mob, it can also be taught as almost a transatlantic collaboration with the American abolitionist.

Chiefly mined today by anti-slavery historians as 'Garrisonian propaganda' or in histories of women's rights, Chapman's reports themselves reveal how anti-slavery women creatively adapted genres to enter public discourse. Rhetorically complex texts, they are part society proceedings, part anti-slavery tracts and anti-clerical critiques like Douglass's later jeremiads, part manifestos on non-violent civil disobedience and 'the holy cause of human rights', part documentary histories enlivened by journalistic reportage. The use of reportage is especially notable in the account of the mob that converged on the BFASS 1835 annual meeting yelling 'Is Mr. Thompson here in petticoats?', out to lynch him and Garrison. As Garrison narrowly escaped, BFASS members formed a phalanx, mixing black with white women, and exited from the meeting amid the crowd's 'roar of rage and contempt' and their townswomen's cries of ' "tar and feather" '.[44] Filled with poetical, biblical, and literary allusions, these generically mixed 'reports' are in effect American instances of what is too narrowly described as 'Victorian sage discourse': written in a Carlylean or Emersonian vein, though with a more activist ethos. 'Narrative is linear – action is solid', as Chapman remarks in the more extended *Right and Wrong in Massachusetts* (1839), citing the challenge Carlyle famously articulated as she produced a comprehensive, if partisan, history of the controversies that split the American anti-slavery movement in 1838–40.[45]

Chapman's reports, disseminated on both sides of the 'pond', shed light on Douglass's transatlantic contexts in numerous ways. First, along with British reports, they indicate how the transatlantic female anti-slavery networks facilitating Douglass's 1845–6 tour were built through racial, religious, and class-mixed alliances, although sometimes fraught ones. Thus Chapman's 1837 report affirms religious ecumenicalism along with racial integration – 'Ask no one's sect, rank, or color' – and includes 'communications' from 'ladies of Liverpool, Manchester, and Darlington', 'Glasgow', and the 'vicinity of Dublin'.[46] Across the Atlantic, an 1837 report of the 'Glasgow Ladies' Auxiliary Emancipation Society' suggests that earlier 'communications' by both coloured and white BFASS members helped to elicit these British 'communications'. The Glasgow report presents a 'communication' from the BFASS 'To the Ladies of Scotland', dated 12 August 1835 and signed by Chapman; a letter from Susan Paul as a BFASS member speaking on behalf of 'the Coloured people'; and an address 'TO THE WOMEN OF GREAT BRITAIN' dated 'BOSTON, *November*, 1836' signed by BFASS President Mary Parker and Chapman.[47]

Secondly, students can analyse how Douglass employed paratexts in the Irish editions of his *Narrative* to extend these female networks and raise the profile of the Boston bazaar: most notably by inserting an address 'TO THE FRIENDS OF THE SLAVE' and listing British ladies standing ready to accept bazaar donations. Sweeney reprints this address, as well as an excerpt from a letter to Chapman in which Douglass describes the bazaar as 'a powerful instrument in affording means to carry on our important antislavery machinery'.[48] The bazaar's own 'machinery' is wittily portrayed by James Russell Lowell in a poem featuring Chapman as its 'coiled up mainspring', while Bennett's innovative staging of 'visit' or verbal tour of the 'National Anti-Slavery Bazaar' documents the material culture of its counterculture ' "resistant consumerism" '.[49]

Thirdly, Chapman's reports and Martineau's 'Martyr Age' illumine the transatlantic contexts of the 'petitions from the north, praying for the abolition of slavery in the District of Columbia' that led to Douglass's discovery of 'abolitionists' as a youth in Baltimore – petitions that he references in a key passage of his *Narrative*.[50] The report for 1835 mentions this petitioning, while the report for 1836 includes a petition to Congress prefaced by an appeal to the 'Women of Massachusetts' dated 'July 13, 1836' and signed by 'M. W. Chapman' and 'M. Ammidon', but authored by Chapman according to Martineau.[51] Susan Zaeske documents the expansion of women's petitioning in the District of Columbia initiative, from twelve petitions in 1834 to eighty-four in 1836, ' "thundering" at the doors of Congress' – an activity inspired by the 1831–3 British campaign against slavery, when Garrison in the House of Commons in 1833 witnessed the London Female Anti-Slavery Society's ' "huge featherbed of a petition" ' with 187,157 signatures.[52] Teaching Douglass's *Narrative* in the context of this transatlantic petitioning furthermore works to counteract the erroneous view in some Douglass scholarship that 'Garrison and his followers . . . largely ignored political debates' or 'eschewed . . . lobbying of legislators'.[53]

Finally, Chapman's reports in conjunction with Martineau's larger-than-life transatlantic portrait of her as the 'most remarkable' of the American women abolitionists in 'The Martyr Age'[54] complicate representations of her in criticism on Douglass's *Narrative* as a (racist) 'grande dame' or 'doyenne' of the 'Boston clique', terms derived from studies by William and Jane Pease.[55] Chapman's sisters, the Westons (all anti-slavery activists), facetiously dubbed 'The Martyr Age' the 'jug' because of the 'eulogies' for Maria that poured from it, like Martineau's phrase ' "beautiful as the day" ', which, one sister quipped, was 'news to' her.[56] But few drops from this 'jug' enter Douglass scholarship. Chapman is sometimes completely unmentioned, as in the *Approaches* collection; more often she enters through accounts of a conflict precipitated by her writing to Webb, worrying that Douglass's tour might expose him to temptations from Garrison's British opponents; Webb indiscreetly read the letter aloud in Douglass's presence and Douglass wrote Chapman a sharp reply, rejecting her ' "overseership" '.[57] The Norton editors, evidently alluding to this incident, mention Chapman only to imply that she had 'racist' attitudes and found Douglass 'too big for any black man's britches'; John Sekora similarly casts her as a managerial racist who kept 'black spokesmen on a very short leash'.[58]

Chapman's role as 'Garrison's lieutenant', the schisms among abolitionists, and the conflicts between Douglass and the Garrisonians resulted in dramatically divergent characterisations of her. On the one hand, Garrison identified her to a British correspondent as 'our celebrated Mrs. Chapman', possibly with Martineau's essay in mind; Edmund Quincy described her to Webb as a 'woman of genius . . . of the keenest sagacity . . . & most invincible integrity'; women's rights activist Abby Kelly saluted her as a 'moral Napoleon . . . qualified to bring the antislavery society into one solid phalanx'.[59] On the other hand, Garrison's opponents, especially those resisting women in management roles, labelled her 'Captain Chapman' or Garrison's 'evil genius'; AFASS leader Lewis Tappan characterised her as 'a talented woman with the disposition of a fiend', who managed the Boston clique 'as easily as she could "untie a garter" '.[60] Influenced by the latter attacks, Henry James may later have based his 'cruel study of female reformers' in *The Bostonians* partly on Chapman.[61] Subsequent conflicting historical interpretations of Chapman replay these nineteenth-century ones. Thus, as second wave feminism emerged, the Peases characterised her as a 'Brahmin' 'bluestocking', attributing the abolitionist activism of anti-slavery women like Chapman to 'personality aberration', while Alma Lutz presented a heroicising portrait akin to Martineau's.[62]

The conflicting impressions of Chapman that emerge from Douglass scholarship, her own reports, Martineau's essay, and scholarship on the abolitionist sisterhood thus furnish ample material for classroom debates. Undoubtedly there was a 'chord of prejudice' in Chapman, Garrison, and other white Garrisonians, subtly explored by Lawrence Friedman, although he also emphasises their progressive racial integration practices.[63] As Valerie Levy observes, Chapman 'worked within the confines of "white gaze" ' in editing and writing for *The Liberty Bell* and in interacting with Douglass.[64] In debating Chapman's treatment of Douglass, however, students may also want to debate the ethics of historical representation reflected in treatments of Chapman. Should she be characterised as a racist 'doyenne' without mentioning that Douglass saluted her among other 'noble' anti-slavery women?[65] Or without mentioning that, with other BFASS members, she was socially ostracised and attacked as deserving 'straight petticoats' for 'consorting with negroes' in intervening against attempts to enslave spirited free women of colour or to assist fugitive slaves, as in the controversial case of the slave child 'Med'?[66] Her report for 1836 vividly portrays the dialogue of a slave woman named Lucile possessing 'uncommon vigor and power of expression', in contrast to the silenced slave women in Douglass's *Narrative*, while her novella *Pinda* (1840), evidently based on an actual incident, depicts a fugitive slave woman (Pinda) who successfully seeks her freedom with her husband Abraham's emotional and financial support, then is followed by her husband: the reverse of what we see in Douglass's *Narrative*.[67]

Like Douglass, Chapman was a forceful personality. She was not the paragon depicted by Martineau or one who, in Mary Ireland's words, 'filled' every female heart with 'admiration'. But neither was she a racist 'grande dame' or 'fiend'. Moreover, she had a keen sense of satiric humour as Douglass himself did, as her poem ' "The Times That Try Men's Souls" ' indicates. Echoing Thomas Paine in its title, this witty parody of conservative clerical attacks on anti-slavery women ostensibly written by the ' "LORDS of CREATION" ' begins, 'Confusion has seized us, and all things go wrong / The women have leaped from "their spheres" '. As the poem proceeds, Chapman evokes the alarm of the Lords of Creation at women insisting on 'their *right* to petition and pray' for the slave, their 'wielding the tongue and the pen', their 'talking to *men*!', and their rising '[l]ike the devils of Milton', despite the clergy's attempts to 'exorcise' the 'turbulent spirits abroad'. Douglass would have heard this poem recited at Seneca Falls and again at the Rochester women's rights convention, even though Chapman herself had set sail across the Atlantic. The poem also appears in full in the report on Seneca Falls in the transatlantic periodical *Littel's Living Age*.[68] It is a work that the parodist who enriched his *Narrative* with his own satiric adaptation of the hymn 'Heavenly Union' must surely have appreciated.

NOTES

1. Clare Taylor, *British and American Abolitionists. An Episode in Transatlantic Understanding* (Edinburgh: Edinburgh University Press, 1974), pp. 243, 247, 244. For Chapman's letters, see also the Boston Public Library Anti-Slavery Collection available at <http://archive.org/details/bplscas> (last accessed 19 January 2014).

2. Debra Gold Hansen, *Strained Sisterhood: Gender and Class in the Boston Female Anti-Slavery Society* (Amherst, MA: University of Massachusetts Press, 1993), p. 13.

3. Taylor, *British and American Abolitionists*, pp. 247–8.

4. Ibid.

5. See Frederick Douglass, *The Frederick Douglass Papers*, ed. John W. Blassingame, C. Peter Ripley, Lawrence N. Powell, Fiona E. Spiers, and Clarence L. Mohr, 5 vols (New Haven, CT: Yale University Press, 1970), vol. 1.

6. John Stauffer, 'Douglass's Self-Making and the Culture of Abolitionism', in Maurice S. Lee (ed.), *The Cambridge Companion to Frederick Douglass* (Cambridge: Cambridge University Press, 2009), p. 19.

7. Frederick Douglass, *Narrative of the Life of Frederick Douglass, An American Slave, Written by Himself*, ed. William L. Andrews and William S. McFeely (New York: Norton, 1997), pp. vii, 96.

8. See ibid., pp. 111, 96; Patricia J. Ferreira, 'Frederick Douglass and the 1846 Dublin Edition of His Narrative', *New Hibernia Review*, 5: 1 (2001), 57–8, 63; and Fionnghuala Sweeney, *Frederick Douglass and the Atlantic World* (Liverpool: Liverpool University Press, 2007), pp. 13–16.

9. See Lee Chambers-Schiller, 'The Value of Female Public Rituals for Feminist Biography: Maria Weston Chapman and the Boston Anti-Slavery Anniversary', *A/B:Auto/Biography Studies*, 8: 2 (Fall 1993), 218; Catherine Clinton, 'Maria Weston Chapman (1806–1885)', *Portraits of American Women from Settlement to the Present* (New York: St. Martin's Press, 1991), p. 153; William Lloyd Garrison, *The Letters of William Lloyd Garrison*, ed. Walter M. Merrill and Louis Ruchames, 6 vols (Cambridge, MA: Belknap Press, 1971–81); Garrison, *Letters*, vol. 2, pp. xxiv, 343, 730; Garrison, *Letters*, vol. 3, pp. 2, 80, 266, 269, 341.

10. Bill Ashcroft, 'Beyond the Nation: Post-colonial Hope', *Journal of the European Association of Studies on Australia*, 1 (2009), 12–22; Gilles Deleuze, and Félix Guattari, *A Thousand Plateaus: Capitalism and Schizophrenia*, trans. Brian Massumi (London: Continuum, 2008), pp. 5–7.

11. Marjorie Stone, 'Elizabeth Barrett Browning and the Garrisonians: "The Runaway Slave at Pilgrim's Point", the Boston Female Anti-Slavery Society, and Abolitionist Discourse in the *Liberty Bell*', in Alison Chapman (ed.), *Victorian Women Poets: Essays and Studies Series* (Woodbridge: Boydell & Brewer, 2003), pp. 39–45; Marjorie Stone, '*A Heretic Believer*: Victorian Doubt and New Contexts for Elizabeth Barrett Browning's Representations of Eve, the Virgin Mary and "The Runaway Slave at Pilgrim's Point"', *Studies in Browning and His Circle*, 26 (Fall 2005): 28–31. For the original opening featuring a male speaker, see Elizabeth Barrett Browning, *Elizabeth Barrett Browning: Selected Poems*, ed. Marjorie Stone and Beverly Taylor (Peterborough: Broadview Press, 2009), pp. 340–1.

12. See Elizabeth Barrett Browning, *The Works of Elizabeth Barrett Browning*,

ed. Sandra Donaldson, Rita Patteson, Marjorie Stone, and Beverly Taylor, 5 vols (London: Pickering & Chatto, 2010), vol. 5, pp. 391–408.

13. Lawrence Hill, *The Book of Negroes* (Toronto: HarperCollins, 2007); *Someone Knows My Name* (New York: W. W. Norton, 2007).

14. Michael Bennett, *Democratic Discourses: The Radical Abolition Movement and Antebellum American Literature* (New Brunswick, NJ: Rutgers University Press, 2005), p. 21.

15. Alma Lutz, *Crusade for Freedom: Women of the Antislavery Movement* (Boston: Beacon Press, 1968), pp. 22–3.

16. William S. McFeely, *Frederick Douglass* (New York: Norton, 1991), pp. 100–1.

17. See R. J. M. Blackett, *Building an Antislavery Wall: Black Americans in the Atlantic Abolitionist Movement 1830–1860* (Baton Rouge, LA: Louisiana State University Press, 1983); Alan J. Rice and Martin Crawford (eds), *Liberating Sojourn: Frederick Douglass and Transatlantic Reform* (Athens, GA: University of Georgia Press, 1999); Benjamin Soskis, 'Heroic Exile: The Transatlantic Exile of Frederick Douglass 1845–1847', *Gilder Lehrman Center for the Study of Slavery, Resistance, and Abolition*, available at <http://www.yale.edu/glc/soskis/fr-3.htm> (last accessed 17 January 2014); Patricia J. Ferreira, 'Frederick Douglass'; Sweeney, *Frederick Douglass*; Paul Giles, 'Douglass's Black Atlantic: Britain, Europe, Egypt', *Cambridge Companion*, pp. 132–45; Ifeoma C. K. Nwankwo, 'Douglass's Black Atlantic: The Caribbean', *Cambridge Companion*, pp. 146–59.

18. James C. Hall (ed.), *Approaches to Teaching* Narrative of the Life of Frederick Douglass (New York: Modern Language Association, 1999).

19. Sweeney, *Frederick Douglass*, pp. 3, 8–9.

20. Stauffer, 'Douglass's Self-Making', p. 28.

21. Giles, 'Douglass's Black Atlantic', p. 133; Ed Folsom, 'Portrait of the Artist as a Young Slave: Douglass's Frontispiece Engravings', in Hall (ed.), *Approaches*, pp. 55–65; see also C. Peter Ripley, Roy E. Finkenbine, Michael F. Hembree, and Donald Yacovone (eds), *The Black Abolitionist Papers*, vol. 3 (Chapel Hill, NC: University of North Carolina Press, 1985), 'Contents', pp. ix–xiii.

22. Giles, 'Douglass's Black Atlantic', pp. 132–3.

23. See, for example, Barbara McCaskill, ' "Trust No Man!" But What about a Woman? Ellen Craft and a Genealogical Model for Teaching Douglass's *Narrative*', in Hall (ed.), *Approaches*, pp. 95–101; Elizabeth Schultz, 'Incidents in the Life of Frederick Douglass', in Hall (ed.), *Approaches*, pp. 102–9; Anne Goodwyn Jones, 'Engendered in the South: Blood and Irony in Douglass and Jacobs', in Rice and Crawford (eds), *Liberating*, pp. 93–114.

24. See Mae Gwendolyn Henderson, '"Speaking in Tongues": Dialogics, Dialectics, and the Black Woman Writer's Literary Tradition', in C. A. Wall (ed.), *Changing Our Words: Essays on Criticism, Theory, and Writing by Black Women* (New Brunswick, NJ: Rutgers University Press, 1989), pp. 16–37.

25. McDowell, in Douglass, *Narrative*, pp. 172–5.

26. McDowell's influential essay itself is also now less often cited: Hall notes that it is cited by 'at least half' of the contributors in his 1999 edited collection *Approaches* (Hall, 'Introduction', p. 10). In contrast, it is referenced only once in Lee's 2009 edited collection *Cambridge Companion* by feminist critic Valerie Smith in 'Born into Slavery: Echoes and Legacies', p. 174.

27. Russ Castronovo, 'Framing the Slave Narrative/ Framing Discussion', in Hall (ed.), *Approaches*, p. 42.

28. See, for example, Jeffrey Steele, 'Douglass and Sentimental Rhetoric', in Hall (ed.), *Approaches*, pp. 66–72; see also Arthur Riis, 'Sentimental Douglass', in Lee (ed.), *Cambridge Companion*, pp. 103–17.

29. Stauffer notes that Griffiths 'not only raised thousands of dollars by organising antislavery fairs', but also taught Douglass 'the art of editing'. Stauffer, 'Douglass's Self-Making', p. 22.

30. See, for example, Lutz, *Crusade*; Blanche Glassman Hersh, *The Slavery of Sex: Feminist-Abolitionists in America* (Chicago: University of Illinois Press, 1978); Shirley J. Yee, *Black Women Abolitionists: A Study in Activism, 1828–1860* (Knoxville: University of Tennessee Press, 1992); Clare Midgley, *Women Against Slavery: The British Campaigns 1780–1870* (London: Routledge, 1992); Kathryn Kish Sklar, *Women's Rights Emerges within the Antislavery Movement 1830–1870: A Brief History with Documents* (Boston: Bedford/St. Martin's, 2000); Jean Fagin Yellin, *Women and Sisters: The Antislavery Feminists in American Culture* (New Haven, CT: Yale University Press, 1989); and Yellin and John C. Van Horne, *The Abolitionist Sisterhood: Women's Culture in Antebellum America* (Ithaca, NY: Cornell University Press, 1994).

31. See Douglass, *Frederick Douglass on Women's Rights*, ed. Philip S. Foner (New York: Da Capo Press, 1992); Frederick Hewitt, ' "Seeking a Larger Liberty": Remapping First Wave Feminism', in Kathryn Kish Sklar and James Brewer Stewart (eds), *Women's Rights and Transatlantic Slavery in the Era of Emancipation* (New Haven, CT: Yale University Press, 2007), pp. 266–78; Sarah Meer, 'Douglass as Orator and Editor', in Lee (ed.), *Cambridge Companion*, p. 50.

32. Douglass, *Life and Times of Frederick Douglass* (New York: Macmillan, 1962), p. 213; Stauffer, 'Douglass's Self-Making', p. 14.

33. One exception is the passing reference to Martineau's impact on British

perceptions of American abolitionism as a 'Manichean struggle' in Soskis, 'Heroic Exile', n. 34.

34. Deborah Logan, 'The Redemption of a Heretic: Harriet Martineau and Anglo-American Abolitionism', in Sklar and Stewart (eds), *Women's Rights and Transatlantic Slavery*, pp. 245–8.

35. Maria Weston Chapman, *Right and Wrong in Boston. Report of the Boston Female Anti Slavery Society; with a Concise Statement of Events, Previous and Subsequent to the Annual Meeting of 1835* (Boston: Published by the Society, 1836), pp. 92–3.

36. See Logan, 'The Redemption'; Constance Hassett, 'Siblings and Antislavery: The Literary and Political Relations of Harriet Martineau, James Martineau, and Maria Weston Chapman', *Signs*, 21: 2 (Winter 1996), 374–409; John Jay Chapman, *Memories and Milestones* (New York: Moffat, Yard & Co., 1915), pp. 218–22.

37. Taylor, *British and American Abolitionists*, pp. 10, 69.

38. Blackett, *Building an Antislavery Wall*, p. 110; Taylor, *British and American Abolitionists*, p. 191.

39. David W. Blight, 'William Lloyd Garrison at Two Hundred: His Radicalism and Legacy for our Time', in James Brewer Stewart (ed.), *William Lloyd Garrison at Two Hundred: History, Legacy, and Memory* (New Haven, CT: Yale University Press, 2008), p. 3; Harriet Martineau, 'The Martyr Age of the United States', *London and Westminster Review*, 32: 1 (December 1838), 15–59; rptd as *The Martyr Age of the United States* (Boston: Weeks, Jordan & Co, Otis, Broaders and Co; New York: John S. Taylor, 1839).

40. Martineau, *Martyr Age*, pp. 7–8.

41. Bennett, *Democratic Discourses*, pp. 8–10.

42. See Ripley et al., *Black Abolitionist Papers*, vol. 3; Lois A. Brown, 'William Lloyd Garrison and Emancipatory Feminism in Nineteenth-Century America', in Stewart (ed.), *William Lloyd Garrison at Two Hundred*, pp. 41–76; D. M. Jacobs, 'David Walker and William Lloyd Garrison: Racial Cooperation and the Shaping of Boston Abolition', in D. M. Jacobs (ed.), *Courage and Conscience: Black and White Abolitionists in Boston* (Bloomington: Indiana University Press, 1993), pp. 1–20; Marilyn Richardson, '"What If I Am a Woman?" Maria W. Stewart's Defense of Black Women's Activism', in Jacobs (ed.), *Courage and Conscience*, pp. 191–206.

43. Martineau, *Martyr Age*, pp. 3–6.

44. Chapman, *Right and Wrong in Boston . . . 1835*, pp. 31–4, 37.

45. Chapman, *Right and Wrong in Massachusetts* (Boston: Dow & Jackson's Anti-Slavery Press, 1839), p. 49; Thomas Carlyle, 'On History', in G. B. Tennyson (ed.), *A Carlyle Reader* (Acton: Copley Publishing Group, 1999), p. 29.

46. Chapman, *Right and Wrong in Boston: Annual Report of the Boston Female Anti-Slavery Society, with a Sketch of . . . Advocates for the Subjection of Women, in 1837* (Boston: Isaac Knapp, 1837), pp. 44, 104–10.

47. Glasgow Ladies' Auxiliary Emancipation Society, *Three Years' Female Anti-Slavery Effort, in Britain and America: Being a Report of the Proceedings of the Glasgow Ladies Auxiliary Emancipation Society, Since its Formation in January, 1834: Containing a Sketch of the Rise and Progress of the American Female Anti-Slavery Societies and Valuable Communications Addressed by them, Both to Societies and Individuals in this Country*, 1837, Samuel J. May Collection. Cornell University Library, available at <Ebooks.library. cornell.edu> (last accessed 19 January 2014). Glasgow, *Three Years*, pp. 17–22.

48. Sweeney, *Frederick Douglass*, pp. 45–6.

49. James Russell Lowell, 'Letter from Boston', cited by Lutz, *Crusade*, pp. 191–2; Bennett, *Democratic Discourses*, pp. 18–44.

50. Douglass, *Narrative*, pp. 33–4.

51. Chapman, *Right and Wrong . . . 1835*, p. 94; Chapman, *Right and Wrong in Boston in 1836. Annual Report of the Boston Female Anti-Slavery Society; Being a Concise History of the Cases of the Child, Med, and of the Women Demanded as Slaves of the Supreme Judicial Court of Mass., with all the Other Proceedings of the Society* (Boston: Isaac Knapp, 1836), pp. 28–32: Martineau, *Martyr Age*, p. 28.

52. Susan Zaeske, *Signatures of Citizenship: Petitioning, Antislavery and Women's Political Identity* (Chapel Hill, NC: University of North Carolina Press, 2003), pp. 43–6; Midgley, *Women Against Slavery*, pp. 65–70.

53. Stauffer, 'Douglass's Self-Making', p. 15; Sweeney, *Frederick Douglass*, p. 49.

54. Martineau, *Martyr Age*, p. 27.

55. Jane H. Pease and William H. Pease, 'Boston Garrisonians and the Problem of Frederick Douglass', *Canadian Journal of History*, 2: 2 (1967), 32; Jane H. Pease and William H. Pease, *Bound with Them in Chains: A Biographical History of the Antislavery Movement* (Westport, CT: Greenwood Press, 1972), p. 57; Sweeney, *Frederick Douglass*, p. 40; Giles, 'Douglass's Black Atlantic', p. 134.

56. Cited by Margaret Munsterberg, 'The Weston Sisters and "The Boston Controversy" ', *Boston Public Library Quarterly*, 10 (1958), 43–5.

57. See Blackett, *Building an Antislavery Wall*, pp. 109–10; Soskis, 'Heroic Exile', n. p.; Clinton, 'Maria Weston Chapman', pp. 156–7; Ferreira, 'Frederick Douglass', p. 61; Sweeney, *Frederick Douglass*, pp. 42–4.

58. William L. Andrews and William S. McFeely (eds), *Narrative*, p. 111; John Sekora, '"Mr Editor, If You Please": Frederick Douglass, *My Bondage and My Freedom*, and the End of the Abolitionist Imprint',

Callaloo, 17: 2 (Spring 1994), 611. For a more historically balanced account, see Blackett, *Building an Antislavery Wall*, p. 109.

59. Garrison, *Letters*, vol. 2, p. 699; Edmund Quincy, cited by Lawrence Friedman, *Gregarious Saints: Self and Community in American Abolitionism, 1830–1870* (Cambridge: Cambridge University Press, 1982), p. 156; Abby Kelly, cited by Lutz, *Crusade*, p. 217.
60. See Clinton, 'Maria Weston Chapman', p. 158; Lutz, *Crusade*, p. 175; Pease and Pease, *Bound With Them*, p. 29. Clinton further notes that 'most' of Chapman's 'enemies within the movement were men'.
61. Clare Taylor, *Women of the Anti-Slavery Movement: The Weston Sisters* (Basingstoke: Macmillan, 1995), p. 15; Yellin, *Women and Sisters*, p. 154.
62. Pease and Pease, *Bound with Them*, p. 28; Pease and Pease, 'The Role of Women', p. 181; Lutz, *Crusade*, pp. 190–206.
63. Friedman, *Gregarious Saints*, pp. 160–95.
64. Valerie Levy, 'The Antislavery Web of Connection: Maria Weston Chapman's *Liberty Bell* (1839–1858)', PhD Dissertation, University of Georgia, 2002, p. 127.
65. Douglass, *Douglass on Women's Rights*, pp. 132, 167.
66. See Chapman, *Right and Wrong in Boston in 1836*, pp. 61, 40–70.
67. Ibid., pp. 41–6; Chapman, *Pinda: A True Tale* (New York: American A. S. Society, 1840).
68. 'Woman's Rights', *Littel's Living Age*, 26 August 1848, p. 424 <http://digital.library.cornell.edu/l/livn/livn.1848.html> (last accessed 19 January 2014). For the full text of the poem as read by Elizabeth McClintock at the Rochester convention, see *Proceedings of the Women's Rights Convention, Held at the Unitarian Church, Rochester, N.Y. (2 August 1848)* (New York: Robert J. Johnston, 1870), <http://www.rochesterunitarian.org/historical_documents/1848> (last accessed 19 January 2014).

CHAPTER 10

'How did you get here? and where are you going?': Transatlantic Literary History, Exile, and Textual Traces in Herman Melville's *Israel Potter*

Andrew Taylor

> The present unfortunate propensity of filling tomes of quartos and octavos with marvellous accounts of the lives of men and women, who, during their existence, produced no impression on the publick mind, and who were not known beyond the circle of their immediate friends, or the mountains, which bounded the horizon of their native villages, is preposterous and absurd.[1]

> Nationalism is an assertion of belonging in and to a place, a people, a heritage. It affirms the home created by a community of language, culture, and customs; and, by doing so, it fends off exile, fights to prevent its ravages.[2]

In a recent essay on Melville's aesthetics, Alex Calder suggests that what characterises this author's style is its deliberate flouting of coherence and measure, what one 1851 reviewer of *Moby-Dick* opined as a 'constant leaning towards wild and aimless extravagance'.[3] This rejection of organic unity, according to Calder, is a result of Melville's being 'saddled with a measure of popularity he came to disdain',[4] so that by the time he writes *Clarel*, a narrative poem of 18,000 lines describing a trip to the Holy Land and published in an edition of only 350 copies, Melville has effected a 'successful adaptation to the role of artist without audience'.[5]

Such an aesthetic strategy, whether or not triggered by Melville's commercial failures, challenges his readers to think beyond the romance of formalist proportion, to consider instead those 'apparently unnecessary and wilful modal discontinuities' in Melville's writing – 'mimicry of other voices, archaic

and far-fetched vocabulary, lurchings into pastiche'[6] – that demand a recon-
sideration of our aesthetic categories and the political valences associated with
them. This essay explores how the aesthetic and the political are inextricably
entangled in Melville's little-read 1855 novel *Israel Potter*, a book whose portrait of the impact of the American Revolution on both sides of the Atlantic
opens up pedagogical possibilities for thinking about the status of nations
within historical narrative and about how coherencies of shape – formal and
national – might be unravelled to reveal their artificially constructed nature. I
read the novel alongside a number of contextual and theoretical perspectives
that, I hope, might offer students a range of approaches for thinking through
its challenges. In its rejection of the monumental in favour of the stylistic and
ontological complexities of disruption, *Israel Potter* is a concentrated interrogation of how the transatlantic space hollows out the cherished shibboleths
of literary and patriotic belonging. Deceptively slight (and until very recently
critically overlooked), the novel's avowedly nomadic structure, its meditation
on exile and return, and its radical decentring of national character deliver
a powerful riposte to the rampant exceptionalism of Melville's Jacksonian
America.

    Israel Potter; or, Fifty Years of Exile: A Fourth of July Story appeared
first, with appropriate timing, in the July 1854 number of *Putnam's Monthly
Magazine*, a journal founded the previous year with the intention, according
to Sheila Post, of being a 'direct contrast to the political conservatism and sentimentalism of *Harper's*', its major competitor for contributors and readers.[7]
Encouraging the submission of 'deliberately ambiguous, multi-layered text',[8]
Putnam's self-consciously set out to interrogate American middle-class assumptions and prejudices. In his first editorial, the editor Charles Briggs asked, 'In
what paper or periodical do you now look to find the criticism of American
thought upon the times?', proposing that his journal would bring together
'the results of the acutest observations, and the most trenchant thought,
illustrated by whatever wealth of erudition, of imagination, and of experience' that American writers could muster.[9] *Putnam's* interest in unsettling the
political and social consensus by challenging complacencies about race, class,
and political power ensured that several important Melville stories – including
'Bartleby the Scrivener' (1853), 'The Encantadas or Enchanted Isles' (1854),
and 'Benito Cereno' (1855) – would find a home in its pages. While, as I go
on to discuss, the sceptical, questioning mode of *Israel Potter* seems perfectly
suited to the intellectual ambitions of *Putnam's*, the economic incentive for
Melville to publish serially could also not be ignored. Walter Bezanson notes
that serialisation allowed Melville to maximise his financial returns in a way
that had largely eluded him for much of his writing career.[10] Melville's assur-
ance to the journal's owner, George Putnam, that his text would 'contain
nothing of any sort to shock the fastidious. There will be very little reflective

writing in it; nothing weighty. It is adventure' was presumably designed to allay any anxieties about the commercial potential of his story.[11] Yet *Israel Potter* is only superficially in the mould of Melville's earlier, and successful, narratives of exotic adventure, *Typee* (1846) and *Omoo* (1847). The romance of encountered otherness to be found in those two novels is recalibrated, in *Israel Potter*, into a more concentrated sense of ontological precariousness, provoked by failures of national affiliation in a time of revolutionary crisis.

How does a nation construct its own coherencies? What textual and extra-textual strategies does it marshal to produce the effect of 'a people' that can attract loyalty and patriotism? The distinction that Michael Hardt and Antonio Negri make between 'the people' and 'a multitude', in their book *Empire*, is instructive here. They write:

> The multitude is a multiplicity, a plane of singularities, an open set of relations, which is not homogenous or identical with itself and bears an indistinct, inclusive relation to those outside of it. The people, in contrast, tends toward identity and homogeneity internally while posing its difference from and excluding what remains outside of it.[12]

It is exactly this tension between enclosure and engagement, between policed sameness and the vulnerability engendered by encounter, that motivates Melville's novel. From America's inception, the founders worried about how 'united' the United States could be. James Madison's *Federalist Paper* No. 10 (1787), for instance, was concerned to shore up the young nation against damaging factions, and in a gothic mode Charles Brockden Brown's novel *Wieland* (1798) had similarly warned of the dangers of disruptive incursion into an American idyll. Paul Giles notes that any sense of 'national triumphalism' in the first sixty years of US history was uncertain, a rhetorical sleight of hand that overlooked 'what many at the time considered to be the dubious theoretical hypothesis of a federal union . . . [T]he country's sense of national identity was as uncertain, as provisional, as its cartography.'[13] As nation-building progressed in the early decades of the nineteenth century, and as the map of America was imaginatively filled in, historical narratives of origin proliferated to authorise a vision of America's exceptionalist mission, the politics of 'Manifest Destiny' so powerfully articulated by the Young America circle of Evert Duyckinck and John O'Sullivan (who coined the term in 1845).[14]

Even *Putnam's*, so proud of its critical editorial remit, was happy to publish, in its March 1853 number, a glowing review of the latest volume of George Bancroft's monumental *History of the United States from the Discovery of the American Continent*. Bancroft's ambitious work (it would be completed with the publication of the tenth volume in 1874) was designed to demonstrate the gradual unfolding of God's purpose for the nation, and its assured moral stance proved very attractive to readers. The *Putnam's* review can usefully be read alongside Melville's novel: it is a fair bet that Melville would have seen it, given his dealings with the magazine at this time, and its lengthy encomium to Bancroft's approach provides students with an effective counterpoint to *Israel Potter*'s demystification of the authorised national narrative. The reviewer is explicit from the outset that Bancroft's credentials to write the story of the nation are as if divinely sanctioned. The 'law of predestination' has gifted America with an author 'born expressly for the fulfilment of this work', in which the task of shaping 'sublime unity' out of the country's 'chaotic nature' has been wondrously accomplished: 'He has redeemed the subject from the repulsive barrenness of the mere annalist, connected its events with the principles on which they depend, [and] evolved the universal laws which underlie the special developments of history'.[15] Bancroft's history is an epic narrative of selection and ordering, in which the rubric of providence is never far from the surface. We read that 'The American revolution was designed to organise social union through the establishment of personal freedom, and emancipate the nations from the authority not flowing from themselves. The battle was fought for the advancement of the principles of everlasting peace and universal brotherhood.'[16] This is a reading of the events of the 1770s and 1780s that, as students can see, Melville's novel will contest when it appears in the pages of the same magazine two years later. One aspect worth noting for now is the reviewer's (and by extension Bancroft's) focus on revolution's ability to promote collective identity via liberated singularities (the dream, of course, of *e pluribus unum*): individual selfhoods willingly cohere into a nation that can then spread its influence globally. The belief that ontology can survive and prosper during revolution is put to the test in *Israel Potter*, where transatlantic shuttling, frequent switches of identity, and performed national alliances all exert pressure on the idea of a discrete, stable character able to be recruited for exceptionalist political ends. America's 'consciousness of a spiritual destiny'[17] gilds a narrative of 'achieved nationalism' that, as Edward Said observed, 'justifies, retrospectively as well as prospectively, a history selectively strung together in narrative form: thus all nationalisms have their founding fathers, their basic, quasi-religious texts, their rhetoric of belonging, their historical and geographical landmarks, their official enemies and heroes'.[18]

The precarious, provisional sense of US identity in the country's first decades, even as it mobilises the rhetoric of exceptionalism, was acutely felt in historical fiction of the revolutionary period. Susan Manning has explored how a dialectic of continuity and difference marks the production of a number of key narratives of the 1770s that explore how national identity is inflected by transatlantic difference. 'National historical fictions are generated in a matrix of spatial and temporal comparison', she argues. 'Historical fiction, that is, accomplished a particular kind of transatlantic thinking.'[19] By paying attention to the degree to which narratives of self-authentification are tangled up in perspectives of difference, students are better able to place readings of American literature within more expansive lines of circulation and exchange. As the subtitle to Melville's novel indicates, it is the dislocation of exile (both geographical and ideological) that structures the vexed iterations of identity that the story performs. The exile may strive to maintain an imaginary relation with the lost home, but the condition is one that, as Said writes, generates its own ontological uncertainties: living 'in a median state, neither completely at one with the new setting nor fully disencumbered of the old', the exile is 'beset with half-involvements and half-detachments, nostalgic and sentimental on one level, an adept mimic or a secret outcast on another'.[20] There is a vast literature on the idea of exile within contemporary critical discourse,[21] and by sharpening students' sense of how displacement can generate, variously, forms of nostalgic adherence, nomadic in-betweenness (as Said understands it), or radical alienation, they are better able to consider how exile is deployed by Melville to show how homes – and homelands – are provisional. The borders and boundaries that we had thought were designed to shore up selfhood can turn out to be exclusionary, to the extent that we are no longer recognised as, or recognise ourselves as, belonging to what Said calls the 'triumphant ideology' of the nation.[22] On finding himself aboard an English warship after a short sea battle, and attempting to pass as an English sailor, Israel Potter is finally confronted by an officer who asks: 'Who are you, any way? How did you get here? and where are you going?'[23] These questions crystallise Potter's inability to secure either his origins or his destination, his past or his future: the providential narrative of exile and return is unavailable to this veteran of the revolution.

* * * * *

The novel's intention to recalibrate the national archive so that it includes figures like Potter is apparent when the reader encounters Melville's 'dedication' 'To His Highness, the Bunker-Hill Monument'. Rather than being directed at an aristocrat, in the tradition of European literary patronage, it is ostensibly designed to celebrate an American monument that commemorates ordinary heroism in the revolutionary war against British monarchical rule. On the surface then, democratic valour is pitted against the imperial yoke, yet such is the switching nature of this text that the ideological lines are not so easily drawn or inhabited:

> Israel Potter well merits the present tribute – a private of Bunker Hill, who for his faithful services was years ago promoted to a still deeper privacy under the ground, with a posthumous pension, in default of any during life, annually paid him by the spring in ever-new mosses and sward.

I am the more encouraged to lay this performance at the feet of
your Highness, because, with a change in the grammatical person, it
preserves, almost as in a reprint, Israel Potter's autobiographical story.
Shortly after his return in infirm old age to his native land, a little
narrative of his adventures, forlornly published on sleazy gray paper,
appeared among the peddlers . . . From a tattered copy, rescued by
the merest chance from the rag-pickers, the present account has been
drawn, which . . . may, perhaps, be not unfitly regarded something in
the light of a dilapidated old tombstone retouched.[24]

The implied critique here is of a historiography unaware of its elisions and
exclusions: the precarious material conditions onto which Potter's life is
inscribed (the 'sleazy gray paper') match the bleakly ironised fate of his life
once it has been written out of American cultural memory.[25] Promotion and
pensions are posthumous, rendered as spiritual (to a higher state) and natural
(with seasonal payment), rather than material and recorded. The book began
as a rewrite of an obscure 1824 narrative, *The Life and Remarkable Adventures
of Israel R. Potter, (A Native of Cranston, Rhode Island,) Who Was a Soldier in
the American Revolution*, which Melville had acquired and read. His rescue of
Potter's biography represents a recuperation of a character, 'dilapidated' but
'retouched', unknown to the monumentalising history of the republic embodied in the proudly phallic Bunker Hill obelisk, a piece of architecture explicitly
designed to stabilise national identity. The dedication works both as a parody
of monarchical regimes, by placing the standard vocabulary of address and the
subject of that address in ironic juxtaposition, and of democratic governments
whose consolidation of national cohesion is mobilised by selective retelling.
When Melville goes on to observe 'That the name [of Potter] should not have
appeared in the volumes of Sparks, may or may not be a matter for astonish-
ment',[26] the reference to Jared Sparks, early nineteenth-century America's
official historian of choice, reminds us of an example of whom and what this
novel opposes. As one of the epigraphs to this essay demonstrates, Sparks's
historiography was resolutely focused on promoting the leading figures in the
national narrative, a practice most famously embodied in his twelve-volume
The Life and Writings of George Washington (1834–7). In his biography of
the American explorer John Ledyard, for example, Sparks declared that the
purpose of biography was 'to bring together a series of facts which should do
justice to the fame and character of a man, who possessed qualities, and performed deeds, that rendered him remarkable'.[27] Israel Potter, a lowly nobody
transplanted transatlantically into a North American revolution being fought
around the coast of Great Britain (a conflict from which he fails to reap any
political or financial reward), is exactly the kind of figure whom Sparks elides
from the authorised secular scripture of the nation. Melville's text conceives of

history instead as a series of serendipities, performances, and imitations, from which the consolations of patriotism are pointedly lacking.

Indeed *Israel Potter* has very little interest in the patriotic possibilities of narrative, for the action at Bunker Hill itself is dismissed with 'But every one knows all about the battle'[28] before the focus settles on Potter's efforts amid the chaos of warfare. The book's most famous military set piece, the naval encounter between John Paul Jones's ship *Bonhomme Richard*, upon which Potter finds himself, and the British *Serapis*, is similarly devoid of any nationalistic lustre, for the narrator confesses that 'Never was there a fight so snarled. The intricacy of those incidents which defy the narrator's extrication, is not ill figured in that bewildering intertanglement of all the yards and anchors of the two ships, which confounded them for the time in one chaos of devastation.'[29] 'Snarled', 'intricacy', 'bewildering intertanglement' – all denote an inability to purify national identity of its intertwined others; the 'extrication' of a comforting tale of patriotic derring-do is thwarted by an aesthetic that, at every turn, works to place romantic American autonomy in a relationship with cultural and geographical difference so as to reveal its own artifice. Paul Giles usefully describes this as a process of 'cross-cultural mirroring that most revealingly backlights the strange and artificial masks endemic to any given set of social customs',[30] and two examples will suffice to illustrate how Melville deploys a disruptive aesthetic to unsettle the political and patriotic valences of his novel. The first returns us to Melville's account of the battle between the *Bonhomme Richard* and the *Serapis*, and a remarkable passage of description:

> Not long after, an invisible hand came and set down a great yellow lamp
> in the east. The hand reached up unseen from below the horizon, and
> set the lamp down right on the rim of the horizon, as on a threshold;
> as much as to say, Gentlemen warriors, permit me a little to light up
> this rather gloomy looking subject. The lamp was the round harvest
> moon; the one solitary foot-light of the scene. But scarcely did the rays
> from the lamp pierce that languid haze. Objects before perceived with
> difficulty, now glimmered ambiguously. Bedded in strange vapors, the
> great foot-light cast a dubious half demoniac glare across the waters,
> like the phantasmagoric stream sent athwart a London flagging in a
> night-rain from an apothecary's blue and green window . . . There
> stood the grinning Man-in-the-Moon, his head just dodging into view
> over the rim of the sea:– Mephistopheles prompter of the stage.[31]

Productive work can be undertaken here by encouraging students to think about how the scene of battle is transformed into an aesthetic spectacle, one replete with textual allusions, that scrambles the conventional coordinates of patriotism. The shift from historical action to a cosmic performance echoes the

'Man-in-the-Moon' of both Shakespeare's *A Midsummer Night's Dream* (V, i) and, most explicitly, of Nathaniel Hawthorne's debunking of political significance in 'My Kinsman, Major Molineux' (1832).[32] The light that is thrown on this theatricalised space mystifies rather than enlightens; it produces a distinct effect that transforms difficulty into ambiguity, thereby replacing the urge to decipher with the spectatorial delights of aesthetic pleasure, as the two ships move 'like partners in a cotillion'. (It's worth noting too that the scene is watched by 'crowds of the islanders' on the Yorkshire coast.)[33] Battle is metaphorised, such that the military specifics of the encounter, and hence its availability for nationalistic reading, are liberated from the historical record and the uses to which that record is put. Melville's repeated crossing of registers generates a creative disorder that acts as a counter-narrative to the simplifications of patriotic history. For example, in the passage above, moonlight is like the strange light emitted from a chemist's window; elsewhere the *Serapis* circles 'like a wheeling cock around a hen' and the ships are like 'Siamese Twins, oblivious of their fraternal bond'.[34] If Mephistopheles is really pulling the strings of this revolution, the belief in human agency inspired by divine sanction begins to look precarious indeed.

One approach for heightening students' awareness of Melville's counter-intuitive approach to questions of patriotism is to consider the representation of historical figures within the text. Israel encounters a number of household names – George III, John Paul Jones, Ethan Allen, Horne Tooke, and Benjamin Franklin. These figures are central to the nation's record, but Melville does not allow them to settle comfortably into such memorialised roles. I want to dwell briefly on the depiction of Franklin, as my second example of aesthetic/political snarling, to show how the novel's placing of this founding father in Paris opens up possibilities of disruptive incursion into his unassailable reputation. In England Potter is recruited by sympathisers of the revolution to act as a courier sending secret messages to and from the Paris-based Franklin, and Melville departs substantially from his source text by devoting several chapters (7–12) to Potter's dealings with him. Franklin is first seen dressed 'in a rich dressing-gown – a fanciful present from an admiring Marchesa – curiously embroidered with algebraic figures like a conjuror's robe', surrounded by the paraphernalia of his intellectual curiosity that combines science and magic. 'The walls had a necromantic look', we read, on which the map of the American continent shows 'vast empty spaces in the middle, with the word DESERT diffusely printed there'. The word, though, has been struck out by Franklin, 'as if in summary repeal of it'.[35] Once again, then, we are exposed to a collision of discursive realms, where the practice of Enlightenment progress seems to be aligned with, or dependent upon, its opposite, the showmanship of the metaphysical. Science and magic combine, too, to enact imperial ambition, for the landscape of emptiness is transformed into a geography fit for national inscription. The benevolent sage of self-reliance – the persona constructed by Franklin's *Autobiography* – is re-imagined as a self-quoting figure of dubious motives, whose character combines duplicity and plain-speaking:

> Viewed from a certain point of view, there was a touch of primeval orientalness in Benjamin Franklin. Neither is there wanting something like a scriptural parallel. The history of the patriarch Jacob is interesting not less from the unselfish devotion which we are bound to ascribe to him, than from the deep worldly wisdom and polished Italian tact, gleaming under an air of Arcadian unaffectedness. The diplomatist and the shepherd are blended; a union not without warrant; the apostolic serpent and dove. A tanned Machiavelli in tents.[36]

The range of reference here is dizzying, and it wrenches Franklin out from his institutionalised mould into someone more complex and less reassuring – in fact, distinctly un-American. 'Primeval orientalness' is pitched against 'Arcadian unaffectedness', and in a double typological move, Franklin's equivalent extends to the biblical Jacob, who stole his brother Esau's birth-right, who, in turn, is likened to Machiavelli, the author of the classic text of political manipulation and intrigue. The incongruity of Jacob's 'polished Italian tact' encapsulates the freedom with which Melville feels able to mix spatial and temporal references, a genealogy that is then added to a few lines later when Thomas Hobbes, the early modern English philosopher of political power, is cited as an early incarnation of Franklin: 'Indeed, making due allowance for soil and era, history presents few trios more akin, upon the whole, than Jacob, Hobbes, and Franklin; three labyrinth-minded, but plain-spoken Broadbrims, at once politicians and philosophers; keen observers of the main chance; prudent courtiers; practical magians in linsey woolsey.'[37] Franklin's exceptionalist credentials collapse when viewed from the broader perspective of global history, where the exercise of power masked by benevolence was ever thus.

After his meetings with Franklin, Potter is confined to his room, causing him at one point to reflect that 'Somehow I'm bound to be a prisoner, one way or another.'[38] The autonomy of the Franklinian self is constantly denied him, and the rhetorical alliance of New World nationality and freedom is also deferred: he is 'doubly hunted by the thought, that whether as an Englishman, or whether as an American, he would, if caught, be now equally subservient to enslavement'.[39] The failure of his eponymous character to acquire the singularity of character is reinforced by Melville's telescoping of Potter's fifty years of exile in London into three brisk chapters (23–5). Working as a brickmaker, 'serving that very people as a slave' whom he had previously fought as a foe, Potter toils in a London wilderness that is Blakean in its wretchedness. Considering for a moment the devastating irony of his exiled status 'in the

English Egypt', Israel resists the easy typology of a providential American return by abandoning national signifiers altogether for a more fundamental scepticism. 'What signifies who we be, or where we are, or what we do?', he asks.[40] In the book's final chapter the exile's return to his homeland is accomplished, as Potter arrives in Boston on the significant date of 4 July 1826 only to be almost immediately run over by a 'patriotic triumphal car' in a procession celebrating the Battle of Bunker Hill.[41] With the solidification of the national narrative and Potter's discovery that all trace of his family in the Berkshires has been forgotten, Melville concludes his novel by reminding us of the proleptic critique in the dedication, in which the reader is prepared to read a narrative of inconsequential failure. It is worth drawing students' attention here to the carefully constructed resonances at work between his dedication and the final, devastating paragraph. While the former had deployed a mode of mocking irony to critique the pretensions of aristocracy and the blindnesses of democracy, the book's last words materialise that for us in a bleak summary of Potter's fate:

> [Potter] was repulsed in his efforts, after a pension, by certain caprices of law. His scars proved his only medals. He dictated a little book, the record of his fortunes. But long ago it faded out of print – himself out of being – his name out of memory. He died the same day that the oldest oak on his native hills was blown down.[42]

The proudly erect monument addressed in the dedication remains standing. The signifier of Potter's America, one tied to the rhythms of nature rather than those of politics, is symbolically felled, as if overcome by the relentless gales emanating from a new, consolidated, but forgetful United States. Textual, ontological and biographical presences are conjoined here in a shattering vision of irrelevance. Yet, as students become increasingly aware as they read through the book, Melville's act of recuperation fights against such definitiveness by granting Potter a spectral presence within the discourse of exceptionalism. Though ultimately its victim, Potter nevertheless haunts the chaos of revolution to reveal the contingency of national identity even as it is being proclaimed.

As this essay has sought to show, the competing vocabularies of exile and exceptionalism, of patriotism and dislocation, provide students with the conceptual framework for thinking about the ways in which Melville's work matters. The transatlantic features in much of his writing – students might want to consider how, for example, *Redburn* (1849) explores transatlantic urban comparison, or how 'The Paradise of Bachelors and the Tartarus of Maids' (1855) uses a transatlantic framework to explore class, gender, and labour. *Israel Potter* is, perhaps, the most explicitly concerned with how the shape and status of identity – both personal and national – are formed and deformed by the transatlantic pressures of revolutionary war. By encouraging students to think about how geographical distance provides the defamiliarising arenas in which the orchestration of an apparently transparent patriotic national consensus can be resisted, *Israel Potter* offers itself as an exemplary text for our patriotic and jingoism-laden times. Melville's aesthetic thrives on the kinds of disruptions, textual allusions, and metaphorical alliances that encourage a suspicion of transcendent transparencies of all kinds. In *Pierre*, his novel of 1852, Melville's narrator meditates on the essential obscurity of character: '[H]e, who, in the view of its inconsistencies, says of human nature the same that, in view of its contrasts, is said of the divine nature, that it is past finding out, thereby evinces a better appreciation of it than he who, *by always representing it in a clear light, leaves it to be inferred that he clearly knows all about it*' (my emphasis).[43] While *Israel Potter* does not succumb to such a radical terminus of unknowability (for its central character is kept in circulation by Melville's efforts), the complexity of personal and national character that it discloses – where the very idea of character itself is put under pressure – chimes with the earlier book's suspicion of the benefits of revelation. In *Israel Potter* the 'clear light' of narrative and historical certainty is hollowed out to reveal an ideologically motivated sham.

NOTES

1. Jared Sparks, *The Life of John Ledyard* (Cambridge: Hilliard & Brown, 1828), p. 294.
2. Edward Said, 'Reflections on Exile', in *Reflections on Exile and Other Essays* (Cambridge, MA: Harvard University Press, 2000), p. 176.
3. Watson G. Branch, *Melville: The Critical Heritage* (London: Routledge, 1974), pp. 285–6.
4. Alex Calder, 'Blubber: Melville's Bad Writing', in Samuel Otter and Geoffrey Sanborn (eds), *Melville and Aesthetics* (New York: Palgrave Macmillan, 2011), p. 29.
5. Ibid., p. 28.
6. Ibid., p. 30.
7. Sheila Post, 'Melville and the Marketplace', in Giles B. Gunn, (ed.), *A Historical Guide to Herman Melville* (Oxford: Oxford University Press, 2005), p. 124.
8. Ibid., p. 125.
9. [Charles Briggs], 'Introductory', *Putnam's Monthly: A Magazine of Literature, Science, and Art*, 1: 1 (January 1853), 2.
10. Walter E. Bezanson, 'Historical Note', in Harrison Hayford, Hershel

Parker, and G. Thomas Tanselle (eds), *Israel Potter: His Fifty Years of Exile* (Evanston: Northwestern University Press, 1982), p. 219.

11. Herman Melville, *Correspondence*, ed. Lynn Horth (Evanston: Northwestern University Press, 1993), p. 265.

12. Michael Hardt and Antonio Negri, *Empire* (Cambridge, MA: Harvard University Press, 2000), p. 103.

13. Paul Giles, 'The Deterritorialization of American Literature', in Wai Chee Dimock and Lawrence Buell (eds), *Shades of the Planet: American Literature as World Literature* (Princeton: Princeton University Press, 2007), p. 41.

14. For more on the Young America movement and Melville's relationship to it, see Edward L. Widmer, *Young America: The Flowering of Democracy in New York City* (New York: Oxford University Press, 1999).

15. Review of George Bancroft, *History of the United States from the Discovery of the American Continent* (1852), *Putnam's Monthly: A Magazine of Literature, Science, and Art*, 1: 2 (March 1853), 300.

16. Ibid., p. 302.

17. Ibid.

18. Said, 'Reflections on Exile', p. 176.

19. Susan Manning, 'Transatlantic Historical Fiction', in Eve Tavor Bannet and Susan Manning (eds), *Transatlantic Literary Studies, 1660–1830* (Cambridge: Cambridge University Press, 2012), p. 260.

20. Edward Said, *Representations of the Intellectual* (New York: Vintage, 1994), p. 49. See, as representative examples, Susan Rubin Suleiman (ed.), *Exile and Creativity: Signposts, Travelers, Outsiders, Backward Glances* (Durham, NC: Duke University Press, 1998); Ada Savin (ed.), *Migration and Exile: Charting New Literary and Artistic Territories* (Newcastle: Cambridge Scholars Publishing, 2013); and Caren Kaplan, *Questions of Travel: Postmodern Discourses of Displacement* (Durham, NC: Duke University Press, 1996).

21. Said, 'Reflections on Exile', p. 177.

22. Said's essay is a complex, ambiguous, and, at times, uncertain meditation on the word. While he recognises the enforced condition of exile (as opposed to, say, expatriation), at times his figure mutates into an unsettling intellectual misfit, perfectly positioned in his or her cosmopolitan worldliness to combat the ideologies of nationalism: 'Exiles cross borders, break barriers of thought and experience' (185). A succinct critique of this conflation of roles can be found in Stefan Collini, *Absent Minds: Intellectuals in Britain* (Oxford: Oxford University Press, 2006), pp. 422–34.

23. Herman Melville, *Israel Potter: His Fifty Years of Exile*, ed. Harrison Hayford, Hershel Parker, and G. Thomas Tanselle (Evanston: Northwestern University Press, 1982), p. 137.

24. Ibid., p. v.

25. Ernest Renan's text, 'What Is a Nation?', is of course a key theoretical companion for its acute realisation of how national imaginaries are dependent upon acts of forgetting. See 'What Is a Nation?', trans. Martin Tom, in Homi Bhaba (ed.), *Nation and Narration* (London: Routledge, 1990), pp. 8–22.

26. Melville, *Israel Potter*, p. vi.

27. Sparks, *The Life of John Ledyard*, p. vi.

28. Melville, *Israel Potter*, p. 13.

29. Ibid., p. 120.

30. Paul Giles, ' "Bewildering Intertanglement": Melville's Engagement with British Culture', in Robert S. Levine (ed.), *The Cambridge Companion to Herman Melville* (Cambridge: Cambridge University Press, 1998), p. 242.

31. Melville, *Israel Potter*, p. 123.

32. In Hawthorne's tale, the 'contagion' of rebellion is undercut by a daring, and unexpected, change of perspective: 'The Man in the Moon heard the far bellow: "Oho," quoth he, "the old Earth is frolicsome to-night!" ' (*Selected Tales and Sketches* (New York: Penguin Books, 1987), pp. 49–50). Michael J. Colacurcio offers a reading of 'My Kinsman' that resonates with the concerns of Melville's novel: 'Here, then, would be the ultimate insult which the deflationist strategy of [the tale] offers to the vaunted claims of American typological historiography: so far from being a unique and climactic event in the unfolding of Divine Purpose, the "majestic" Revolution is not more remarkable, "structurally," than any other local resistance to local authority' (*The Province of Piety: Moral History in Hawthorne's Early Tales* (Cambridge, MA: Harvard University Press, 1984), p. 149).

33. Melville, *Israel Potter*, p. 124.

34. Ibid., pp. 122, 125.

35. Ibid., p. 38.

36. Ibid., p. 46.

37. Ibid., pp. 46–7.

38. Ibid., p. 52.

39. Ibid., p. 152.

40. Ibid., p. 157.

41. Ibid., p. 167.

42. Ibid., p. 169.

43. Herman Melville, *Pierre; or, The Ambiguities*, ed. Harrison Hayford, Hershel Parker, and G. Thomas Tanselle (Evanston: Northwestern University Press, 1971), p. 70.

Americans, Abroad: Reading *Portrait of a Lady* in a Transatlantic Context

Sandra A. Zagarell

Until recently, I read and taught Henry James's *The Portrait of a Lady* (1881) as most people do: as the high point of James's treatment of the 'international theme' during his 'early' period. *Portrait*, I assumed, stages encounters between innocent or naive 'New World' Americans and the Old World, or Europe, and especially the latter's sophisticated, often devious inhabitants. But when I taught *Portrait* in a new course, 'Transatlantic Currents: Nineteenth-Century English and US-American Literature', I found, to my surprise, that this reading seemed off-base. The English literature in the course reminded my students and me that the very notion of 'Europe' is provincial. The English, like most western Europeans, thought of themselves in terms of their nationality and national culture; in fact, they tended to distinguish themselves from inhabitants of 'the continent'.[1] More significantly, my class realised that there are very few 'Europeans' in *Portrait*; the only important one is Isabel Archer's English suitor Lord Warburton. Every other major character is American; most are upper-class. Was this novel about such Americans, not about Americans' collision with the Old World? As this essay develops the proposition that one can plausibly read *Portrait* as a novel that characterises a certain kind of American, it will sometimes describe how that reading emerged in my class and sometimes develop my own subsequent analysis. The second was made possible not simply by teaching *Portrait* in this new context but because class members were inquiring, imaginative and very smart. While I will avoid the awkwardness of distinguishing among what actually transpired when I taught the novel, what I have arrived at after teaching it, and what my future pedagogical approach will be, I want to highlight the most significant outcome of this experience: its testimony to how mutually enriching teaching and scholarship can be.

That much of the literature we read in 'Transatlantic Currents' had a national focus proved valuable for recognising how deeply concerned with

Americans *Portrait* is. It was obvious that *Uncle Tom's Cabin* insists on the collusion with raced slavery of Americans in the north as well as the south, that *Bleak House* takes the measure of key aspects of England as the industrial revolution and modern notions of class, gender and property were taking hold, and that *The Garies and Their Friends* exposes the entrenchment of racial apartheid and racial violence in Philadelphia (supposedly the city of brotherly love) and the resilience of the city's African Americans. Reading these novels prompted students to note that, in contrast, *Portrait* is not set in the country of which its characters are citizens. This led us to explore how the novel portrayed England, Paris, Florence and Rome. Not in much detail, we noted. Close examination of even the passage which features Isabel Archer's excursions to 'old Rome' to remind herself of the 'smallness' of her own unhappiness given the sadness of the 'human lot' throughout history revealed that Rome functions as background.[2] Indeed, comparisons with a *Baedeker's* or a *Murray's* suggest that *Portrait's* England, Italy and France rarely exceed what contemporary travel guides featured. It thus becomes apparent that the novel takes advantage of its non-American, or 'European', settings, not, as so many critics have taken for granted, because European countries provided the social, cultural and historical texture which the United States lacked,[3] but because 'Europe' allows it to distil what was particularly American about the Americans it features. Freed from their immediate socio-cultural coordinates – as Isabel is not when she lives in Albany or visits in New York City – characters could be featured as quintessentially American, without attention paid to supporting props which might distract from that core. And what, we asked, do James's Americans exhibit? In particular, habits of mind about the accessibility of other nations that the novel casts as exceedingly American and, coexisting with those, equally American assumptions about the superiority, even uniqueness, of Americans themselves.

Viewed from this perspective, *Portrait* emerges as a very American novel whose Americanness is inseparable from its transatlanticism. If students take this proposition to imply that James is simply appropriating European countries by using them as settings for studies of Americans and that he is thereby figuratively colonising them, countering the oversimplification of such inferences could involve asking them to examine James's history and his writing. He had been living mainly in England or France or Italy since 1872 and he was immersed in aspects of these countries' histories, cultures, and geographies. He had also long associated closely with French, Russian, English, and American writers and with other 'Europeans' of his own class. His knowledge of the countries he lived in far exceeded that of a tourist and also of many American 'expatriates', and he drew on it when he chose to: in well-informed essays about Florence, Venice, and elsewhere for the *Nation*, the *Atlantic Monthly*, the *Independent*, and other US magazines as well as his 1877 novel

The Americans, with its nuanced representations of parts of France and of French aristocrats, and his 1870 story 'An International Episode', which deftly satirises English provincialism.

What his transatlantic residency also afforded James was something such a residency has afforded others as well: a cosmopolitan perspective on his own country. In suggesting this, it is worth noting that the fiction of most post-bellum US-American writers, realist and regionalist alike, was concerned with who Americans were as the nation regrouped in the wake of the Civil War and Reconstruction, and industrialisation and other aspects of modernisation became conspicuously irreversible. In this light, the unusualness of James's standpoint for an American writer becomes especially clear, for whereas post-bellum US-American literature was normally written by American authors who lived in the United States, living 'abroad' gave James special purchase on Americans. It underwrote the particular insider-without perspective from which *Portrait* is written: the position of a sometime participant who had observed Americans closely from within, then continued to do so from across the Atlantic. James, moreover, was not merely living outside the US, but was doing so in countries to which genteel Americans were travelling in increasing numbers, giving him ample opportunity to continue to observe this class of Americans. Still further, his insider-withoutness is enhanced by a particular kind of queerness: a sceptical, analytic view of heterosexual arrangements which Americans generally took to be givens, namely the conflation of gender and sex and both with selfhood.[4]

A student in 'Transatlantic Currents', an English major, noticed that last dimension of *Portrait*. It occurred to him because he compared the mutual attentiveness of male and female characters in Jane Austen's novels and in *Jane Eyre* to *Portrait*'s men and women and saw that the latter are not intensely oriented towards one another. His observation led me to explore *Portrait*'s sustained dissociation of gender, self, and desire in a companion piece to this essay entitled '*Portrait of a Lady*: "No intention of deamericanising"'.[5] 'Americans, Abroad' focuses on aspects of the novel which complement this disaggregation. My subject here is *Portrait*'s exposé of Americans' penchant for assuming that other nations and cultures can be known synecdochally, by characterising people who stand for them, while Americans themselves are exceptions to this rule: Americans, the thinking goes, are individual and they can create themselves as they will.

There is nothing particularly American about thinking in terms of types or samples; it is a form of generalisation, of how we make sense of the sheer magnitude of life. But what I will call synecdochal thinking became increasingly common during and after the Enlightenment, as the known world continuously expanded. Reference to European exploration and colonisation of the 'New' World makes this clear: encountering unfamiliar people, cultures, flora and fauna, and geographies, Europeans familiarised these as they colonised them, partly by employing Europe-based systems of classification.[6] Moreover, newer and newer technologies of observation and examination, ever-growing opportunities for travel, the mechanisation of print, the spread of literacy and of international commerce, the rise of industrial production, the continual increase in available goods – all this and more also encouraged both categorisation and a tendency to conceive one member of a class as a stand-in for the entire class.[7]

By the early nineteenth century, Americans were relying more and more on synecdochal thinking to secure knowledge of their own vast and changing country. It took forms as varied as the US Census and other numerical forms of information that circulated in print, in government-issued material or magazines, newspapers and books, in the proliferation in popular culture of regional or racial types – the Sambo, Paul Bunyan, the Yankee peddler, and the like – and, in 1876, in the Centennial Exposition in Philadelphia, where exhibits like 'the' Colonial Kitchen and 'the' Swedish Cottage purported to capture lifeways past and present. Americans relied on synecdochal thinking to gain purchase on newly 'discovered' places in Africa, Latin America, and the Middle East, and also on 'Old World' nations. Likewise, Washington Irving used it to convey the essence of 'John Bull' in the *Sketch-Book* and, as Emerson's title indicates, he employed it in *English Traits*, parts of which we read in 'Transatlantic Currents'. Such thinking intensified as steamships, increased means and leisure, and the thirst for knowledge of 'Europe' converged in the post-bellum era. It also appeared in the travel literature and tourist guides which proliferated over the course of the nineteenth century and, by mid-century, often featured visual representations of national or regional types.

James was not resistant to synecdochal thinking, as is evinced by the titles of two novels which preceded *Portrait*, *The American* and *The Europeans*, and his effort to characterise 'the' American girl in 'Daisy Miller'. *Portrait*'s commitment to characterising Americans sometimes exhibits it as well, but the novel also plumbs its drawbacks, specifically Americans' excessive use of it to attain what they took to be epistemological command of the European countries to which so many of them were gaining physical access in the decades after national reunification. *Portrait* suggests that while characterising 'Europeans' using the shorthand of types presumes that 'Europeans' are static and provides little or no insight into them, what it says a good deal about are the Americans who engage in it. *Portrait* not only exposes the epistemological narrowness, bordering on materialism, which inheres in the assumption that assembling a mental museum of types or exemplars is tantamount to understanding cultures and peoples; it also backlights the deceptions and self-deception that such thinking can lead to in those who practise it.

Having established what synecdochal thinking is and suggested that *Portrait* scrutinises it, I asked students whether it might figure in *Portrait*'s initial characterisation of Isabel Archer. They quickly recognised it as an expression of her early naive arrogance. Shortly after she arrives in England, for example, she tells Ralph Touchett that she wants to see ' "specimens": it was a word that played a considerable part in her vocabulary; she had given him to understand that she wished to see English society illustrated by eminent cases'.[8] Although Ralph lightly mocks this nearly perfect description of synecdochal thinking about national types by noting, as Lord Warburton comes into view, that he is 'a specimen of an English gentleman', Isabel persists in it.[9] When, in her first encounter with Madame Merle, she hears the mixture of French with English that characterises Merle's speech, she thinks, 'She's a Frenchwoman . . . [;] she says that as if she were French.'[10] Once Madame Merle makes it clear that she is American, Isabel simply re-conceives her as an exception which proves the rule that national identities (including those of other Americans, though not herself) are generally amenable to being summed up by types: ' "Ah then she's not French . . . " ' she says to herself, and proceeds to romanticise Madame Merle as an unusual American – 'Rarer even to be French seemed it to be American on such interesting terms.'[11] In doing this Isabel is not merely simplifying; she is making herself susceptible to Madame Merle's poses and her machinations, just as later, in idealising Gilbert Osmond as a man who 'belonged to [none of the] types already present to her mind . . . he was a specimen apart', [12] she falls prey to his very American performance as a unique individual who commands admiration as such.

How else might *Portrait* problematise Americans' synecdochal thinking? Henrietta Stackpole's pre-formulated mission to observe manifestations of the inferiority of 'European' life and institutions and report them to her American readers is fairly obvious, but it calls attention to subtler instances. Madame Merle herself is one of these. Her display of her supposed command of the English is multiply significant. It is a pose designed to convey her sophistication to the still-naive Isabel and it exemplifies how she herself thinks. The scene in which the two women walk in the rain at Gardencourt illustrates this. Madame Merle declares that 'in England the pleasures of smell were great . . . there was a certain mixture of fog and beer and soot which, however odd it might sound, was the national aroma, and was most agreeable to the nostrils, and she used to lift the sleeve to her British overcoat and bury her nose in it, inhaling the fine, clear scent of the wool'.[13] While Merle's flamboyant gesture slyly mocks Isabel's zeal for understanding England through specimens and betrays limits to her own knowledge of cultures and countries, it also mocks readers who do not take note of it until they later understand that Merle specialises in manipulating others' predilections – and, perhaps, that they too have fallen for her pronouncements about 'the [English] national aroma'.

Recognising how brilliantly *Portrait* satirises synecdochal thinking is rewarding, but the resonance of its satire becomes more apparent when its conjunction with other habits of mind is identified. Isabel is particularly susceptible to Merle's performance because of her assumption that she herself can observe without being involved, can 'look about [her]', 'taste for herself', without 'tasting the cup of experience'.[14] Is there anything especially 'American' about this presumption of being able to look and take in without having to experience – about being so free that one can determine one's own experiences? Many students could recognise this expectation as an expression, on a personal level, of American exceptionalism. Referencing Emersonian self-reliance can illuminate this point and can encourage recognition of *Portrait*'s complementary suggestion that this sense of entitlement coexists with Americans' supposition that although people of other nationalities could be accounted for by types, they are free to choose simply to be themselves. Lydia Touchett's response when Isabel objects that her criticism of almost every country 'doesn't seem to be American' at once exemplifies that stand-point and slyly shows that Americans could in fact be typified – by their sense of individualism. 'American? Never in the world: that's shockingly narrow. My point of view, thank God, is personal',[15] she says, demonstrating that the claim to high individualism could shade into being inured to anyone or anything but oneself and one's own preferences.

Having seen this, students are also ready to see that *Portrait* goes much farther in its exposé of Americans' faith in their ability to be or create themselves.[16] I invite them to consider the proposition that many of its Americans are genteel, in some cases wealthy, analogues to the pioneers who were settling the American West in the decades after the Civil War. The West offered the supposedly virgin land from and on which many settlers would re-create themselves as successful farmers and ranchers. Europe offered genteel and would-be genteel Americans something comparable. It was a 'world' to which they could travel readily, and where they could enjoy historic atmosphere, acquire polish, and more generally increase their cultural prestige. For many of *Portrait*'s Americans 'Europe' also offers material opportunities: former Vermont farm boy Daniel Touchett profits from international finance, while Mr and Mrs Luce, Edmond Rosier, Madame Merle, and Gilbert Osmond can live in relative opulence without great expense. But whereas pioneers in the West often touted their Americanness, Gilbert Osmond and Madame Merle's pretensions to gentility preclude such an affirmation. They display their Americanness nevertheless, for both are extreme instances of the vaunted American practice of self-invention. The novel makes much of the pains both take to downplay their Americanness and present themselves as 'European' and of the unintentionally American character of those efforts. Their performances are pitched so conspicuously to how they want others to see them that both can be regarded as subtle versions of an American exaggeration of self-invention, the con artist.

Since Madame Merle's efforts are more obvious than Gilbert Osmond's, it's productive to explore hers first. Erasing both her original surname and her proper name, she wields the conventional cognomen of a married Swiss woman as though it signified nobility. Similarly, she introduces herself to Isabel as though she were announcing her own pedigree: 'I am an old friend of your aunt's. I've lived much in Florence. I'm Madame Merle.'[17] Everything she says and does can be traced to her strained self-characterisation as a woman who belongs to 'the old, old world',[18] as she puts it, from the linguistic mélange in which she speaks to her collections of exquisite 'things' to her flaunted musical accomplishments. As she affirms her 'Europeanness', Merle also betrays her eagerness not to be counted as American ('I was born under the national banner', she edgily says to Isabel) while referencing the 'old World' in a manner which marks her Americanness.[19] 'I think I know my Europe',[20] she declares, using a phrase which is not only crude but goes against the grain of European countries' intensifying nationalism during the 1870s and 1880s.

Seeing Merle as a patently American impersonation of a 'European' fosters understanding that Gilbert Osmond's American self-fashioning as a 'European' is no less self-betraying. Like Merle's, his collections are studied displays of cultural capital. His tasteful and uncommon objects assert his sophistication and knowledge as well as the leisure to look for them. (This is his message when he talks about discovering a sketch by Correggio 'on a panel daubed over by some inspired idiot' in a dusty Florentine shop.)[21] Like Merle's, his pose as a European unintentionally broadcasts Americanness. Who but an American could declare, with an irony which does not disguise the essential truth of the sentiment, that 'there were two or three people in the world I envied – the Emperor of Russia, for instance, and the Sultan of Turkey! There were even moments when I envied the Pope of Rome – for the consideration he enjoys.'[22] When Isabel says that Osmond always seems to be envying someone he replies, 'I don't want to destroy people – I only want to *be* them.' He adds, disingenuously but with a truth which the novel notes though he does not, 'You see it would destroy only myself.'[23] Isabel's late realisation that Osmond thinks of himself as 'the first gentleman of Europe' perfectly captures the man he has striven so self-consciously to create, its core Americanness, and its inappropriateness to the circumstances for which he devises it.[24] Aspiring to the status of 'first' bespeaks the ambition that often fuels Americans' self-creation, while 'the first gentleman of Europe' situates 'gentleman', a word Osmond uses frequently about himself, within the context of his contempt for actual Europeans. Nowhere is that contempt more evident than when, during their engagement, Osmond explains to Isabel that he could not become an Italian patriot because he liked Italy as it was,[25] the implication being that Italians' efforts to create a unified Italian republic threaten to mar the 'Italy' he likes as he likes it.

Are there counterpoints to these Americans who reinvent themselves as (faux) Europeans? Asking this question can turn students' attention to the Americans who have followed the more familiar path of self-creation in America. Determined to remain American, they are staunchly impervious or hostile to European countries and what they offer. The novel invites identification of Henrietta Stackpole as a self-made woman. Isabel regards Henrietta as having something of the 'strong, sweet, fresh odour' of America itself while Ralph comments that 'she does smell of the Future – it almost knocks one down'.[26] Henrietta's disdain for European countries contributes to her success as a journalist; she offers up accounts of their hidebound traditionalism for her American readers. Caspar Goodwood affords perspective on her male counterpart in a form masculine self-creation was taking in the post-bellum United States. Unlike the rough-edged protagonist of William Dean Howells's *The Rise of Silas Lapham* (1885) Goodwood combines the modern capitalist with a kind of physically accomplished masculinity whose Americanness was being celebrated in the latter decades of the nineteenth century (and which would have one apogee in Teddy Roosevelt and his Rough Riders). Goodwood is canny about markets and management; he likes 'to organize, to contend, to administer'; his intelligence is practical – he is an inventor; he is athletic, renowned at Harvard as 'a gymnast and an oarsman'; he is 'of supremely strong, clean make', as Isabel acknowledges.[27] Gilbert Osmond, whose perversity and keen intelligence fertilise one another, captures something subtler about Goodwood's masculinity: 'The whole American world was in a conspiracy to make you [narrowly commercial]. But you've resisted; you've something about you that saved you. And yet you're so modern, so modern; the most modern man we know!'[28] What 'saves' Goodwood and makes him a 'modern man' is, Osmond implies, his romanticism, his love of Isabel. Undeniable and intense, this love is also informed by Goodwood's driving purposefulness: he wants her and only her. His insularity is so extreme that when he travels to Europe in pursuit of her he rarely takes in anything about the countries in which she is living and almost always returns immediately to the United States after seeing her.

Considering the lights *Portrait* shines on many of its Americans' attitudes towards 'Europe', 'Europeans', and themselves is invaluable for recognising the complexity with which Isabel Archer exemplifies American self-fashioning. Some recent readers have regarded the pre-marriage characterisation of Isabel as a critique of American, indeed Emersonian, self-reliance and have maintained that in her later development she grows beyond self-reliance. In my view, this flattens James's assessment of Americans. Situating Isabel's 'portrait' within the novel's cool-eyed assessment of the forms of provincial, sometimes destructive self-fashioning that most of its Americans practise can bring into focus James's emphasis on the remarkable capacity for growth and depth that self-fashioning, or self-reliance, also makes possible.[29] Indeed, *Portrait* goes further than Emerson, for while Emerson's self-reliant American enjoys privileges that were generally reserved for men, *Portrait* indicates that they were available to some American 'girls'. The narrator empha- sises that '[l]ike the mass of American girls, Isabel had been encouraged to express herself' and 'believes her own thoughts'; even a moderately well-read American could discern that, like Emerson's self-reliant man, she is also 'origi- nal and not conventional'.[30] Emersonianly, she has profound regard for her own 'Supreme Soul', and she trusts herself so entirely that while she assumes she will make mistakes, she also assumes she will be able to learn from them. Additionally, she takes for granted that she has extraordinary 'independence', can guide her own 'development', and can enjoy her 'liberty'.[31]

Asking students to explore the implications of the association of Isabel with 'independence', self-development, and 'liberty' helps them recognise these American watchwords as signifiers of her unexamined American sense of indi- vidual freedom. This sense can be linked to an arrogantly complacent sense, also discernible in 'Self-Reliance', that she can be exempt from suffering.[32] Close attention to the sections in which Osmond woos her also shows them that Isabel's presumption of enjoying the liberty of free choice is precisely what causes her the suffering to which she thinks she can remain immune: she cannot imagine that she could be manipulated. The same level of attention to the chapter devoted to her long examination of her marriage, her husband, and herself (chapter 42) reveals that it is also her self-reliance that enables her to face the full nature of all three, and, in the process, to redefine her concept of liberty. In this dark night of her soul, her self-trust is essential to the depth of her reflections and realisations. Relying on her own clarity of mind and emotion, she is able to identify her fundamental incompatibility with Osmond as a matter of 'attach[ing] such different ideas, such different ideas and associa- tions, to the same formulas'. In coming to terms with this incompatibility, she re-conceives her own once individualistic concept of liberty to associate it with responsibilities that come with privilege. 'Her notion of the aristocratic life was simply the union of great knowledge with great liberty; the knowledge would give one a sense of duty and the liberty a sense of enjoyment.' This, she under- stands, is fundamentally at odds with Osmond's view of liberty as 'altogether a thing of forms, a conscious, calculated thing'.[33] Significantly, and, again, most Emersonianly, as she travels to Gardencourt to be with Ralph when he dies, she understands that her own life is an ongoing process, and she can foresee 'the quick vague shadow of a long future' which may include happiness as well as the kind of suffering she currently experiences.[34]

This future lies beyond the novel's last page, but in foreclosing on a conventional romantic resolution by making it clear that Isabel could not maintain her sense of self if she were to unite with Caspar Goodwood, *Portrait* charges those readers who want to imagine her life after she returns to Rome with the task of engaging with the sombre sense of liberty and the tragic sense of self-reliance she has developed. Imagining this – Isabel living within the framework of the choices she has made, however unaware she was of their ramifications when she made them – entails accepting the embedded form of liberty which she herself has formulated, with its attendant limits and suffering as well as the internal sovereignty it preserves. In contrast, imagining a future for Isabel free of the marriage that encumbers her amounts to a return to the individualistic, detached concept of liberty and self which she had once embraced and had significantly deepened. Choosing any path for Isabel thus involves much more than envisioning the future of a beloved character. It requires grappling with what the novel poses as very American questions – questions about the character of self-reliance and of liberty. Put differently, both *Portrait*'s own transatlantic location and James's transatlantic insider-without perspective are fundamental to the novel's charge to its designated readers – American but also English, since James published it virtually simultaneously in the US and England – to contemplate afresh what it is to be an American, and what, for better and for worse, Americans have the potential to become.[35]

ACKNOWLEDGEMENTS

Many thanks to Ana Cara, Eve Sandbeg, and Bethany Schneider for suggestions and feedback.

NOTES

1. British novelist and essayist Margaret Oliphant, in her 1882 review of *Portrait*, draws the distinction as follows: James's 'studies have their scenes laid on the Continent, or in this island'. Margaret Oliphant, 'Recent Novels', *Blackwood's Edinburgh Magazine*, 131 (March 1882), 374.
2. Henry James, *The Portrait of a Lady*, 1908 (New York: Barnes & Noble, 2004), p. 537.
3. Michael Gorra, *Henry James and the Making of an American Masterpiece* (New York: W. W. Norton, 2012) is prominent among these.
4. I use 'queer' to refer to a standpoint, not as a biographical characterisation. Although, whatever James himself was, he was surely 'not straight', to

borrow Siobin B. Somerville's phrase, the queerness of much of his fiction through *Portrait* lies in the coolly analytic eye it trains on heterosexuality and gender and their accompanying institutions, but for the most part not in subtextual themes or subtly referenced attractions or relationships. See Siobin B. Somerville, 'Queer', in Bruce B. Burgett and Glenn Hendler (eds), *Keywords for American Cultural Studies* (New York: New York University Press, 2007), pp. 187–91.

5. Sandra A. Zagarell, '*The Portrait of a Lady*: "no intention of deamericanising"', *Henry James Review*, 35: 1 (Winter 2014), 23–33.

6. My thanks to Professor Ana Cara for this observation.

7. References to Linnaeus's creation of his system of botanical classification would help make this point, as would information about the emergence of such national icons as flags and trees, the systematisation of museums and collections, and the emergence of ethnography. James Clifford, *The Predicament of Culture: Twentieth-Century Ethnography, Literature, and Art* (Cambridge, MA: Harvard University Press, 1986); Eric Hobsbawn, 'Introduction: Inventing Traditions' and 'Mass-Producing Traditions: Europe, 1870–1914' in Eric Hobsbawm and Terence Ranger (eds), *The Invention of Tradition* (Cambridge: Cambridge University Press, 1983), pp. 1–14, 263–307; and Mary Louise Pratt, *Imperial Eyes: Travel Writing and Transculturation* (London: Routledge, 1992) could prove useful. A premise of museums' exemplification of synecdochal thinking was articulated by George Brown Goode (1851–96), creator, in 1881, of the Division of Arts and Industries and Material Media of the National Museum (which would become the Smithsonian): objects were a window to the past because '. . . the people of the world have left their history most fully recorded in the works of their hands' <http://siarchives.si.edu/history/exhibits/baird/bairde.htm> (last accessed 22 May 2014).

8. James, *Portrait*, p. 78.

9. Ibid., p. 78.

10. Ibid., p. 186.

11. Ibid., p. 187.

12. Ibid., p. 277.

13. Ibid., p. 203.

14. Ibid., p. 164.

15. Ibid., p. 73.

16. In his fine reading of Isabel Archer, Gorra has recently identified her flawed assumption that she is at liberty to fashion herself as a critique of American exceptionalism. Gorra uses the concept to characterise *Portrait*'s evaluation of the utopian Emersonianism endorsed by Henry James, Sr, but in his view the critique centres on Isabel, whereas I see it to be both broader and more nuanced, and maintain that James considers

the strengths of self-reliance as well as its many faults; see Gorra, *Henry James*.

17. James, *Portrait*, p. 188.
18. Ibid., p. 210.
19. Ibid., p. 188.
20. Ibid., p. 208.
21. Ibid., p. 281. *Portrait* is quite obvious in its commentary on this. Edward Rosier, a great collector of lace and porcelain, tells Isabel that antiques in Paris are better and 'cheaper, too, if you know the right places', as he does (p. 229).
22. James, *Portrait*, p. 281.
23. Ibid., p. 318.
24. Ibid., p. 449.
25. Ibid., p. 281.
26. Ibid., p. 107.
27. Ibid., pp. 130–1.
28. Ibid., pp. 524–5.
29. Gorra has given currency to this reading and it has been picked up in reviews by Jean Strouse, 'Why Did Isabel Go Back', *New York Review of Books*, 22 November 2012, pp. 27–9, and James Wood, 'Perfuming the Money Issue', *London Review of Books*, 11 October 2012, pp. 3–6.
30. James, *Portrait*, p. 68; Ralph Waldo Emerson, 'Self-Reliance', *Essays and Lectures*, ed. Joel Porte (New York: Library of America, 1983), p. 259.
31. James, *Portrait*, pp. 65, 67, 129.
32. Ibid., pp. 62, 164–5.
33. Ibid., p. 450.
34. Ibid., p. 583.
35. That *Portrait*'s English readers were less appreciative of its ending than its American readers shows the former's reluctance to give themselves over to such questions, and that is itself another affirmation of the novel's Americanness.

PART IV

Teaching Genres in Transatlantic Context

CHAPTER 12

Making Anglo-American Oratory Resonate

Tom F. Wright

The long nineteenth century was a high water mark for spoken elo-quence in transatlantic culture. 'This century', proclaimed one popular Boston anthology of speeches in 1857, 'may be called, with strict propriety, the Golden Age of American Oratory.'[1] Two decades later, the London *Times* observed that 'in the course of these fifty years we have become a nation of speech-makers. Everyone speaks now.'[2] From the Senate floor to the Mechanics' Institutes of Scotland, from abolition speeches at London's Exeter Hall to the labour rallies of industrial Chicago, and through acres of newspaper and print transcriptions, the age resounded with spoken words whose role in shaping a shared cultural and literary imagination is too often overlooked. Because oratory of the period was simultaneously a literary form and a form of power, a world of expression both functional and artistic, it sits uneasily at the crossroads of modern disciplinary traditions. Yet any account of modern literature that ignores the importance of this expressive world of voices reduces our understanding of the period. Equally, any understanding of these traditions that presents Edmund Burke or Wolfe Tone apart from Sojourner Truth and Mark Twain diminishes the network of stylistic, insti-tutional, and discursive bonds that make this shared spoken culture so vibrant and contentious.

To contemporary sceptics like Thomas Carlyle, this oratorical world was at times an 'epoch . . . of babblement'.[3] To the twenty-first-century literary scholar and teacher, however, this fertile body of speech offers unique pos-sibilities for developing transnational curricula. This essay focuses on the classroom potentials offered by new understandings of this 'babblement' and by transatlantic approaches to its traditions, and considers possible approaches to some varied examples of suitable texts. The speeches, lectures, and sermons of the period, I suggest, represent not just a neglected rich trove of verbal art, but also an exemplary way of encouraging reflection on the intersections of language, performance, and history, while making fundamental transnational and multicultural currents tangible.

RETURNING SPEECH TO LITERARY STUDIES

Thinking about oratory as part of a teachable literary tradition represents one chapter in the broader ongoing enlargement of English studies. In a discipline that is moving beyond circumscribed definitions of the 'literary', speech texts are merely one of many types of artifacts now being brought into reading lists to provide a fuller sense of the history of creative expression. But this attempt to bring speech back to the classroom faces particular obstacles. Though spoken eloquence had lain at the heart of both humanistic education and artistic endeavour for hundreds of years, over the last hundred years a combination of post-Romantic conceptions of art and the professionalisation of higher education helped effect a separation of oral language and literature proper. By the late nineteenth century, oratory had already become more prominently associated in the literary and intellectual mind with the political marketplace and statecraft, more concerned with matters of ideology than with permanent artistic values. This division duly exerted sway over canon formation during the founding moments of British and American literary studies, with speeches, sermons, and lectures seen as detached from the main strands of the novel, drama, poetry, and the essay. Gradually, the two subjects of 'Rhetoric and Communication' and 'English' developed separate institutional identities, the one having surprisingly little to do with the other.

A series of intellectual trends contributed to the persistence of English studies' neglect of oral forms. The New Criticism distrusted the ephemeral, contextual nature of the spoken word and the kinds of questions that emerge from rhetorical situations. The influence of social history encouraged literary scholars to label bodies of work that survive the processes of public historical memory as elite discourses. History of the book scholarship, with its emphasis on the materiality of texts, also tended to marginalise the spoken word. Most momentously, Jacques Derrida's powerful poststructuralist critique of Western overemphasis on the 'presence' of speech raised the ideological stakes involved in the very act of contemplating spoken texts. The combination of these wide-ranging and overlapping tendencies enabled a generation of scholars to view oratorical expression with suspicion.

During recent years, however, there has been something of a return to the world of speech. The New Historicism advocated a less sharp divide between 'literary' and 'rhetorical' and made possible the study of a wider range of texts, while multicultural literary studies has encouraged scholars to explore the archives of non-literate or working-class peoples often denied access to print discourse. As a result, speeches and ideas about voice have re-emerged as themes in nineteenth-century literary studies. From the perspective of Victorian Britain, critics such as Ivan Kreilkamp and Matthew Bevis have positioned the works of writers from Charles Dickens to Joseph Conrad back alongside the popular and Parliamentary oratory and speech traditions that served as the aesthetic foil and inspiration to literary creation. From an American perspective, Jay Fleigelman and Christopher Looby have made it clear that US literary emergence must be understood in terms of its unique relation to speech and performance, and Sandra Gustafson has encouraged a powerful new sense of what the 'emerging media' of multicultural oratorical history can teach us.[4]

Nonetheless, teachers of this material must still make a compelling case for the lasting importance of elusive moments of public speech. For some, the oratory of the past will always seem more historical or instrumental than literary and disconnected from the rest of the literary landscape. Since by definition only the voices of the more powerful actors from history tend to survive the process of historical erasure, the study of oratory cannot avoid seeming to be the connoisseurship of elite male discourse. For others, taking this material into the literary classroom involves submitting unsuitable artifacts to improper criteria. Students faced with important but unwieldy political speeches may well concur with Herbert Wichelns's wry observation that 'the statesmen who dominate a crisis, to rouse and mold the mind of senate or nation, has something else to think about than the production of literary masterpieces'.[5]

The most successful approaches would work to show how this material illuminates fundamental questions: what role does speech play in culture and society? What kinds of social relations does public speech stage? How differently do we need to think about oral and written languages, and how do we understand the relation of speech to literary expression? An ideal approach allows for a double focus – to understand the workings of isolated oratorical examples, and to grasp the history of ideas surrounding speech and rhetoric. In light of that primary goal, the teaching of oratory will involve training in close-reading skills, imparting terminology sufficient for students to speak meaningfully about rhetorical appeals, tropes, and parts of oratory (deliberative, epideictic, and forensic). It will also entail asking the kind of questions intrinsic to rhetorical analysis that are not always obvious to students of literature, thinking about what arguments mean on both conceptual and historical levels, the reasons for the adoption of any particular approach, and how spoken utterances can be understood in terms of drama or performativity. Attempting to bring speech back to the classroom through a transatlantic frame allows these questions to be explored through two distinct but intertwined sets of historical, social, and aesthetic contexts, multiplying the possibilities for instructive juxtaposition.

NINETEENTH-CENTURY CONTEXTS AND THEMES

The body of speech between the American Revolution and the death of Victoria provides ideal ground upon which to undertake this kind of seminar-room exploration. To some, however, this is a surprising claim. It seems intuitive to argue, as many have done, that the Romantic period and the onset of mass print media marked a transition from orality to literacy. In one of the most famous of such claims, Walter Ong argued that this moment marked a 'new state of consciousness associated with the definite interiorisation of print and atrophy of ancient rhetorical traditions'.[6] This notion of a watershed moment has become central to influential accounts of nationalism and literary emergence in both British and American contexts.

For a number of reasons, the turn of the nineteenth century was in fact a fertile moment for speech cultures. Intellectually, the influence of the Scottish Enlightenment and the elocutionary movement helped foster new self-conscious engagement with the power of oratory. Politically, the conditions involved in the uneven rise in democracy necessitated new opportunities for deliberation, testimony, and advocacy, helping make popular oratory one of the characteristic genres of transatlantic modernity. Technologically, developments in transport and communications infrastructure also helped catalyse the growth in civic and religious institutions based around live voice, from the reformist clubs, lyceums, and the popular lecture circuit to new types of evangelical camp meetings. These shifts all helped to promote new speech genres and functions for resurgent public oratory in this age of mass print, forms, and opportunities that attracted some of the most compelling and creative minds of the age.

This loquacious age demands to be understood in transatlantic terms for a number of reasons. For one thing, this is how it was understood at the time in schoolrooms where textbooks passed traditions of Anglo-American eloquence to new generations. Moreover, the key intellectual discourses of the period – from abolition and women's suffrage to science and spiritualism – were collaborative, explicitly transatlantic affairs, reliant upon a shared network of settings, speakers, goals, tropes and discourses that frequently dispel notions of a homogenous racial or gendered public sphere. Commentators on both sides throughout the century made much of this shared tradition, even if they eagerly noted points of departure between the eloquence of the two nations.[7] As with all of the topics discussed in this volume, integrating consideration of these two speech worlds helps clarify illuminating dissonances and points of connection.

Nonetheless, factors such as the lack of an established canon make this classroom topic somewhat different from other newly transatlantic subjects. No selection can do justice to a diffuse and shapeless historical record that stretches across multiple arenas, geographic areas, and forms, but in assembling a course suitably representative and rich for the modern seminar room, a balance can be made between well-known and more unexpected and unjustly neglected orators. Classic nineteenth-century speech anthologies remain of use for illuminating the kinds of figures students of the period studied, for clarifying the transatlantic canon of (overwhelmingly male) political oratory in English from Charles James Fox through Daniel Webster to Benjamin Disraeli, and for putting readers in touch with some unavoidable settings and discourses such as American and Irish nationalisms. Building on this familiar terrain, we must also draw upon increased historical knowledge of other oratorical traditions: the women's rights discourse of Frances Wright, Sarah Grimké, Josephine Butler, Frances Power Cobbe, Anna Dickinson, and Elizabeth Cady Stanton; the transatlantic abolitionism of William Wilberforce, Frances Ellen Watkins Harper, Frederick Douglass, and Wendell Phillips; the diverse array of Native American oratory; and speeches from beyond Anglo-America engaging with the British and American empires.

A sample syllabus that offered a pairing of speeches from either side of the Atlantic each week for detailed analysis might run as follows. Following an introductory session on the classical inheritance in eighteenth-century rhetoric, the course could begin with the pairing of Edmund Burke's 'Speech on the Conciliation with the Colonies' (1775) and Thomas Jefferson's final draft of 'The Unanimous Declaration of the United States of America' (1776) to explore the debate over American independence. A week devoted to the theme of nationalisms could place the two Dublin courtroom speeches of Irish republicans Wolfe Tone (1798) and Robert Emmett (1803) in dialogue with Patrick Henry's 'Give Me Liberty or Give Me Death' (1775) oration in Richmond, Virginia. William Wilberforce's parliamentary speech on 'Resolutions Respecting the Slave Trade' (1789) would be an instructive parallel to John Calhoun's senate speech 'Slavery, A Positive Good' (1837) in a seminar on debating slavery.

For a week on testimony and oppression, Feargus O'Connor's 'Chartist Petition' parliamentary address (1848) could be juxtaposed with Sojourner Truth's 'Speech to the Women's Rights Convention' (1851). Theodore Parker's Boston sermon 'The Transient and Permanent in Christianity' (1841) could help clarify the equally challenging sermons of Cardinal John Newman such as 'On the Present Position of Catholics' (1851). A highlight of the module might remain entirely within the United States, pairing Abraham Lincoln's 'House Divided' (1859) speech with Frederick Douglass's '4th July to the Negro' address. For a special week on literary performers, Mark Twain's 1860s talk 'Our Fellow Savages of the Sandwich Islands' could be placed against Oscar Wilde's 'Lecture to Art Students' from his 1880s American tour. For a week thinking about the idea of civil rights, William

Gladstone's 'Government of Ireland Bill' speech to the House of Commons (1886) could provide instructive contrast to Elizabeth Cady Stanton's late speech to Congress, 'Solitude of Self' (1892).

Such pairings would facilitate the tracing of overarching themes or narratives between the weeks. Topics for discussion could include the relationship of speech to republicanism, nationalism, and reform; the changing role of classical rhetorical models; the relation of rhetoric to gender; the relation of public speech to theology and belief; and the evolution of rhetoric over time. Students would be encouraged to discuss the tension of the Romantic focus on authenticity with the neoclassical demand for unity, and to try to think through the role of oratory as entertainment. Above all, students might be encouraged to think of the very act of reading oratory from the past as a problematic endeavour, reliant as it is upon partial and damaged texts and the reconstruction of ephemeral moments of performance. Students should be trained to develop a healthy scepticism towards the very notion of the 'transcribed voice'. No print record of an oral performance is ever transparent, and it can only ever represent a fallible version of one rendition, a fact that can be explored through discussion and exploration of the problematic textual afterlife of speeches by Sojourner Truth and others, where the agenda of the 'scribe' or recorder looms large in the process of documentation. Perhaps the most effective way of addressing these conceptual challenges is to turn textual issues into opportunities for discussing these methodological issues relating to the ethics of historical reconstruction.

To address these themes, brief readings specific to each orator, discourse, or genre can be accompanied by a survey of brief pieces providing a history of rhetorical ideas. These could begin with important excerpted passages from Aristotle, Cicero, or Quintilian, early modern and Scottish Enlightenment sources such as Francis Bacon or Hugh Blair – a shared currency of school and college rhetorical education on both sides of the nineteenth-century Atlantic – before moving to nineteenth-century commentators such as Ralph Waldo Emerson. Students could then be introduced to short selections from twentieth-century rhetorical theorists such as Kenneth Burke, communication studies work by Marshall McLuhan, and more philosophical discussions by Derrida and Brian Vickers. In addition, a useful means of reconnecting these ideas back to the literary world might be to use depictions of oratory in other nineteenth-century writing, in texts ranging from Dickens's *Martin Chuzzlewit* (1843–4) to Douglass's accounts (1845, 1855, 1881) of his experience as a pre-eminent transatlantic orator. Working backwards from novelistic, essayistic, or autobiographical depictions can help establish the social and psychological stakes at work in the primary texts under discussion, and allow students to think about the complex ways in which public speech can be embedded in literary texts.

PUBLIC MORALISTS: JOHN RUSKIN AND EMERSON

Two sets of examples – one canonical pair, one less well known – can help demonstrate how this pedagogical approach can work. For the first, a session on 'Public Lectures and Public Morality' would begin by looking at the notoriously adversarial opening to John Ruskin's lecture 'Traffic' (1864), in which he greets his audience of businessmen at Bradford Town Hall:

> My good Yorkshire friends, you asked me down here among your hills that I might talk to you about this Exchange you are going to build: but earnestly and seriously asking you to pardon me, I am going to do nothing of the kind . . . I cannot speak, to purpose, of anything about which I do not care; and most simply and sorrowfully I have to tell you, in the outset, that I do not care about this Exchange of yours.

He then turns to his real subject a paragraph later:

> All good architecture is the expression of national life and character; and it is produced by a prevalent and eager national taste, or desire for beauty. And I want you to think a little of the deep significance of this word 'taste;' for no statement of mine has been more earnestly or oftener controverted than that good taste is essentially a moral quality. 'No,' say many of my antagonists, 'taste is one thing, morality is another. Tell us what is pretty; we shall be glad to know that; but preach no sermons to us.' Permit me, therefore, to fortify this old dogma of mine somewhat. Taste is not only a part and an index of morality – it is the ONLY morality.[8]

This celebrated rhetorical flourish tends to puzzle and appeal to students, who enjoy the unsettling tension it creates. They could be encouraged to explore why and how this tension is created: for example, how Ruskin's *exordium* (or introductory gesture) contravenes expectation by becoming an effective appeal to ethos based both on his own character ('I cannot speak, to purpose, of anything about which I do not care') and on refutation of a volume of enmity towards him from his 'many . . . antagonists'. In other words, Ruskin asks forgiveness for rejecting and contravening the terms of his invitation in order to strengthen his subsequent moral claims. From a literary perspective, students might note how the elegance of the parallel constructions ('earnestly and seriously . . . simply and sorrowfully', 'natural life . . . natural taste') contrasts with the abrasive content, and might be asked how this relates to his argument about the moral dimension of 'taste'. From a social or historical perspective, since Ruskin voices a popular impatience with moralistic discourse ('preach no sermons'), students might wonder: what kind of discourse or 'dogma' is he claiming to offer instead?

This question would bring us to an instructive parallel, the similarly themed opening of Emerson's key lecture 'The Poet' (1841):

> Those who are esteemed umpires of taste, are often persons who have acquired some knowledge of admired pictures or sculptures, and have an inclination for whatever is elegant; but if you inquire whether they are beautiful souls, and whether their own acts are like fair pictures, you learn that they are selfish and sensual. Their cultivation is local, as if you should rub a log of dry wood in one spot to produce fire, all the rest remaining cold. Their knowledge of the fine arts is some study of rules and particulars, or some limited judgment of color or form, which is exercised for amusement or for show. It is a proof of the shallowness of the doctrine of beauty, as it lies in the minds of our amateurs, that men seem to have lost the perception of the instant dependence of form upon soul.[9]

This 'hidden truth', he proceeds to argue, 'draws us to the consideration of the nature and functions of the Poet, or the man of Beauty, to the means and materials he uses, and to the general aspect of the art in the present time'.[10] Like Ruskin's, Emerson's talk addresses the complex relationship between taste and morality, but students may likely find this approach at once more difficult and more appealing. They might observe that this *exordium* is actually a *refutatio* from the outset, relying upon a strident antithesis between those listeners present and the third-person self-appointed cultural gatekeepers who are both 'umpires' and 'amateurs'. The anaphora, the network of rich similes, and the strategic vagueness of the pronouns may also be points of comment, as might be the illogical but strangely seductive process by which he 'draws' the reader from *refutatio* to proof. The actual argument – that beauty is all about soul, not about 'study' – may take some time to leap out, and students might be asked to reflect on why this is so and how successful they find this elusive rhetorical approach.

Students may grasp the similar theme and can be encouraged to note that both deal with the role of culture under industrialism, the creation of national tastes, and an Anglo-American debate over ethics and aesthetics. However, the key questions would probably centre on the theme of authority and the role of the public lecture form. If these texts are not in fact 'sermons', what do the audience and speaker believe their respective roles to be? It would be useful to gloss a very broad history of the Mechanics Institute and Lyceum movements, and explore how the moral essay comes to occupy a new place as oratory in mid-century life, reaching a new audience of mercantile business-men and aspirational workers. Transatlantic distinctions might also be usefully addressed here, reflecting perhaps on how the passage from the 'The Poet' is also a cultural nationalist argument directed against an 'esteemed', 'cultivated', and implicitly Europhilic elite. These aspects could be used to think through the distance between the apparently levelling and democratic agenda of 'The Poet' and the seemingly patrician 'dogma' of 'Traffic', and a seminar might want to unpack these simplifications. In literary-historical terms, students could be encouraged to think about the influence of Emerson's idiosyncratic oral prose on later literary experiments in organic form, and to discuss the importance of Walt Whitman's attending and writing about this very 1841 lecture.[11] They might also be asked to think about the potentially less ingratiating shrillness of Ruskin in terms of how similar or different they find him from Dickens's satire of mid-century pedagogical rhetoric in *Hard Times* (1854). To provide a usefully sceptical assessment of what lectures meant to the culture, contemporary newspaper and magazine accounts from London could be used or short passages from Henry James's depiction of mid-century lecture culture in *The Bostonians* (1888).

RADICAL WOMEN: BESANT AND PARSONS

A second pairing from the end of the century would consider the discourse of speakers advocating fringe beliefs. In a session entitled 'Radical Women', the first text would be 'Theosophy' (1888) by the British reformer, atheist, and colonial rights activist Annie Besant, a piece first delivered at the South Place Ethical Society in London and repeated worldwide including India and the United States. About five minutes into the talk, Besant offers the following narrative:

> Passing strange is it to note how the minds of men have changed in their aspect to the guardians of the Hidden Wisdom. Of old, in their passionate gratitude, men regarded them as well nigh divine, thinking no honours too great to pay to those who had won the right of entrance into the temple of the Unveiled Truth. In the Middle Ages, when men, having turned from the light, saw devils everywhere in the darkness, the Adepts of the Right Hand Path were dreaded as those of the Left, and wherever new knowledge appeared and obscure regions of nature were made visible, cries of terror and wrath rent the air, and men paid their benefactors with torture and with death. In our own time, secure in the completeness of our knowledge, certain that Our philosophy embraces all things possible in heaven and earth, we neither honour

the teachers as gods nor denounce them as devils: with a shrug of
contempt and a sniff of derision we turn from them, as they come to us
with outstretched hands full of priceless gifts, and we mutter, 'Frauds,
charlatans!' entrenched as we are in our modern conceit that only the
nineteenth century is wise.[12]

Besant is making the case for a type of spiritual belief – 'theosophy', an esoteric
revealed religion – far out of the mainstream of British cultural understanding.
Her task at this moment is to meet the criticisms of a potentially sympathetic
but perhaps wary audience. The seminar students would be encouraged to see
how she opts in this passage for a form of judicial oratory, offering a judgemental narrative of intellectual history that offers an ironic comparison between the
'modern conceit' of the 1880s and the apparently similar small-mindedness of
an imagined Middle Ages. Students may note how she rhetorically navigates a
third course between two antithetical historical responses. They may also note
how her narrative relies for its effect on her troubling key words – 'secure',
'certain', 'wise' – for her audience. Sowing seeds of doubt about the complete-
ness of knowledge, she nonetheless very clearly claims the mantle of 'guardian'
and 'teacher' in the London auditorium.

Another speech from the same period provides an illustrative parallel of
historical narrative as justification. The much-repeated speech 'The Principles
of Anarchy' by Mexican-African-American radical orator and writer Lucy
Parsons was first delivered in Chicago in the 1890s. Defending her claim
that 'we, as a race, are growing' towards a moment of anarchist takeover, she
observes that:

The idea of less restriction and more liberty, and a confiding trust that
nature is equal to her work, is permeating all modern thought. From
the dark year –not so long gone by – when it was generally believed
that man's soul was totally depraved and every human impulse bad;
when every action, every thought and every emotion was controlled
and restricted; when the human frame, diseased, was bled, dosed,
suffocated and kept as far from nature's remedies as possible; when
the mind was seized upon and distorted before it had time to evolve a
natural thought – from those days to these years the progress of this
idea has been swift and steady. It is becoming more and more apparent
that in every way we are 'governed best where we are governed least'
. . . Still unsatisfied perhaps, the inquirer seeks for details, for ways
and means, and whys and wherefores. But anarchism is not compelled
to outline a complete organization of a free society. To do so with any
assumption of authority would be to place another barrier in the way
of coming generations. The best thought of today may become the

useless vagary of tomorrow, and to crystallize it into a creed is to make it unwieldy.[13]

As in Besant, students might find the broad synoptic historical narrative used here by Parsons an effective appeal to ethos. Her argument against confining ideas of Calvinist depravity is conducted through a present tense modality ('growing . . . permeating . . . becoming') that helps to underpin her claim to the proof of the famous line quoted from Thomas Jefferson. The most interesting thing that students will likely note here is that Parsons' is a rhetorical approach that rejects claims to her own authority, displacing the energies from oratorical leadership towards audience reflection and action. In this appeal to logos rather than pathos, she presents herself as 'not compelled' by traditional rhetorical assumptions, and informs the audiences (in the figure of the imagined 'inquirer') that the proofs and guidance they seek after are wrong. Students could be asked how paradoxical or effective they find such a gesture for political argument, and how far removed it is from the promise of the 'teacher' or 'guardian' offered by Besant's rhetoric.

These two passages would allow the seminar to consider the rhetorical stakes involved in framing non-mainstream views. They also offer examples of problematic belief systems – anarchism, the bogeyman of the *fin de siècle* world political landscape; theosophy as a combination of non-Christian and potentially anti-Imperial energies – that allow us to trace the threat of disruptive speech in international terms. Besant's speaking career and agitation are bound up with global politics, and since 'theosophy' is anchored by Indian culture, her argument is one that implicitly champions the dignity of the beliefs colonialism oppressed. Parsons, a mixed-race insurgent, condemned by Illinois authorities as 'more dangerous than a thousand rioters' for her prolific public speaking, speaks as part of a formidable network of mostly Francophone and German-speaking international anarchists.[14] Both therefore emerge from discourses and milieus that crossed linguistic, national, and continental barriers. Both were transnational figures that toured extensively in several countries, feted and condemned for their gender and ideas by audiences stretching from Britain and the United States to Asia.

Getting students to reflect upon the performances of Besant and Parsons allows them to grasp some ways in which what had been a relatively cohesive transatlantic tradition of Emerson and Ruskin had begun to fracture by the end of our period into a more complex picture. It is a world in transition that could be contextualised for students through the fictional depictions of Chicago radical oratory in the climactic scenes of Upton Sinclair's *The Jungle* (1904). Equally, this newly globalised world of speech could be traced through the depiction of the power of mutinous voices and the diseased eloquence of Kurtz in Conrad's *Heart of Darkness* (1899), where fractured speech confronts proto-Modernist technique. These and other sources can prompt students to think about the ways in which American and British culture grappled with unsettling ideas, new modes of expression, and the emergent force of demagogic oratory at the start of a new century.

CONCLUSION: VOICE AND PEDAGOGIC PRACTICE

Immersion in the journey of public speech from Burke to Parsons provides students with a range of critical, linguistic, conceptual, and contextual tools that can illuminate a diverse range of unrelated texts. A repertoire of terms for technical analysis will allow for meaningful commentary on the workings of prose. Reflection on issues of argument and performance will establish what it means to think of texts as 'rhetorical'. Thinking about the ideals and imagery of public speech will encourage students to see thematic and formal configurations of oral expression – dialogue, ventriloquism, oration – as a means through which to read British and American literary history. Consideration of how public speech changed in formal and institutional ways and exposure to an innovative range of contexts and speakers will broaden a sense of depth and complexity of the nineteenth-century Anglo-American imagination.

Bringing the richness of Anglo-American oratory back to the literary classroom also allows us to address barriers in institutional and intellectual practice. Scholars and teachers of English can learn a great deal from the wide-ranging work undertaken in rhetoric and communication studies, and from a versatile pedagogy that never loses sight of real-life skills. Whether or not the study of oratory involves practical speaking assessment (and why not?), exposure to this world of speech cannot help but impact upon our students. Confronting the voices of the past helps us reflect upon our own values and potential in powerful ways. To an extent that is surprising and counterintuitive, our contemporary digital media ecology continues to generate fresh fascination with human presence and seems destined to retain a key role for the agency of face-to-face persuasion. Reflecting upon the power of voice is therefore by no means merely a nostalgic task. Ideas about voice and rhetoric provide a unique route through politics, culture, and literary history, and by making Anglo-American oratory resonate, we reconnect students to the power and fascination of a timeless human activity.

NOTES

1. Edward Parker, *The Golden Age of American Oratory* (Boston: Whittemore, Niles & Hall, 1857), p. 1.

2. *The Times* (1873), quoted in Mathew Bevis, *The Art of Eloquence: Byron, Dickens, Tennyson, Joyce* (Oxford: Oxford University Press, 2007), p. 3.

3. Thomas Carlyle, 'The Stump-Orator', in H. D. Traill (ed.), *Latter-day Pamphlets* (New York: C. Scribner's Sons, 1901), p. 175.

4. Sandra Gustafson, 'American Literature and the Public Sphere', *American Literary History*, 20: 3 (2008), 465–78.

5. Herbery A. Wichelns, 'The Literary Criticism of Oratory' (1925), in Martin J. Medhurst (ed.), *Landmark Essays on American Public Address* (Davis, CA: Hermagoras Press, 1993), p. 131.

6. Walter J. Ong and John Hartley, *Orality and Literacy: The Technologizing of the Word*, 30th anniversary edn (London: Routledge, 2012), p. 162.

7. For a good example of comparative assessments of oratorical traditions, see Edward Everett, 'Speeches of Henry Clay', *North American Review*, 25 (October 1827), 425–51. Also see the commentary in John Q. Adams, *Lectures on Rhetoric and Oratory* (Cambridge, MA: Hilliard & Metcalf, 1810), pp. 10–27, and Charles Dickens, *American Notes* (London: Chapman & Hall, 1850), pp. 141–5.

8. John Ruskin, *The Crown of Wild Olive: Three Lectures on Work, Traffic and War* (London: Smith, Elder, 1866), pp. 79–80.

9. Ralph Waldo Emerson, 'The Poet', in Joseph Slater et al. (eds), *The Collected Works of Ralph Waldo Emerson*, vol. 2, *Essays, First Series* (Cambridge, MA: Harvard University Press, 1979), p. 12.

10. Ibid., p. 13.

11. Available at <http://www.whitmanarchive.org/published/periodical/aurora.html> (last accessed 1 August 2013).

12. Annie Besant, 'Theosophy', in South Place Institute, *Religious Systems of the World: A Contribution to the Study of Comparative Religion. A Collection of Addresses Delivered at South Place Institute* (London: Swan Sonnenschein, 1904), p. 641.

13. Lucy E. Parsons, *The Principles of Anarchism: A Lecture* (Chicago: L. R. Parsons, 1890), pp. 6–7.

14. Quoted in Carolyn Ashbaugh, *Lucy Parsons: An American Revolutionary* (Chicago: Haymarket, 2012), p. 2.

CHAPTER 13

Genre and Nationality in Nineteenth-Century British and American Poetry

Meredith L. McGill, Scott Challener, Isaac Cowell, Bakary Diaby, Lauren Kimball, Michael Monescalchi, and Melissa Parrish

Meredith L. McGill: In the fall of 2012, hoping to draw students of American and British poetry into dialogue with one another, I offered a graduate course on nineteenth-century poetry in transatlantic context. Rather than hewing closely to national traditions for the purpose of comparison, I designed the course around the trajectory of particular verse genres, asking whether and how national culture makes a difference for major genres such as pastoral, georgic, and epic, as well as for minor ones such as elegy, ballad, and, ode – genres that over the course of the nineteenth century seemed to loosen the ties between formal definition and social or cultural function.

Constructing the syllabus proved daunting, in part because tracking poetic genres from their eighteenth-century roots through their appearance in nineteenth-century poems, in explicit or occulted form, on both sides of the Atlantic involved a formidable amount of reading. Taking such a broad over-view of poetic history liberated us from norms of historicist critical practice in ways that felt both thrilling and neglectful. I worried that graduate students in the process of developing period-field expertise would rightly think that the syllabus included both too much to read and numerous unexplained omis-sions. The course stretched across two (or three) conventional periods and two national literatures, and was structured by a series of asymmetries that could not – and, I decided, should not – be made even. Some of these asymmetries were inherent to our object of study, the product of comparing a metropolitan with a provincial or early national poetic tradition. Others emerged from the histories of the verse genres themselves. For instance, the genres comprising the Virgilian career were well covered in the criticism and relatively easy to trace. The only real challenge in reconstructing the transatlantic history of pastoral, georgic, and epic was the sheer number and length of the sprawling epic poems, which I accommodated by assigning a handful of First Books and Cantos for the purposes of comparison.[1]

The minor verse genres, however, posed all kinds of interesting difficulties. Given the contemporary debate over the historicity of the lyric and the difficulty of separating what we have come to call lyrics from ballads and songs, I decided to teach the debate itself, turning the class on the lyric into a class on lyric theory (students chose their own 'lyrics' to use as testing grounds for a variety of theoretical assumptions). Ballads brought with them the challenge of describing the entanglement of folk traditions, aristocratic antiquarianism, and a burgeoning mass culture; in this context, the high-literary tradition inaugurated by Wordsworth and Coleridge's *Lyrical Ballads* (1798) seemed only one strand of a significantly broader and more perplexing cultural phenomenon. And the dramatic monologue, long considered a Victorian invention, felt less stable and assured of definition once we began exploring its roots in circum-Atlantic drama and its kinship with what M. H. Abrams called the 'greater Romantic lyric'.[2]

Class discussion was extremely lively and always seemed to spill over the bounds of the particular sessions. And so I invited students from the course to reflect with me on its successes and limitations. What follows is an Internet-mediated conversation, six months after the conclusion of the class, about our attempt to interpret nineteenth-century poetry through the prism of the history of verse genres. How useful was the transatlantic framework for students of British Romanticism, Victorian literature, and early national American literature? What kinds of insights did our serial focus on poetic genres produce, and what perspectives or conversations did it inhibit?

Lauren Kimball: I'm not certain that transatlantic exchange turned out to be our object of study. The prevalence of 'exchange' and its synonyms ('travel', 'crossing', 'traffic') in recent criticism suggests an inclination to be literal-minded. The actual movement of materials and bodies within this broad geographic space is arguably what concretises transatlantic projects and keeps us honest in the attempt to think outside the nation. But these terms have limitations we may be glossing over to conceptualise the equally imperfect term 'transatlantic'. 'Exchange' and 'traffic' both connote commerce, and yet we also use these terms to talk about figurative or imaginative exchanges occurring in sites of reading and writing.

The commercial success of particular genres was certainly part of the story we uncovered. For instance, the New World often figured as a *locus amoenus* of British pastoral during periods of imperial expansion, while georgic poems disseminated information about the colonies. The choice of genre could be a political one: the American poet Joel Barlow made his epic ambitions unmistakable in recasting his nationalist poem, *The Vision of Columbus* (1787), as *The*

Columbiad (1807). Ballads and elegies in particular opened doors for women poets because these genres favoured anonymous authorship. While the commercial viability of specific nineteenth-century genres is one of their *raisons d'être*, it does not tell us what nineteenth-century writers felt they could do with genre. Among other motivations, poets turned to particular verse genres out of ambition, in order to instruct, or to tell local or national histories.

We might have treated genre as a collection of tropes, as Benjamin Franklin does in his satire on elegy in *Silence Dogood No. 7* (1722). In the persona of a middle-aged housewife, Franklin gives readers a do-it-yourself recipe for writing elegy that pokes fun at popular elegy and poets' opportunism in practising it.[3] The 'Receipt' vividly illustrates poetic composition as a process of inserting miscellaneous raw material into a body and ejecting a profoundly impersonal, generic poem.[4] With this editorial, the young Franklin demonstrates elegy's shortcomings: as a literary art, it has been reduced to a formula; as a cultural practice of communal grief and consolation, it has become an outlet for quick local fame. In the light of Dogood's 'Receipt', elegy looks like a genre that just did not work in the age of Lockean empiricism.

Ultimately, however, I think it is more productive to consider genre as a structure of meta-poetic idealisation. What I mean by 'meta-poetic' is the announcement, in a poem or its editorial framing, that 'this is poetry': evidence of an ambition to get beyond tropes or generic traditions to a higher aim – what might have been called Poesy, or the work of Imagination. At the same time, the metaphysical sense was not the only or perhaps even the most important sense of *meta-* in the periods we were studying. The Greek prefix μετα (*meta-*) can also mean 'together with', a usage that captures what it means to practise as well as to study genres historically and transatlantically, taking into account genres' spatial and temporal multiplicity and how and why poems reflect on their own genres.

Isaac Cowell: I agree with Lauren that metaphors of commerce emphasise texts' material journeys at the expense of more abstract movements of influence and lineage. Perhaps this is why 'transatlantic' questions and 'genre' questions go hand in hand. To investigate transatlantic literary movements is already to question the genre classifications that make dialogue and exchange possible in the first place. Indeed, nineteenth-century poetic genres already contain within themselves the potential for their own unmasking, exposing the artifice of the critical limits we set for them. After all, genre takes its conceptual unity from the fundamental premise of the transgression of boundaries: between country and city; between the ancients and the moderns; between oral culture and print culture; and between the 'folk' purveyors and the 'elite' collectors and patrons of cultural tradition. To think of genre, then, is to think of mediation, inequality, and compromise – the process of self-complication by which many of the texts we read distance themselves from their ostensible genres.

Scott Challener: You're suggesting that nineteenth-century poets distance themselves from generic features that, by widespread cultural use, came to be perceived as stale or over-used? I agree that poets such as Pope and Wordsworth but also Anna Laetitia Barbauld and Lydia Sigourney distance themselves from what Raymond Williams called 'structures of feeling' that became ossified as they attached to particular generic boundaries, sequences, and dispositions.[5] But if nineteenth-century poets distance themselves from such features, they don't forsake them, their rubrics, or their staying power. Would it be more accurate to say that many of the texts we read take advantage of the more predictable or expected generic limits they are heir to and in conversation with?

Cowell: The *Lyrical Ballads*, for instance, might be read not only as a series of lyric poems masquerading as ballads, but as deliberate attempts to reconcile conflicting models of knowledge, to mediate between the introverted self-reflection of the lyric and the extroverted, dialogic wisdom of the ballad. When the speaker in 'We are Seven' fails to grasp the mathematical logic of the 'little Maid', or when the speaker in 'The Leech-Gatherer' listens without hearing, the result is a troubling of lyric epistemology that seems to align us, as readers, with the provincial subject (the girl, the old man) and to place us in opposition to the metropolitan speaker and his obtuseness. Nonetheless, Wordsworth resists this easy realignment of readerly sympathies. In the 'Preface' to the 1802 *Lyrical Ballads*, Wordsworth self-consciously distances himself from the 'superstitious man' – his speaking persona. We are instructed from the get-go to regard what might seem to be a sympathetic reconciliation between country and city – and, in generic terms, between ballad and lyric – as an unnatural process, 'altogether slavish and mechanical'.[6] By thinking of nineteenth-century poetic genres as structures of mediation, then, we remain open not just to the successes of such mediation, but also to its failures, to the generative possibilities latent even in the impasses between, say, lyric and ballad.

Kimball: What Isaac seems to be describing is the internal disunity or unevenness of all genres. Here, then, are a few provisional premises about the compatibility of transatlanticism and genre criticism: (1) The two critical perspectives are always (already) comparative ones; (2) they play along a 'boundary' that is ideological and contingent rather than actual, one that can help us to understand, for instance, what nineteenth-century intellectual communities thought poetic genres were; (3) the conceptualisation of nation and genre happened analogously and concurrently. We can think of nation and genre as on parallel conceptual tracks but also as intersecting with and informing each other in historical time.

Cowell: That's why I think about genres as structures of mediation. Indeed, genres do not seem to become visible as such until they have *already* gone through a self-conscious process of mediation. In the nineteenth-century 'literary ballad', for instance, the position of the 'folk' is not one that the author or editor can simultaneously preserve *and* inhabit; in preserving it, he has to treat it as foreign, as 'other'. The codification of the ballad as literary genre therefore involves an uncanny doubling of the 'folk' – from an authentic subject-position to a museum-like cultural 'object' – that parallels an imaginative doubling in the lyric speaker, who must pretend to speak from an imagined subject-position that he does not yet fully inhabit, and perhaps never could.

McGill: So you're suggesting that the process by which popular poetry gets identified as literary – passing over the threshold from low to high culture – is key to understanding how nineteenth-century genres work more broadly?

Cowell: Yes. Part of the inherent interest of the *Lyrical Ballads* derives from the epistemological break between the uneducated purveyors of culture and the educated consumers or patrons of culture. Wordsworth continually reconfirms this imagined difference, as if to lose sight of it would be to lose the structuring principle of the work as a whole.[7]

Melissa Parrish: For me the course clearly divided into halves. The Virgilian genres led us to consider the endurance and the evolution of genre, in part due to the interpretive models provided by critics such as Michael McKeon and Kevis Goodman.[8] But our study of genres such as the lyric, the ballad, and the dramatic monologue, with inspiration from critics such as Theodor Adorno and Virginia Jackson,[9] encouraged us to think about genre in terms of illusion, self-consciousness, and a drive toward self-effacement. Genre norms seemed less stable, more uncertain as the course progressed.

Kimball: Part of the inherent instability of the latter group is that they were considered minor – that is, not ancient, and so lacking in Aristotelian authority. They were also considered belated: always seeking ground on which to found themselves (hence editors' repeated reframing of verse ascribed to Sappho and Ossian as ancient lyrics).[10]

   Although we were acutely aware of the instability of the minor genres, we were not as worried about the boundaries of pastoral, georgic, and epic – but perhaps we should be. Pastoral's 'firstness' in the imagined chronology of genres does not make it any less susceptible to dominating and colonising the other genres than lyric. Perhaps because it attempts to do the work of epic in compressed form (for example, the carved cup of Theocritus' *Idyll I* is Achilles' shield in miniature), pastoral appears to be self-contained and self-generating. Pastoral's dialectically interacting binaries – its 'simple' and 'complex' elements and its 'representative anecdotes'[11] – can act like typologies for our reading of pastoral across time. The danger is that we can find the types of pastoral poetry all over the poetic field, if we want to. Should we be more wary of critics' tendency to explode pastoral, so that it can become a key for reading almost any poem?

Challener: It's also worth acknowledging that the genre system in Virgil's day was no more stable or less ideological than it was at any other period: Virgil embeds allusions to the *Eclogues* and to the *Aeneid* within the *Georgics*, and it's not impossible to see the *Georgics* in the *Aeneid*, in which, as our classmate Julie Camarda pointed out, soldiers regularly 'plough' through bodies. Genres have always been more permeable, strange, and irresolvable than the systematicity most theories suggest.

McGill: I wonder if we might have read the nineteenth-century investment in the Virgilian genres differently had we read the syllabus in reverse. There is a strong tendency to read the history of poetic genres, particularly at the turn to the nineteenth century, as a narrative of decline or dissolution. David Duff's description of the post-neoclassical genre-system is helpful here. For Duff, the Romantic critique of neoclassicism is a 'self-serving polemic . . . concealing important continuities between neo-classical and Romantic thought'.[12] Duff argues that the widely accepted story of British Romantic poets' rejection of neoclassical genres gives too little credit to eighteenth-century poets' generic innovations and obscures the Romantics' fascination with genre. Duff claims that what critics have taken to be a breakdown of the system is not an abandonment of genre but a radical expansion of generic possibilities.[13]

Bakary Diaby: Indeed, genre hardly seems to disappear, especially given the continuing importance of the Virgilian career, a set of consecrated genres attempted in order of increasing poetic difficulty by later poets for their own literary consecration. The Virgilian career emphasises rather than effaces genre: Pope titles his early poems 'Pastorals'; Milton affixes a subtitle to 'Lycidas' describing it as a 'Monody . . . [bewailing] a learn'd Friend, unfortunately drown'd'. The examples go on: Gray's 'Elegy written in a Country Churchyard', Poe's 'Bridal Ballad' or 'Ulalume – A Ballad', Emerson's 'Threnody' (for both Ode and Elegy), Browning's 'Dramatic Lyrics'.

Challener: Consider too Keats's 'Hyperion: A Fragment'. Keats's epic, like many of these examples, clarifies a basic but often confounding question: what exactly is being emphasised by these genre-tags? The turn to Virgil is more than 'a set of consecrated genres attempted in a particular order of increasing poetic difficulty' – at least if you believe Kevis Goodman, who points out that the *Georgics*, ostensibly a poem about how to be a better farmer, is actually the most densely allusive and glitteringly adorned of Virgil's works.[14] (And if by 'difficulty' you mean something like T. S. Eliot's definition – complexity, allusiveness, artifice or the conspicuous 'madeness' of the verbal object.) Our course gave the lie to the fictions of the Virgilian career and of genre, but it also revealed why these fictions were useful and important to nineteenth-century writers. Gray's 'Elegy written in a Country Churchyard' is a cento with a swain in it; in a certain sense, a 'dramatic monologue' is an oxymoron, but in all senses, it is a blurred or mixed genre, and as Herbert Tucker points out, it has proved quite durable. And did we settle, ever, on what 'lyric' was or is? I was persuaded by Virginia Jackson's theory of lyricisation, which helped us to understand how genre systems are more than a stable set of consecrated genres.[15] If we assume that genres have a kind of agency, then genre might seek its own effacement, but only in order to ensure that its generic conditions or parameters continue to thrive.

Diaby: I'm still not persuaded that genre effaces itself or that it – qua concept – has agency. How can it? What about the reader or the audience? Jackson's account is a theory of lyric *reading*; she argues that the lyricisation of Dickinson's poetry was a long-term process brought about by various agents (institutional, editorial, curricular, and more). It seems that much more than the will of a genre keeps its generic conditions or parameters thriving.

Challener: Good point, Bakary: readers do matter. In 'On the Uses of Literary Genres', Claudio Guillén argues that genres 'incite or make possible the writing of a new work', but also that it is often hard to disentangle this process from the critical endeavour to 'search for the total form of the same work'.[16] Critics, Guillén suggests, tend to make genres appear more total and stable than they are. You also suggest that we failed to consider the institutionality or sociology of genre. That is, we tended not to historicise or investigate the social reasons for literary genres, the values produced by readerships and cultural institutions that developed around certain literary genres, or the particular cultural practices associated with these genres. For instance, we did not discuss how and why *Aurora Leigh* (1856) became a bestseller that readers treated as a kind of scripture. Nor did we try to account for the popularity of the genre system itself; in fact, in choosing to follow the Virgilian career, and then diverge from it into ballad, elegy, ode, and dramatic monologue, we avoided some of the problems of the popularity and business of genre altogether. (I recall Meredith saying at one point that there could be a companion class exclusively focused on popular verse genres.) Our study of the ballad did, however, address some of the problems that go along with pairing the sociology and institutionality of genre with the category of nation. Our conversations about the changing meanings of the complex binary of country and city – present in pastoral and georgic but also in epic, elegy, ode, and dramatic monologue – highlighted how poets took advantage of generic tradition, updating it for their own ends and times. Think, for example, of the impress of slavery on the georgic: James Grainger's *The Sugar Cane* (1764) opens with a discourse on how to achieve the most efficient system of slave labour on the sugar plantation, while William J. Grayson's *The Hireling and the Slave* (1854), a pro-slavery georgic written in the style of 'the school of Dryden and Pope', compares the living conditions of manumitted European 'hirelings' with those of slaves in the United States.

McGill: Does a transatlantic framework for the analysis of poetic genres get us anywhere national critical traditions do not or could not? Do transatlantic comparisons risk reifying the very national narratives they seek to transform or displace?

Challener: What emerges from transatlantic accounts of poetic genre is a different kind of story. For instance, Adela Pinch has shown that it is impossible to understand George Meredith's 'Modern Love' *as* modern without taking into account its transatlantic reception.[17] Robert Frost's career, too, is illuminated by a transatlantic approach. Even before he returned from England, Frost's first two books were being released and marketed – unbeknownst to him – by the American publisher Henry Holt. Their dust jackets proclaimed Frost a successful poet coming home, an American Theocritus who lived somewhere North of the city. Frost's brief poem 'The Pasture' quickly became the epigraph to all of his selected and collected editions. The more pastoral Frost became to his readers, the more what Kevis Goodman calls the 'georgic underpresence and discipline' alive in his work became obscured, as georgic itself had done by the late eighteenth century.[18]

By reading the georgic back into Frost's work, we can see not only how Holt's casting of Frost as a pastoral poet helped him achieve his goal of reaching 'the general reader who buys books in the thousands', but also more generally how poets, publishers, and readers respond to the genre system as they write, revise, and edit their work.[19] Frost was cannier about the genre system than many critics give him credit for. What's more, the example of Frost makes clear that georgic never really disappeared in the nineteenth century: even when a genre appears to disappear or become unpublishable, it continues to function as a poetic resource that informs and even constrains the practices of composition and revision. For example, Frost's well-known sonnet 'Design' can arguably be read as part of a series of georgic mill sonnets occasioned by Frost's experience in the mills in Lawrence, MA – a meditation as much on industrial design as on a theological argument from design.[20]

With few exceptions, critics do not talk about georgic in the twentieth century, and as a result, we've missed out on how deeply twentieth-century poems engage with problems of labour, industrialisation, global capitalism, and so forth as *poetic* problems. This, as Goodman provocatively argues, is the real generic power of georgic: not its supposed didacticism, but the way in which its structural, processual poetics showcases what she calls 'the labor of representation'.[21] When we miss how poems themselves actually engage labour as labour, we fail to see how poems have always been used to engage the problem of how to know, as Philip Levine puts it, 'What work is'.[22] From poems as different as William Cowper's 'The Task' (1785) and Lydia Sigourney's 'To A Shred of Linen' (1838), from *The Sugar Cane* to *The Hireling and the Slave*, georgic offered poets a durable and flexible means of writing about work.

Michael Monescalchi: I think the study of American poetry stands to gain quite a bit through transatlantic comparison, in part because dialogues between British and American poems allow us to see American poetry as both imitative and innovative. Phillis Wheatley's *Poems on Various Subjects, Religious and Moral* (1773) has been criticised for being a 'colorless imitation of Alexander Pope'.[23] Timothy Dwight's 1794 response to Oliver Goldsmith's 'The Deserted Village' (1770) – the second part of the long poem *Greenfield Hill* called, fittingly enough, 'The Flourishing Village' – could have similar accusations levelled against it. But these texts are also important *because* they are not wholly original.

Both Dwight and Goldsmith model their poems on Virgil's *Georgics*, but the way in which each poet describes agrarian labour differs. When Dwight's speaker first encounters the flourishing village, he hears 'The bee, industrious, with his busy song, / The woodman's axe, the distant groves among' (II: 15–16).[24] The figure of the industrious bee recurs throughout Virgil's *Georgics*, so it is no surprise that bees can be found in Dwight's poem. But there are no 'industrious, busy songs' in Goldsmith's poem, for when his speaker revisits his 'Sweet smiling village, loveliest of the lawn, / Thy sports are fled, and all thy charms withdrawn' (ll. 35–6).[25] Dwight inverts the conditions of the rural community in Goldsmith's poem. As Larry Kutchen notes, 'Goldsmith imagines a thriving community of virtuous, property-owning farmers that can only be accessed through nostalgia, and Dwight celebrates this flourishing community in the present.'[26]

McGill: So, one of the benefits of a transatlantic history of poetic genres is that it encourages us to stop thinking in terms of British original and American copy, and to focus instead on how both British and American poets found in classical poetry a template for understanding the violence of modernity. It strikes me as a new kind of challenge for Americanist critics to be undeterred by poetic imitation – of either British or classical poetry.

Monescalchi: Dwight's imitation of Goldsmith is crucial to understanding what's innovative about his poem. If in 'The Flourishing Village' Dwight imagines that virtuous American farmers might be able to stave off the enclosure, depopulation, and concentrations of wealth that have ruined Goldsmith's Auburn, in the poem's fourth part, 'The Destruction of the Pequods', Dwight describes a desolate field that resembles the grounds of Goldsmith's poem: a 'weeping field', a place 'Where silence swims among the moulder'd walls' (IV: 23, 27).[27] Though the descriptions of the fields echo each other, the speakers' responses to their environments do not.

   Looking at these poems as productions of a specific national context helps to clarify why Dwight's speaker is hopeful when he finds himself standing on a decimated field and Goldsmith's is not. Unlike Great Britain, the American nation is only beginning to conceive of itself as an independent empire. Dwight claims that the Pequots prevented the land from reaching its full potential, and so instead of mourning the environment's depopulated condition, Dwight rejoices at the destruction of the indigenous population. Toward the end of 'The Flourishing Village' Dwight notes that 'Labour's axe resounds' as forests fall, and 'the savage shrinks, nor dares the bliss annoy' (II: 693, 705).[28] The last sound that can be heard on the 'weeping fields' in 'The Destruction of the Pequods' is also of labour: 'In yon small field, that dimly steals from sight, / Turning the sluggish soil, from morn to night, / The plodding hind, laborious, drives his plough, / Nor dreams, a nation sleeps, his foot below' (IV: 109–13).[29] By plowing over the land where the Pequot 'nation sleeps below', and by working where 'the Indian creep no more', the agrarian labourer becomes a figure of American imperialism; as he labours on the land, he erases the traces of colonial violence (II: 724).[30]

McGill: Understanding depopulation as a national opportunity is a pretty grim position for Dwight to take, although it was a common white response to Native American 'removals' in both poetry and prose: witness Bryant's astonishing poem 'The Prairies' (1832), and much of the debate preceding the expulsion of the Cherokee from their lands. But you're right to insist that it's a complex conversation about the uses and the limits of genre that makes Dwight's chilling optimism possible. In this example, differences in the deployment of georgic conventions mark the phases Great Britain and the US

have reached in a stadial theory of empire, somewhat like the individual paint-
ings that comprise Thomas Cole's *The Course of Empire* (1833–6).

Diaby: Genre seems intimately tied to nation-building. But if genres are no
more than discourses with certain historically contingent terms and conditions, how can they be so easily turned to nationalistic ends? Genre is more
than simply a descriptive taxonomy of works (or a prescriptive rubric for
future ones); it has ideological uses. We make our genres, but then it seems we
want our genres to help make us.

For example, multiple poems we read, particularly on the American side,
took the epic as one of the pillars of national identity-formation. This is an old
story: we know the importance of nation-building to the *Aeneid*, and critics
have long taken the Homeric epic to define Greek identity. This history,
including Milton's defence of Protestantism in *Paradise Lost* (1667), is in
fact what the nineteenth-century American epic may seek to conjure, but
even Tennyson's *Idylls of the King* (1859–85) is the 'cultural alibi'[31] of white
Christian English history. What exactly lies within any poetic schematisation
of culture that can aid in the construction of national identity? Does genre aid
nation-building? I wonder, with all sincerity, if the reverse is true: does nation-
building aid genre?

McGill: That might explain the energy behind foundational American epics
such as Barlow's *Columbiad* and Henry Wadsworth Longfellow's *Evangeline*
(1845), though most Americanist critics would track the synergy between
nationalism and genre through the history of the novel. But your comment
importantly points to a residual uneasiness around literary nationalism that,
despite our general embarrassment, continues to structure literary study.

Kimball: One of the reasons why Americanists may need the nationalist
framework is that we are still in the process of making early American poetry
available for scholarship. There is still an enormous amount of recovery to
do. At the same time, this national project may obscure the actual transatlantic and trans-historical work required to appreciate early American poetry.
Antebellum poets understood themselves to be part of a British-centred literary tradition and marketplace. They were thinking *trans-*, and so should we.
While transatlanticism is very important to postcolonial studies and other
fields influenced by the cultural turn, transnational perspectives are curiously
less common in scholarship on the history of literary form.

Diaby: I find it helpful to view the transatlantic as a mid-level concept
between the national and the global. What the transatlantic approach to genre
provided me was an opportunity to push beyond nationalist lines without

being wholly lost in the world republic of letters. By looking at the similarities and differences in nineteenth-century Anglophone poems, and thinking about and then beyond exchanges between nations on both sides of the Atlantic, we can transcend potentially myopic nationalist assumptions while still accounting for the important role nation and nationalism play in the literary arts.

McGill: One of the advantages of the transatlantic study of nineteenth-century poetry, then, is that it produces different groupings of texts, which forces us to put our reflex critical narratives under scrutiny. Not all of our critical commonplaces will be dislodged by this broader framework, not all of the idols will spontaneously fall. And yet transatlantic perspectives encourage us to ask anew about the range of evidence on which these narratives have been built, productively returning us to first principles. I'm also intrigued by Lauren's suggestion that the transatlantic framework invites a return to questions of poetic form as well as a questioning of the temporal markers we use to establish and give shape to our literary histories. Transatlantic differences in the uptake of particular genres keep us attuned to genre's historicity, resisting the critical impulse to regard genre as a kind of transcendental logic of literariness. It is difficult, however, to keep our eyes on the shifting parameters of the genre system as a whole, particularly as it is challenged and transformed by galvanising works of art. Is it possible to imagine a social history of poetic genres that wouldn't minimise the shaping power of individual works?

Challener: For one answer, we might return to our discussion of the Virgilian career. The enormous popularity of Dryden's translation of the *Georgics* (1697) depended in part on the appeal of the *Georgics* as a poster-poem for scientific and agricultural reform, and in part on the appeal of its perceived teachability. As a result, the classics curriculum quickly grew flush with new grammars built around the *Georgics* as a didactic poem of discipline, of labour for labour's sake. But over the course of the long nineteenth century, the genre system became less stable or resolvable in new or different ways, not only as institutions, technologies and readerships changed with changes in print culture, but also as poets' and readers' expectations about nation, history, gender and genre shifted.

For instance, if epic typically embeds other genres within it, this is no less true in the nineteenth century's many longer poetic experiments, from the *Lyrical Ballads* to Elizabeth Barrett Browning's *Aurora Leigh* to George Meredith's *Modern Love*. But now genre's very instability and porousness become formal targets. For example, in Barrett Browning's verse novel, pastoralism is first associated with the paternalistic heavy-handedness of her father, who, not knowing what to do with Aurora Leigh after her mother dies, takes her into Nature to be educated. Aurora's authoritarian English aunt then tries to dominate and discipline the 'Italian-ness' out of her by confining her to

> a little chamber in the house,
> As green as any privet-hedge a bird
> Might choose to build in, though the nest itself
> Could show but dead-brown sticks and straws; the walls
> Were green, the carpet was pure green, the straight
> Small bed was curtained greenly, and the folds
> Hung green about the window, which let in
> The out-door world with all its greenery.
> You could not push your head out and escape
> A dash of dawn-dew from the honeysuckle . . .
>
> (First Book, 567–76)[32]

Pastoral functions in these instances as a kind of generic prison, an instrument of English discipline, and a means of domesticating nature. But Barrett Browning also turns to the hills of Italy in later sections as a source of freedom – all in the same blank verse.

McGill: You're suggesting, then, that we can trace the shifting fortunes of poetic genres within the bounds of individual works? That the critic's role is not to place a particular poem within a larger system, but rather, that poems themselves allow us to glimpse the system as a whole as it adapts to and is transformed by new works?

Parrish: The *ars poetica* in the Fifth Book of *Aurora Leigh* provides particularly rich ground for considering form, genre, and *poïesis* within a single work:

> . . . While Art
> Sets action on the top of suffering:
> The artist's part is both to be and do,
> Transfixing with a special, central power
> The flat experience of the common man,
> And turning outward, with a sudden wrench,
> Half agony, half ecstasy, the thing
> He feels the inmost – never felt the less
> Because he sings it.
>
> (365–73)[33]

Here, Aurora relates the everyday thrust of contemporaneity to the poet's craft rather than to poetic tradition; her references to 'the common man' and a 'sudden wrench' distort the expectation of heroic action and an epic past. Instead, she links self-conscious instruction in what art 'should' do to a larger, melancholy narrative that crosses both geographic and generic borders. I wonder what such an expansive, self-reflexive poem about a trans-border journey can tell us about permeability and poetic form. I'm particularly drawn to Aurora's engagement with almost grotesque forms of nature in the second half of the poem. The Seventh Book, for instance, unites her with the 'dead' Marian Erle in part elegy, part eerie pastoral. This turn in the poem reimagines the world as 'something wonderful / For sorrow' (1047–8); fellowship with lizards, snakes, and frogs become the norm because 'the birds were grown too proud for [her]' (1107). These strange images, finally, merge with the death of her past to bring her back to 'the perfect solitude of foreign lands' (1194).[34] Pastoral retreat, a georgic instructiveness about what one 'should' do, and an elegiac lamentation come together in foreign territory, suggesting that a twisting or even inversion of established traditions is necessary to bring the experiential vision of a woman artist into visibility. The 'sudden wrench' of permeable strangeness is itself a way – perhaps the only way for both Aurora and Barrett Browning – of achieving this grand 'turning outward' within the bounds of poetic conversation.

Cowell: Like Melissa, I'm less interested, finally, in tracking the development of genre from work to work than I am in describing the generic ambiguities and contradictions within a single work. This would involve thinking about genre less along the teleological lines of the Virgilian career and more along the lines of simultaneous interaction and recombination, remaining mindful that genre often emerges only in the individual work's internal contradictions, its misaligned or irreconcilable premises and goals.

McGill: So, what's the takeaway for our thinking and writing, but also for our teaching of nineteenth-century poetry? Does a focus on poetic genres produce new kinds of genealogies? Did the transatlantic scope of the course produce new critical narratives you'll want to pursue, or will we all snap back to thinking about nineteenth-century poetry in the usual ways, as Romanticists, Victorianists, or Americanists?

Cowell: I'm on board with Melissa's argument for the 'permeable strangeness' of genre in *Aurora Leigh*, the narrative's powerful openness to temporal and spatial slippage. Melissa insightfully characterises Browning's representation of generic intermixture in *Aurora Leigh* as a deliberate literary coup – a reflection of the heroine's more general resolution to upset social and artistic conventions. But I want also to think about texts in which the troubling of genre is less the means of poetic triumph – an occasion for showcasing the artist's intellectual coming of age – than the means of deliberate poetic frustration or even strategic failure.

Challener: The transatlantic approach to genre gave me a way to see how nineteenth-century poets responded to the moving target of the genre system. As institutions, technologies, and readerships changed with changes in the culture at large, and writers' and readers' expectations shifted, the poets we read seemed to become more aware of the system *as* a system – as a formalised, modern construction with a formidable, vexed history. Further, the transatlantic framework also helped me to see how these poets worked with and across genres. In other words, they wrote not so much in the shadow of this system as a singular entity, but with a lively sense of how the genre system's boundaries might open onto new poetic possibilities. Read this way, many of the nineteenth century's longer poetic experiments turn the ideological work of the genre system into potent formal opportunities and occasions to consider the nature of the system's instability and porousness.

McGill: We have put literary periodisation and the geographical framework of the transatlantic under a good deal of pressure here. Our focus on genre made salient how the strong, if residual, presence of the classical past disrupts clean lines of influence and indebtedness, while the imaginary geographies and social fantasies of the poems we studied turned out to be far stranger than the imagined communities literary nationalist critics ordinarily invoke to sort and contain them. Transatlantic literary studies will have to invent new critical approaches to account for the odd temporalities and strange trajectories of nineteenth-century poetic genres. But the field will be more interestingly internally divided, more '*trans-*', for thinking across as well as along with these generic histories.

NOTES

1. The syllabus (McGill et al., Appendix 1) is available on the website associated with this volume.
2. M. H. Abrams, 'Structure and Style in the Greater Romantic Lyric', in *The Correspondent Breeze: Essays on English Romanticism* (New York: W. W. Norton, 1984), pp. 76–108.
3. Benjamin Franklin, 'A Receipt to Make a New-England Funeral Elegy', in J. A. Leo Lemay (ed.), *Franklin: Writings* (New York: Literary Classics of the United States, 1987), pp. 21–2. Although Franklin himself studied, composed, and admired poetry, he valued it primarily as a pedagogical tool – a means to refine one's writing – rather than as an expressive

medium. See Max Cavitch, *American Elegy: The Poetry of Mourning from the Puritans to Whitman* (Minneapolis: University of Minnesota Press, 2007), pp. 3–10, 42–8, 60–1.

4. After acquiring the ingredients, including a title, a neighbour 'who has died suddenly', and a bunch of estimable traits, the reader is instructed to 'mix, strain, season with melancholy expressions', 'put them into the empty Scull of some young Harvard', take them out, add double-rhymes, affix one's name to the bottom – and *Presto*. Franklin, *Franklin: Writings*, pp. 21–2.

5. Raymond Williams, *Marxism and Literature* (Oxford: Oxford University Press, 1977), pp. 128–35.

6. William Wordsworth, 'Preface', in *Lyrical Ballads* (London: Longman & Rees,1802), vol. 1, p. xxx.

7. As Wordsworth writes in the note to 'The Thorn', he sees it as his responsibility to mediate between the uneducated and the educated: while 'adhering to the style' of 'superstitious men', he '[took] care that words, which in their minds are impregnated with passion, should likewise convey passion to Readers who are not accustomed to sympathise with men feeling in that manner or using such language' (*Lyrical Ballads*, vol. 1, p. 202).

8. Michael McKeon, 'The Pastoral Revolution', in Kevin Sharpe and Steven Zwicker (eds), *Refiguring Revolutions: Aesthetics and Politics from the English Revolution to the Romantic Revolution* (Berkeley: University of California Press, 1998), pp. 267–89; Kevis Goodman, *Georgic Modernity and British Romanticism: Poetry and the Mediation of History* (Cambridge: Cambridge University Press, 2004).

9. Theodor W. Adorno, 'On Lyric Poetry and Society', in Rolf Tiedemann (ed.), *Notes to Literature: Volume One*, trans. Shierry Weber Nicholsen (New York: Columbia University Press, 1991), pp. 37–54; Virginia Jackson, *Dickinson's Misery: A Theory of Lyric Reading* (Princeton: Princeton University Press, 2005).

10. See Yopie Prins, *Victorian Sappho* (Princeton: Princeton University Press, 1999) for one version of this history.

11. Frank Kermode (ed.), Introduction, *English Pastoral Poetry: From the Beginnings to Marvell* (London: George G. Harrap & Co., 1952), pp. 11–32; Paul Alpers, 'What is Pastoral?' *Critical Inquiry*, 8: 3 (1982), 437–60.

12. David Duff, *Romanticism and the Uses of Genre* (Oxford: Oxford University Press, 2009), p. 40.

13. Duff summarises the 'modifications made to the neoclassical genre-system over the course of the eighteenth century' as follows: a 'relaxation of generic rules; loosening of generic boundaries; acceptance of generic

mixture; enlargement of the genre-spectrum; shifts in the hierarchy of genres; recognition of the historical variability of genres; and integration of literary genre theory into larger rhetorical or aesthetic systems' (*Romanticism*, p. 41).

14. Kevis Goodman, 'Georgic', in Roland Greene et al. (eds), *The Princeton Encyclopedia of Poetry and Poetics*, 4th edn (Princeton: Princeton University Press, 2012), pp. 556–7.

15. Herbert F. Tucker, 'Dramatic Monologue and the Overhearing of Lyric', in Chaviva Hosek and Patricia Parker (eds), *Lyric Poetry: Beyond New Criticism* (Ithaca, NY: Cornell University Press, 1985), pp. 226–43; Jackson, *Dickinson's Misery*.

16. Claudio Guillén, 'On the Uses of Literary Genre', in *Literature as System: Essays Toward the Theory of Literary History* (Princeton: Princeton University Press, 1971), p. 109.

17. 'Transatlantic Modern Love', in Meredith L. McGill (ed.), *The Traffic in Poems: Nineteenth-Century Poetry in Transatlantic Context* (New Brunswick, NJ: Rutgers University Press, 2008), pp. 160–84.

18. Goodman, *Georgic Modernity*, p. 10.

19. Robert Frost, *Collected Poems, Prose & Plays* (New York: Library of America, 1995), pp. 667–8.

20. See, for example, 'The Mill City' (1906) and 'When the Speed Comes' (1907), in Robert Frost, *Collected Poems, Prose & Plays*, pp. 509, 511.

21. Kevis Goodman, 'Georgic', p. 556.

22. See Philip Levine, *What Work Is: Poems* (New York: Alfred Knopf, 1991), pp. 18–19.

23. Quoted in Marsha Watson, 'A Classic Case: Phillis Wheatley and her Poetry', *Early American Literature*, 31: 2 (1996), 104.

24. Timothy Dwight, *Greenfield Hill: A Poem in Seven Parts* (New York: Childs & Swain, 1794), p. 31.

25. Oliver Goldsmith, *The Deserted Village* (London: W. Griffin, 1770), p. 8.

26. Larry Kutchen, 'Timothy Dwight's Anglo-American Georgic: *Greenfield Hill* and the Rise of United States Imperialism', *Studies in the Literary Imagination*, 33: 2 (2000), 114.

27. Dwight, *Greenfield Hill*, p. 94.

28. Ibid., p. 51.

29. Ibid., p. 96.

30. Ibid., p. 52.

31. Roland Barthes, *Mythologies* (New York: Hill & Wang, 2012), p. 76.

32. Elizabeth Barrett Browning, *Aurora Leigh* (New York: Norton, 1995), p. 22.

33. Ibid., p. 155.

34. Ibid., pp. 245–6, 249.

CHAPTER 14

Teaching 'Transatlantic Sensations'

John Cyril Barton, Kristin Huston, Jennifer Phegley, and Jarrod Roark

In the fall of 2008 Jennifer Phegley, a Victorianist, taught a course with John Barton, an Americanist, on transatlantic sensation literature to a mixed audience of graduate students and advanced undergraduates. Through the class they hoped to begin mapping the development of the sensation novel on both sides of the Atlantic over the long nineteenth century; they also hoped to trace the commonalities and divergences between the national manifestations of this bestselling genre. The course was conceived a year earlier over lunch when the two talked about how important sensationalism was to both British and American literature and culture during this period. Comparing notes, they were surprised to learn that scholars in both fields had largely neglected the interrelated traditions of sensation in the two nations.[1] This curious oversight in transatlantic scholarship invigorated their research and prompted them to design a course on the subject. That work has recently borne fruit in the publication of an edited collection of scholarly essays titled *Transatlantic Sensations*.[2]

The purpose of this essay is to discuss the course, 'Transatlantic Sensations', that inspired the research project. In doing so we describe not only the actual class we taught – with its successes and misfires – but also how our subsequent research has enabled us to re-imagine an improved version of the course that could be taught again at our university or comparable institutions. We also advocate teaching the course collaboratively and promoting an ongoing dialogue between instructors and students as they renegotiate a national tradition with which they are more familiar in light of its transatlantic counterpart – in our case, the relation between British and American culture. Such a conversation exposes students to the value of interdisciplinary (or 'inter-field') thinking and faculty to the valuable pedagogical practices of colleagues working in closely related fields. In the spirit of collaboration, Jennifer and John are joined in this essay by Kristin Huston and Jarrod Roark – two doctoral students working primarily in Victorian and US literature respectively – who took 'Transatlantic Sensations' in the fall of 2008. Culminating with Kristin's and Jarrod's reflections on how the course shaped their dissertations and professional identities, the essay begins with Jennifer and John's rationale for the course re-imagined in light of subsequent research and concludes with thoughts for a reboot of the course in the context of recent transatlantic scholarship.

WHY 'SENSATION' IN TRANSATLANTIC NINETEENTH-CENTURY LITERATURE? (JENNIFER AND JOHN)

As an advertisement for a recent book series notes, transatlantic studies typically address topics such as travel and exploration, migration and diaspora, slavery, aboriginal culture, revolution, colonialism, and anti-colonial resistance.[3] Those subjects, of course, are important ones that can figure into a transatlantic investigation of almost any period since the 'discovery' of the Americas. We argue, however, that sensation is an especially rich subject for a transatlantic approach to teaching Anglo-American literature and print culture over the long nineteenth century. To begin with, 'sensation' as a theme is intrinsically interesting, with its connections to mystery and intrigue, crime and punishment, and a host of hot-button topics of the time. Most twenty-first-century students become as engrossed in the mystery or crime-related plots that typically drive sensation fiction as nineteenth-century readers did. More importantly, the activity of locating clues and piecing together evidence to uncover a sensation plot's mysteries provides instructors with a heuristic for activities often expected in the humanities classroom, which involve critical awareness of social context and careful analysis of relevant evidence.[4] In addition, the ripped-from-the-headlines subject matter rife in sensation fiction enables instructors easily to connect particular literary works to a broader cultural conversation about race, class, and gender as well as particular social or political issues garnering wide press coverage of the day.

'Sensation' also constitutes a style, historical category, and genre that emerged at the turn of the nineteenth century – with the rise of the sensational press and the popularity of early gothic and crime literature – and culminated in the 1840s in the United States and the 1860s in England. Thus, in addition to facilitating a discussion of current events and contemporaneous cultural practices, instructors can use sensation to foster understanding of a new aesthetic and literary sensibility that developed transatlantically. To promote such study, we recommend grounding the course in intense investigation of popular print media of the day. Indeed, by tracing certain rhetorical threads of sensation through online periodical databases, instructors can highlight for students the myriad and conflicting ways sensation as a style and genre was assessed on both sides of the Atlantic. To this end, we offer one demonstration of how debates over sensation's aesthetics (as well as its ethics) played out, while acknowledging that many other rich veins of material remain in the archives for students to discover and for instructors to use for teaching transatlantic sensationalism.

Literary scholars today usually study sensation in isolation, as a discrete national product of British or American culture. But for nineteenth-century critics and novelists alike, it was a transatlantic phenomenon. For some, such as Mary Elizabeth Braddon, George Lippard, William Harrison Ainsworth, and E. D. E. N. Southworth, it was a harbinger of a new and more energetic age. For others, it was a sign of cultural decline, with many detractors pointing fingers at their transatlantic counterparts for originating this 'vulgar' form. In England, for instance, W. Fraser Rae famously criticised sensation novels – Braddon's in particular – for blurring class boundaries by 'making the literature of the kitchen the favourite reading of the drawing-room'.[5] The central role of women – as readers, writers, and criminals – was thus a prominent part of English disparagement of the genre. Such censure was also present in American criticism, although US critics were often more concerned with the 'sinful' nature of sensation and frequently deployed religious or moral arguments against it. George Thompson, one of the genre's most prolific and profane American practitioners, indulged the public's interest in sordid crimes while simultaneously warning against them. He also made his worst criminals of foreign extraction, including a French pickpocket who ingeniously hides her booty in her genitals, and an English thug in New York who rapes and murders a disfigured woman after forcing her to star in his freak show. Similarly, Lippard – who in his international bestseller *The Quaker City* championed the work of Ainsworth ('whom all the starch-and-buckram critics have been abusing so heartily for years' as 'understand[ing] the art and theory of the *plot* of a story better than any living writer') – nonetheless blamed English novelists for doing 'more to corrupt the minds of American children than any sort of bad literature that ever cursed the world'.[6] Charles Dickens, as if in response to Lippard from across the Atlantic, would later take the opposing side, declaring that 'sensations are epidemic. . . . We at home have our insanities, but I think the Americans run madder, and suffer oftener.'[7]

Dickens's declaration took poetic form in 'Sense vs. Sensation', published in *Punch* in 1861. The poem established a stark contrast between the nations, portraying sensation as a problem with American origins:

Some would have it an age of Sensation,
If the age one of Sense may not be –
The Word's not *Old* England's creation,
But New England's over the sea.[8]

The poet's claim makes some 'sense', given the massive popularity of execution sermons and ballads as well as crime narratives that, as Daniel Cohen has demonstrated, can be seen as the origins of popular culture in America.[9] Yet crime literature was just as popular in England during this time and influenced some of the most famous eighteenth-century English novels, including Fielding's *Jonathan Wild* and Defoe's *Moll Flanders*. Moreover, the British *Newgate Calendar*, beginning publication in 1773, would become one of the most widely read periodicals in both England and America – its transatlantic success providing a formula for many publications. Thus, introducing students to such early forms of popular literature alongside transatlantic debates over sensation over the long nineteenth century enables instructors to highlight the partnership between popular fiction and the periodical press in shaping a thriving transatlantic culture.

USING SENSATIONALISM AND THE POPULAR PRESS TO FOSTER ORIGINAL RESEARCH (JENNIFER AND JOHN)

In addition to sustained examination of literary works in relation to the popular press, we strongly recommend having students work closely with scholarly definitions of both transatlanticism and sensationalism during the first several weeks of the course. To this end, we began our fall 2008 class by having students work in small groups with key excerpts from important critical or theoretical works in both fields. Their task was to work through collaborative analysis of excerpts within groups and then teach them to the class. Getting students engaged from the get-go with this scholarship is crucial, since there is little established criticism bringing the two national sensation literatures together. In this respect, students have a unique and exciting opportunity to break new ground in an emerging field of study. Some students, however, may feel frustrated given that there is so little critical work examining sensationalism in a transatlantic framework. Thus, one of our pitfalls in designing our course was not exposing students to enough criticism on sensationalism and transatlanticism. Indeed, having students engage more with scholarship would help them learn how to adopt, apply, and modify critical or theoretical methodologies and arguments to suit their own goals. Such work in the classroom would, in turn, better prepare students for our course's two major assignments: (1) a critical research paper and (2) a collaborative public wiki project. The term paper, familiar to us all, needs no explanation here but the team wiki project merits further discussion.

To promote active collaborative learning outside the classroom, we designed a print culture group project that involved primary source research. In a collaboratively taught course intended to model the productivity of back-and-forth exchanges between national literatures as well as specialists in each field, the wiki project provided a way for students to continue such exchanges in a public forum. The first step in our wiki assignment involved students working individually to locate an article, poem, story, advertisement, or image from an online newspaper or periodical database (*Nineteenth-Century British Newspapers*, *Nineteenth-Century American Newspapers*, *British Periodicals I & II*, and *American Periodicals* among them) that illuminated transatlantic sensationalism. We divided students interested in similar texts, themes, or ideas into groups of three or four and provided each team with feedback about how to organise their ideas and workload, pursue further research, and draw conclusions from their analyses. About a month later, each team submitted a research proposal that addressed our first round of feedback, the group's subsequent research and discovery of primary-source material, and their objectives and plans for completing the project. We then provided teams with another round of comments, from which each group selected a final artifact to contextualise, annotate, and interpret for their final wiki project and class presentation. The projects (to which hyperlinks are provided in the online supplementary material for this collection) included the following: (1) an 1848 announcement, from *Lloyd's Weekly London Newspaper*, of a theatrical adaptation of Lippard's *The Quaker City* at London's Royal Standard Theatre; (2) an 1865 article, 'Ye Mother Superior' in *The London Review*, concerning the trial and later life of Constance Kent, a sixteen-year-old girl accused of brutally murdering her four-year-old brother; (3) an 1870 cartoon, 'The Ovation of Murder', depicting the riotous public funeral of John Real, a controversial figure who was executed for the murder of a New York police officer, though he claimed self-defence; and (4) an 1845 illustration, ' "Parties" for the Gallows' in *Punch*, which lampooned popular bloodlust for public executions.

Not only did the wiki projects give students valuable experience in using online databases, but they also encouraged collaboration on writing original research. Moreover, the assignment demonstrated the extent to which sensation was a transatlantic phenomenon by requiring students to identify artifacts in both English and US periodicals. However, students struggled to develop truly transatlantic topics. In fact, the project focusing on the London playhouse production of Lippard's novel was the only one that fully achieved this goal. Nonetheless, students created the kind of transatlantic context we had hoped to foster through the dialogue and exchanges that transpired among groups during the final week of classes when each team presented its wiki for discussion. To this extent, the project helped meet one of our main goals by immersing students in primary-source research and having them, through active and collaborative learning, situate a particular artifact within a transatlantic framework. To improve the course for a reboot, however, we believe it would be more productive to have each group choose one document from each nation on a particular theme or issue and to analyse them in relation to one another. Putting these two documents in dialogue and finding common ground for analysing them in terms of a transatlantic culture of sensation would take our course to the next level. All things considered, the print culture wiki project and the course as a whole, despite some shortcomings, met with much success – as Jarrod and Kristin help explain in what follows.

TRANSATLANTIC SENSATIONS IN THE AMERICAN LITERATURE CLASSROOM AND BEYOND (JARROD)

In the fall of 2008, two years after I began teaching American Literature at a college-preparatory school in Kansas City, Missouri, I returned to graduate school and began working on my PhD. My first class, 'Transatlantic Sensations', transformed the ways in which I conceived of literary studies, both as a graduate student and as a teacher. The wiki project, in particular, helped me identify literary problems and formulate more creative ways to deal with them than I could have done on my own. My wiki team chose an image and accompanying article published in 1845 in *Punch* titled ' "Parties" for the Gallows', which was a response to the murder by John Tawell, an excommunicated Quaker and ex-convict, of Sarah Hart, his former mistress. While awaiting trial, he was placed on display to crowds of morbid thrill-seekers. We divided our research into four main categories. 'Notes on the Text' included annotations, definitions, and descriptions of settings and people in the article for twenty-first-century readers. 'Commentary on the Text' contextualised our article among the British magazine's many years of social commentary and the writer of the 1845 article. 'Sensation News and Sensation Literature' offered an overview of sensational literature and illustrated how the *Punch* cartoon and text fit within this tradition. The final section, 'Cross Classes and Cultures', provided a scholarly overview of literary criticism and concluded that the simultaneous popularity and critical rejection of sensation fiction appeared on both sides of the Atlantic.

When our group of four students began discussing the wiki project, we decided to divide the work according to our strengths and interests. While we all performed research and writing and formulated arguments about our document, two of the group members dealt little with the wiki tool. They were uncomfortable navigating the site, which was sometimes buggy and cumbersome. Instead, they compiled and assembled our research while the other group member and I edited the text and uploaded content to the site. While working, and disagreeing, with other students can be frustrating, ultimately we celebrated our opposing positions, concerns, and philosophies. For example, some of us opposed capital punishment, and others supported it. This ideological tension strengthened our project, for we had to convince each other that our research included an unbiased view of the topic, as well as replicate a scholarly exchange of ideas to challenge and inform our readers. Such a tension existed in sensation fiction and sensational journalism: while it might have instructed readers to be vigilant against seduction, for example, sensational texts often celebrated such sexualised scenes and invited readers to thrill in the sensational aspects of class conflict or crime.

As a result of this experience, I now assign collaborative research and presentation projects to my students each year. For one such assignment related to Kate Chopin's *The Awakening* (1899), I ask small groups to focus on one issue each: how setting reflects a character's social situation, personal growth, or cultural conflict; how fashion and beauty standards for female characters illustrate a particular set of gender expectations for women; and how male vocation and power dynamics illustrate ways to view manliness and masculinity, especially in relation to femaleness and femininity. My students wrestle with similar questions that I pondered when I began the wiki project in 2008. Because of my experiences then, and because I have continued to work collaboratively since, I offer details and advice that I hope answer their questions and challenge their assumptions about research and writing. Most students agree that while they learned much about their topics, they learned even more about how to work with others. For example, when a project has unsuccessful arguments or other weaknesses, individuals must learn how to solve the problem for the group's success.

'Transatlantic Sensations' also caused me to view my dissertation research in new ways. My dissertation discusses Mark Twain's early sensational journalism and hoaxes within a transatlantic, sensational publication history. I argue that Twain uses similar methods to portray Western culture in the 1860s that sensational writers of the 1840s, 1850s, and 1860s use to depict Eastern urban culture. Like sensationalists Lippard, Thompson, Emerson Bennett, and Collins, Twain wrote sensational journalism and sensation hoaxes that exploited literary depictions of violence. Such writing appeared in daily, weekly, and monthly periodicals, which entertained but also encouraged readers to critique politics, crime, justice, and gender performance. Because Twain was influenced by earlier sensational writers, I view Twain's early writing as a continuation of sensational, socially relevant writing birthed in the antebellum metropolis and in the mining towns of the West rather than as an example of Twain's humour or style as learned from fellow Western journalists.

Studying Twain's early Western writing within the context of transatlantic sensationalism thus allows for new interpretations of his approaches to justice and gender. Though most research on these topics employs evidence from his Realistic novels, or more recently from his later work, Twain's negative view of abusive men, for example, appears much earlier. This periodical publishing enabled Twain to enter the transnational and transatlantic publishing marketplace. Focusing on Twain's sensational journalism has allowed me to gain professional attention at conferences, and, more importantly, has decentred Twain's famous novels as the primary sources for understanding his often subversive and satirical views of nineteenth-century American culture. Indeed, reading his sensational periodical writing that dwells 'beneath' the canon of his realistic fiction against transatlantic sensational literature from the 1840s to the 1870s reveals that Twain participated in creating, rather than wholly rejecting, popular, sometimes didactic, often sensational literature.

TRANSATLANTIC SENSATIONS AND THE DEVELOPMENT OF A NEW PROFESSIONAL IDENTITY (KRISTIN)

The semester that I enrolled in 'Transatlantic Sensations' was near the end of the coursework in my Interdisciplinary PhD programme. While I did not have a particular interest in transatlantic studies, I soon found that the transatlantic lens challenged me to rethink the literature I knew and loved and provided me with an exciting new framework for my scholarship. 'Transatlantic Sensations' struck me immediately as a refreshing change from typical literature classes. It was clear from the first meeting that we were being asked not simply to read American works and British works and compare and contrast them, but instead to think deeply and critically about how the two traditions were operating in conversation with each other. The class was an attempt to work through Jennifer and John's ideas about transatlantic sensation and to contribute to their initial conceptions of the field and definitions of the genre. While this was exciting and enriching, it was also frustrating at times.

We worked through the American material first, and I must say my greatest irritation came from the fact that the American works we read made the British ones seem tame by comparison. While Mary Elizabeth Braddon and Wilkie Collins certainly were sensational, their novels were not filled with the graphic sex and violence of George Lippard and George Thompson. I felt that some of my peers in the course were favouring the American fiction and that saddened me because of my deep love for British sensation. Once I moved past that initial gut reaction, I realised that the issue of the different modes of sensation was an interesting one for further study. My desire to read more transatlantic scholarship was also a challenge. My peers and I soon found that there were few resources specific to the study of sensation literature in a transatlantic context. In one respect, that helped us to feel like we were part of a groundbreaking new area of study, but it also left us wading into what felt like murky territory as we conducted research. Many of us ended up enjoying the transatlantic aspects of the course, but our final papers still came down to a strictly British or American approach. Even after a semester of residency in a transatlantic world, we still felt safest writing in familiar paths.

While I wrote a primarily British paper to complete the course, the lessons learned were a catalyst, months later, for a change in dissertation topic. My new topic, nineteenth-century representations of Creole women in transatlantic novels and periodicals, married my love of British literature with my excitement for the Creole culture of Louisiana. It would never have occurred to me that I could take such an approach had it not been for the course. Because of the knowledge I gained in the classroom I suddenly had a way of seeing material, like Brontë's *Jane Eyre*, with new vision. As I began to search Victorian periodicals for representations of Creole women, I felt a sudden shift in my understanding of nineteenth-century life. Though there are some significant differences among the British and American representations of Creole women, the similarities let me see a unity and synchronicity that I had not experienced before. For example, while I originally organised my dissertation chapters around specific periodicals, I quickly found that it was far more interesting and exciting to organise them thematically. This change was directly influenced by my desire to articulate a transatlantic literary experience rather than one with clear boundaries. Through this thematic approach, I have been able to identify striking commonalities in the portrayals of Creole women in both the United States and the British Empire, specifically with regard to their (often dangerous) sexuality, the fears they provoked regarding racial purity and the sanctity of national identity, and the feminisation (and sometimes demonisation) of the New World territories they inhabited. Transatlanticism and Creoles seem to go hand in hand, but there is very little work focused specifically on the plight of Creole women and the similarities in their experiences transgressing national boundaries.

'Transatlantic Sensations' also shaped my teaching, informing the ways I teach my Women and Literary Culture courses as well as survey courses like British Literature II. I now emphasise the relationship between British and American history, literature, and philosophy in those courses. For example, I incorporate abolitionist rhetoric from both sides of the Atlantic in British Literature, to help the students see that a dialogue about slavery was taking place and to help them better understand that the abolition of slavery had a severe impact on the British colonies in the West Indies and beyond. I find this approach especially useful when I teach *The Journal of Dora Damage*, a contemporary novel set in nineteenth-century Britain that features a pornography-publishing heroine who becomes involved with a former slave from America. While *The Journal of Dora Damage* is fiction, it presents students with a clear opportunity to see how Britain was actively engaged in the fight for abolition in the United States, and many excellent transatlantic student projects have resulted.

Finally, my experience has shaped my professional identity and my preparation for the job market. No longer thinking of myself as a strict Victorianist, I bring versatility to the table. While I do have specialisations – gender studies, nineteenth-century studies, etc. – my background in transatlanticism, coupled with my interdisciplinary degree, means that I can teach a variety of courses and that my research interests are varied. There are challenges ahead, and I may not fit well in universities where the goal is to fill one specific niche, but as academia works to meet the shifting needs of our student population, there will hopefully be many opportunities for professionals like me, who are comfortable standing with one foot on either side of the ocean.

RETHINKING 'TRANSATLANTIC SENSATIONS' (JENNIFER AND JOHN)

Examining sensation literature in a transatlantic context in this course enabled each of us to begin to redefine the field in both national traditions. On one hand, American sensation literature is usually seen as peaking in the 1840s, with the massive popularity of the city-mysteries and urban-gothic novels of Lippard, George Thompson, Ned Buntline, and others. The English sensation novel, on the other, is said to begin in the 1860s with Wilkie Collins's *The Woman in White*, Braddon's *Lady Audley's Secret*, and Ellen Price Wood's *East Lynne*. There is little acknowledgement among scholars that the genre predated the 1840s and 1860s, respectively, and developed simultaneously and matured over the century on both sides of the Atlantic. While Andrew Maunder recognises that the genre extends well beyond the decade of the 1860s in England and David S. Reynolds points to the English and European origins of the genre in the US in the early nineteenth century, placing sensation fiction in its transatlantic context in our course allowed us to begin to map the evolution of sensation across the century as well as across the Atlantic.[10] As a result, we began to see more clearly how both American and English traditions developed in a reciprocal relationship, while realising that sensationalism has a long historical line with many branches firmly grounded on both sides of the Atlantic.

We were only beginning to understand this narrative when we ventured into the course. In fact, we made some predictable choices that actually thwarted our efforts to chart sensation as a unified phenomenon. John's experience with American sensationalism led him to choose working-class sensation novels such as Lippard's *Quaker City* (1845) and Thompson's *City Crimes; or Life in New York and Boston* (1849). Jennifer's understanding of English sensation fiction, in contrast, led her to focus on more middlebrow novels: Collins's *The Woman in White* (1861) and Braddon's *Lady Audley's Secret* (1862). These choices set up a dichotomy that emphasised America's sensation fiction as more violent, graphic, and proletariat, and England's as more refined and bourgeois. Kristin's experience testifies to the ways this dichotomy challenged her as a devotee of British sensationalists. As one classmate wrote in an evaluation of the course, the British sensation novels were 'more demure' while the American novels were more 'graphic and "in your face"'. Yet even this student recognised that each nation's sensationalism was similar in its notoriety and popularity. Another student likewise concluded that 'Transatlantic sensationalism, while involving much give and take between the two countries and showing how they are alike, exposes much more of the differences in what each society considered sensational. The interesting part is that while the US literature is more graphic . . . the effect each had on its corresponding society was the same.' These astute summaries certainly reflect the novels we read in the course, yet they only begin to gesture towards some of the nuances that we hoped to convey. In an effort to better map the connections and disconnections in the two national literatures, we realised a few weeks into the course that we should counter the overly simplistic national divisions suggested by our chronological organisation.

We anticipated this challenge early on and tried to address it by tracing many of the elements of the 1840s American sensation novels of Lippard and Thompson back to British gothic fiction of the 1790s and Newgate novels of the 1830s as well as forward to detective tales of the 1880s. We also discussed the connections between American middle-class sensationalists Louisa May Alcott and E. D. E. N. Southworth and the typical English sensation novelists of the 1860s, while linking their brand of sensationalism to later-century realists, New Woman novelists, and romance and adventure writers. We hoped these broader discussions would challenge the narrow vision of the sensation novel as either an 1840s American or an 1860s English phenomenon. However, we later realised we needed to offer a more diverse range of texts from both national literatures to drive this point home. Our focus, as it evolved throughout the semester, was attentive to what Paul Giles calls 'points of transnational convergence and interference that arise out of works incorporating their own particular local perspectives'.[11] But if we were to teach the course again, we would probably pay more attention to the convergences by making different textual selections that would reinforce connections among national literary traditions. We might pair Braddon's *Lady Audley's Secret* with Louisa May Alcott's 'Behind a Mask' or E. D. E. N. Southworth's *The Hidden Hand* to emphasise the similar forms of feminine, middle-class sensation fiction. Likewise, we could couple Lippard's *Quaker City* with G. W. M. Reynolds's *The Mysteries of London* (or one of the many Ainsworth novels Lippard admired) to show the commonalities among English 'penny dreadfuls' and American working-class sensational forms. We could also place issues of sensational crime magazines from both sides of the Atlantic in conversation. For example, we could assign the *London Journal*, founded by Reynolds and known for its sensational stories and serials, the *Illustrated Police News*, which tracked crime stories in a sensational manner in England or, from the United States, any number of popular court reports from capital trials that competed with novels in the literary marketplace or books and pamphlets on notorious criminals such as *The Record of Crimes in the United States* (one of Hawthorne's favourite books), or the *Quaker City Weekly*, a working-class magazine that Lippard founded and edited following the success of his bestselling novel.

Regardless of the course's shortcomings, we believe that teaching sensationalism in a transatlantic context provided us and our students with valuable new ways of understanding the interconnected world of nineteenth-century reading, writing, and publishing. Since much of the literature in American periodicals was copied from English magazines, there was an obvious interdependence between the two national literatures. Likewise, English publishers reprinted American books, with *and* without permission, since there was no international copyright law until 1891. In the past decade, the emergence of many new electronic databases containing nineteenth-century periodicals has facilitated the exploration of transatlantic connections while at the same time contributing to the overwhelming abundance of readily available primary source material from both nations. As Meredith McGill points out, bringing the culture of transatlantic periodical exchange into focus allows critics to 'take up the question of the cultural coherence of the nation rather than assuming the existence of a national literature as a threshold condition for literary study'.[12] This shift from a nationalistic to a transatlantic perspective, then, transforms the conversations about English and American literary culture in profound ways.

Transatlantic studies has indeed emerged as a vibrant new field of inquiry that has become the focus of numerous conferences, scholarly journals,[13] book series,[14] and job postings.[15] With the publication of the *Transatlantic Studies Reader*, the field has certainly come into its own, though it remains eclectic and diverse in its approaches and parameters. Studies using a transatlantic framework invite scholars and students to shift away from a microscopic examination of individual texts within distinct national literary traditions toward a telescopic view of cultural practices, authorial identities, publication systems, and literary exchanges across national boundaries. This move from a micro to a macro vision of literature and culture fosters new ways of seeing familiar authors and works that lead to an integrated understanding of a single transatlantic cultural realm. Particularly in regard to the Anglo-American world, nationalistic frameworks can obscure cultural connections that would have been taken for granted by nineteenth-century readers, including the transatlantic traffic in all things sensational.

NOTES

1. Exceptions tend to exist more among Americanists such as David S. Reynolds (*Beneath the American Renaissance: The Subversive Imagination in the Age of Emerson and Melville* (Cambridge, MA: Harvard University Press, 1998)) and Michael Denning (*Mechanic Accents: Dime Novels and Working-Class Culture in America* (London: Verso, 1987)), who make passing but consistent references to British and European sensation writers in their exploration of US sensation literature. Shelley Streeby (*American Sensations: Class Empire, and the Production of Popular Culture* (Berkeley: University of California Press, 2002)) engages an explicitly transnational approach but does not extend her study across the Atlantic. At the time we taught this class, few scholars in Victorian studies offered a sustained study of transatlantic sensations. Audrey Fisch's *American Slaves in Victorian England* is a notable exception (Cambridge: Cambridge University Press, 2000).

2. See Jennifer Phegley, John Cyril Barton, and Kristin N. Huston (eds), *Transatlantic Sensations* (Farnham: Ashgate Press, 2012).

3. Ashgate Press's call for papers, to which we responded when proposing our edited collection, 'Transatlantic Sensations', defined transatlantic studies in these terms.

4. For a discussion of how detection serves as a heuristic analogy for academic analysis, see John Cyril Barton, Douglass Higbee, and André Hulett, 'Reading Detectives: Teaching Argument and Analysis in First-Year Composition', in Judith H. Anderson and Christine R. Farris (eds), *Integrating Literature and Writing Instruction: First-Year English, Humanities Core Courses, Seminars* (New York: Modern Language Association, 2007), pp. 174–92.

5. [W. Fraser], 'Sensation Novelists: Miss Braddon', *North British Review*, 43 (September 1865), 198.

6. George Lippard, 'English Novels', in David S. Reynolds (ed.), *George Lippard, Prophet of Protest: Writings of an American Radical, 1822–1854* (New York: Peter Lang, 1986), pp. 260, 253.

7. Charles Dickens, 'American Sensations', *All the Year Round*, 5 (4 May 1861), 132.

8. 'Sense Vs. Sensation', *Punch*, 20 July 1861, p. 31.

9. See Daniel A. Cohen, *Pillars of Salt, Monuments of Grace: New England*

Crime Literature and the Origins of American Popular Culture, 1641–1860 (Oxford: Oxford University Press, 1993).

10. See Andrew Maunder (ed.), *Sensationalism and the Sensation Debate, Varieties of Women's Sensation Fiction, 1855–1890*, 6 vols (London: Pickering & Chatto, 2004), vol. 1, and Reynolds, *Beneath the American Renaissance*. Since we taught the class and published our edited collection, the publication of Pamela K. Gilbert (ed.), *A Companion to Sensation Fiction* (Chichester: Blackwell, 2011), has demonstrated the connections between sensation fiction of the 1860s and earlier Newgate novels and penny dreadfuls. Likewise, Lynn Pykett explores this relationship in 'The Newgate Novel and Sensation Fiction, 1830–1868', in Martin Priestman (ed.), *The Cambridge Companion to Crime Fiction* (Cambridge: Cambridge University Press, 2003), pp. 19–40.

11. Paul Giles, *Transatlantic Insurrections: British Culture and the Formation of American Literature, 1730–1860* (Philadelphia: University of Pennsylvania Press, 2001), pp. 8–9.

12. Meredith McGill, *American Literature and the Culture of Reprinting, 1834–1853* (Philadelphia: University of Pennsylvania Press, 2003), p. 4.

13. See, for example, *Symbiosis: A Journal of Anglo-American Relations* and the *Journal of Transatlantic Studies*. While not solely transatlantic, *Nineteenth-Century Contexts*, *Nineteenth-Century Literature*, and *Nineteenth-Century Studies* also publish articles on both British and American literary topics.

14. Ashgate Press has a series in Nineteenth-Century Transatlantic Studies and Edinburgh University Press has Studies in Transatlantic Literatures.

15. The job Jennifer Phegley was hired for was advertised in the fall 1998 Modern Language Association *Job List* as a position in transatlantic nineteenth-century literature. More recently, jobs in eighteenth- and nineteenth-century transatlantic studies have begun to appear regularly.

CHAPTER 15

Prophecy, Poetry, and Democracy: Teaching Through the International Lens of the *Fortnightly Review*

Linda Freedman

The prophetic mode is important to discussions about democracy and nationhood in the nineteenth century because self-styled prophets frequently assumed national status and were concerned with the fate of the nation. But there was an international modality to ideas about prophecy and democracy which nationally bounded studies inevitably overlook.[1] The prophet's claim to national status was often championed by those abroad. Walt Whitman found supporters in William Michael Rossetti and his crowd. The Italian radical, revolutionary, and self-styled prophet Guiseppe Mazzini, who devoted his life to the cause of Italian Unification, lived in exile in England from 1837 where he worked as a journalist and activist seeking help from sympathetic republicans in both England and America. The English prophet-artist William Blake was made modern and relevant to contemporary democratic debates when Algernon Charles Swinburne compared him to Whitman. Swinburne's own turn towards democratic prophet-artist was a direct result of Mazzini's influence and sought inspiration in Whitman's American example. This transatlantic current was a two-way exchange that made prophecy the lifeblood of a literary, democratic ideal. My essay starts to map the ground for a transatlantic network and exchange of prophet-artists and suggests how students of nineteenth-century culture and literature might use the *Fortnightly Review* as a basis for classroom investigation and discussion.[2]

John Holloway makes a gesture of acknowledgement to transatlantic influence and relationships in his early seminal work *The Victorian Sage* when he says that Ralph Waldo Emerson might have been included if space in his book had permitted it.[3] Transatlantic scholarship has since developed. Robert Weisbuch's work on American literature and British influence in the age of Emerson has produced illuminating readings of transatlantic connections. Weisbuch finds enmity the most important tone, arguing that the need for

American writers to overcome British influence is real and strong. He acknowledges that this is often counter-personal. Emerson loved and admired Thomas Carlyle but had to see him, as an American viewing an English writer, in terms of 'the magnificence of his genius and the poverty of his aims'.[4] Weisbuch argues that the commonality between Emerson and Carlyle can be found in the integral connection both men forge between prophecy and poetry. He suggests that this arises out of opposing temporal concerns whereby America is associated with earliness and Britain with cultural lateness. Thus Emerson's 'Representative Men' has a stronger sense that every man is potentially great than Carlyle's 'Heroes and Hero-Worship'. For Weisbuch, Carlyle's work is indicative of the late Romantic discordance that defines cultural lateness, whereas Emerson's more inclusive title defines the democratic optimism of cultural earliness.

I am hugely indebted to Weisbuch in my readings of transatlantic connections and antipathies in this period. His dominant sense of the child struggling to free itself from the literary modes of the parent country offers compelling readings of major American writers such as Whitman and Nathaniel Hawthorne. But Weisbuch's American perspective underestimates the value of post-civil war America to British and European ideas of the democratic prophet-artist. America and America's representative bard, Walt Whitman, were particularly important to an avant-garde group of international, liberal, and democratically minded individuals who congregated in London in the mid-1860s. Weisbuch's conception of American cultural earliness and British cultural lateness also becomes quite complicated, and somewhat altered, in the context of the transatlantic discussions about prophecy, democracy, and nationhood that took place after the end of the American Civil War. Prophecy forces us to think about space and time since the idea of timeliness is essential to the prophetic mode. Prophets appear at a moment of crisis and at a time of need. Their voices are urgent. Their mission is change. Yet there is another quality equally belonging to prophecy that deals in open-endedness and the vatic. Prophecy tends to battle a tension between what is and what will be. This makes it especially appropriate to emergent ideas of nationhood and the formation of a democratic poetic which needs to open up processes of becoming as well as signal the onset of change. Prophets occupy an equally strange geographical position in relation to their societies. They are situated in a kind of liminal no man's land – this is the legacy of the biblical 'voice crying in the wilderness' – and yet they take centre-stage. They are the most responsible, arguably over-responsible, people in their society, taking it upon themselves to remedy social ills and to open the eyes of their followers.

The transatlantic context of the democratically minded prophet artist brings some of these spatial and temporal considerations to the fore. It is the paradoxical centrality and removal of prophet-artists in relation to their societies that makes them internationally interesting – and important subjects and figures for transatlantic pedagogy, as well as scholarship. It is because he both belongs to, and stands apart from, his society that Whitman becomes relevant to British ideas of the democratic prophet-artist. Transatlantic context also introduces a time lag. Transatlantic publishing and print culture strongly affected the speed at which ideas about prophecy and democracy spread. In the years following the American Civil War, the 1867 edition of *Leaves of Grass*[5] was eagerly devoured by Rossetti, Swinburne, and other London-based avant-garde liberals, and Rossetti produced a selected edition of Whitman's works in 1868.[6] Whitman was known as an optimistic visionary, but the image was ten years out of date. Back home the disillusioned American was busy writing *Democratic Vistas*,[7] a far more chastened text, but this wouldn't be known in England until 1871. While Whitman was working through his own doubts as to the possibility of a democratic prophet-artist and national poet, pro-American and pro-republican left-wing, liberal, and avant-garde readers in England were holding him up as a shining example of success, even as other British readers reacted with hostility. In *Democratic Vistas* and *Songs of Parting*, a collection included in later editions of *Leaves of Grass*, Whitman's prophetic tone frequently tips into a kind of lamentation for things unrealised. This is Whitman's sense of 'years prophetical'[8] in *Songs of Parting* where he wanders in futurity, as if through Hades, able to see only strange phantoms of things-to-be, insubstantial and hauntingly comparable to his own approaching death. Yet Swinburne titled his collection of poems on Italian Unification *Songs before Sunrise*, in deliberate homage to his American hero.[9] As the title suggests, *Songs before Sunrise* anticipates a new dawn of democratic republicanism in Europe. He included a poem titled 'To Walt Whitman in America', which was laudatory in tone:

> Heart of their singer, to be for us
> More than our singer can be[10]

In his desire to capitalise on American associations with freshness and new beginnings, Swinburne either didn't notice, or deliberately reversed, the haunting and unwelcome sense of lateness in Whitman's current writing.

It is difficult to teach such transatlantic connections within nationally defined courses. One way to expose students to transatlantic currents is through national and local periodicals as periodicals frequently acted as forums and loci for the international avant-garde. This is now possible in the classroom because of the large number of nineteenth-century periodicals that are available as digital archives. This essay follows the group that gathered around the London-based *Fortnightly Review* in the years immediately following its inception in 1865. The *Fortnightly* was modelled on the French *Revue des deux mondes* with a commitment to bipartisan democracy and free speech. It was established by George Henry Lewes and taken over in 1867 by John Morley. The *Fortnightly* is available digitally through the *British Periodicals Online* archive, which means that students and researchers do not have to turn dusty pages at the British Library but can access material from wherever in the world they happen to be. For those who do not have a subscription, full pages of selected volumes are available on Google Books.

As the *Fortnightly* was one of the first periodicals to oppose the principle of anonymity and encourage its contributors to publish articles signed with their own names, students in a cluster room can track the presence of specific individuals in particular discussions and come across variety and contradiction that make for interesting debate. For example, students tracking the way America was perceived immediately after the civil war will likely arrive at an understanding of sympathy for the North and optimism for the future that would accord with the editor's perspective. But they will also encounter some oddities. A striking example can be found in the 15 August 1865 issue. The editor, Lewes, was anti-slavery, but the edition featured an article entitled 'The Last Six Days of Secessia', which recounted the retreat of Lee from Petersburg and Richmond and the surrender at Appomattox with romantic sympathy.[11] Students could be encouraged to compare this piece with Moncure Conway's equally romantic but politically opposed article entitled 'Personal Recollections of President Lincoln', which was published in the 15 May 1865 issue.[12] Students might think about the way these differently oriented contributors both use elements of prophetic style to inflect their political discourse.

NEW AMERICA

America was relevant to nineteenth-century European discussions about democracy for obvious reasons. During the first half of the period, it appeared as a republican experiment, laughable for many, precarious for almost all, and symbolic of hope and futurity for a few. After the victory of the North in 1865, its status understandably changed. Those who had long been supporters of American democracy now had firmer ground on which to base their arguments. Pro-American London liberals felt that Britain's relationship with America might be set to change for the better, and they were keen to shed the violent associations of New World democracy in favour of a more peaceful, progressive ideal. But America's recent violence simultaneously presented itself as an inspiration and practical resource to the more militant advocates for democratic change.

In June 1865 the 'Public Affairs' column in the *Fortnightly Review* began:

There are no events to be recorded in the history of the last fortnight which can distract attention from the grand operations carried out on the American continent . . . Scarcely has the sound of the last cannon shot died away ere 400,000 victorious soldiers hasten to lay down their laurel-wreathed arms, and seek their peaceful homes. Is that not a glorious spectacle? Ought it not to re-assure those who fear the fierce democracy, and who believe in the mastering influence of a once-gratified tasting for blood?[13]

The image of a new, peaceful, and democratic America clearly continued to grow in the pro-American columns of the *Fortnightly*. An article published in March 1867 claimed that, before the war, the assumption was that 'the Republican bubble was to burst, and that the fitting penalties were to fall on the vulgar, democratic, spitting, and caucusing mob who, for the moment, were permitted to outrage by their existence all our refined and gentlemanly feelings'.[14] The author, J. Cotter Morrison, takes his argument largely from W. Hepworth Dixon's *New America*, a book published in London in 1867.[15] He is enthused by the idea that British ridicule of their former colony might now be turning into admiration. America is mythologised as a land of ready opportunity and character-building necessity. The 'caucusing mob' have now become a multitude of enterprising individuals: 'Men are thrown upon their own resources, and the dullest are driven to strike out a new idea sooner or later.'[16]

An editorial in the following issue was keen to separate the American ideal from recent violence. In an article entitled 'Young England and the Political Future', the new editor, John Morley, comments on the vague and disorganised state of democratic thought and misguided ideas about democracy in England, which are fuelled by fears of French- and American-style uprisings and violence. Morley claims that there is a group of clearer-thinking people in Britain (by which he seems to imply his own contributors) to whom the future belongs even though the 'sectarians' and 'obstructionists' of church and state may have their 'little day'.[17] Old associations with tobacco-chewing, pistol-firing hooligans are deliberately discouraged in favour of a more rationalist, progressive approach.

By tracking particular voices in the *Fortnightly* over multiple issues, students studying nineteenth-century print culture can identify recurring themes that mark this shifting relationship between Britain and America. For instance, the American minister Moncure Conway, who had been living in London since 1863, was a regular contributor to the *Fortnightly* as well as other London-based periodicals. He helped fuse notions of prophetic insight and rational intellect, lending an Emersonian tone to many of his articles. Deeply influenced by Emerson, he envisaged democratic advancement as a process of internal revelation. In an article on a utopian community in Long Island, he wrote:

> If there is any revelation for us, it is sheathed in the human mind; let the bud expand under the light, and at its heart will appear the true religion, wherever it is. At present all but the ignorant must be sceptics, though they have also sacred, prophetic whispers of the heart. When true methods of thought are adopted by all thinkers; when Science is enthroned; when all the rays of intellect are freed from the obscurations of dogmas and timidities, and brought to a focus upon the great problems of the universe, the world will have a prospect of having a religion, – a rich, ripe, sustaining fruit, with no worm of unbelief and misgiving gnawing at its heart.[18]

Conway's description of revelation is strongly reminiscent of Emerson's instruction in 'Self-Reliance': 'a man should learn to detect and watch that gleam of light which flashes across his mind from within'.[19]

Like Emerson, Conway expresses the birth of reason in prophetic terms. This passage illustrates the importance of the prophetic mode in realising an international democratic ideal. Conway's sense of space is global and cosmic. His example is American but his subject transcends national concerns. His sense of time works in the same way. Revelation matters to the progress and prospects of individual nations, but it draws meaning from a cosmic frame of time and space. It is a change in perception relevant to 'all thinkers', a prophetic breakthrough rather than a logical progression. The merits of intellectual debate become absorbed but not effaced by prophetic rhetoric when scientific method unseats traditional hierarchies. Conway believes that all people are capable of true thought if they will only listen to their own instincts. He wants to make prophecy democratically available. Listening to one's instincts and utilising the intellectual scientific method is something every thoughtful person can potentially do. The messages could subsequently be heard or read by anyone.

To the Italian revolutionary Guiseppe Mazzini (a favourite and almost cult-like figure for the enthusiastic readership of the *Fortnightly*), the end of the civil war signalled the beginning of America's greater international democratic responsibility. In 1865 Mazzini sent Conway a letter exhorting him to engage America in the democratic struggle of all peoples everywhere and specifically to lend Italy financial assistance. His opening was apocalyptic; peacetime brings responsibility to act: 'The heroic struggle in your native land is at an end. Ought it not to be the beginning of a new era in American life?'[20] Mazzini's language is openly religious, giving cosmic significance to the idea of emergent nationhood. Crucially, for Mazzini, nationhood is not the end in itself – though it may appear so to countries beset by internal conflict – but a means towards the greater end of the redemption of humanity:

> The life of a great nation is twofold; inward and outward. A nation is a mission – a function in the development of mankind – or nothing. A nation has a task to fulfil in the world for the good of all, a principle it represents in a mighty struggle which constitutes history, a flag to hoist in the giant battle – to which all local battles are episodes – going on in the earth between justice and injustice, liberty and tyranny, equality and arbitrary privilege, God and the devil. The non-interference doctrine is an atheistic one. To abstain is to deny the oneness of God and of mankind.[21]

This is a good example of Mazzini's ability to harness religious language for political ends. His characteristically prophetic mode was the keystone of his popular appeal. As Jonathan Steinberg has argued, Mazzini's contemporary, the less well-known Italian revolutionary Carlo Cattaneo, was a much better political and economic analyst but thoroughly ineffective as an agitator because he lacked the religiosity that framed Mazzini's political vision.[22] Mazzini clearly imagined the struggle for nationhood as religious and saw himself as Italy's prophet. He absorbed the violence of the American Civil War and Italian uprising into a conceit of martyrdom founded in the dual movement of sacrifice and resurrection. Young men who died fighting for their nation died fighting for God. In the same way that Christian resurrection required the sacrifice of God's son, national resurrection required the sacrifice of the nation's sons. Conway admitted later that he never showed Mazzini's letter to anyone. He could not stand as a supporter of violent revolution after the bloodshed of the American Civil War. But as an American in London, and a regular contributor to magazines, Conway was clearly an important figure in channelling ideas of the new America and its role in leading the way for international democracy.

Students could be presented with extracts from Conway's *Autobiography*, some of which are available on the website associated with this volume, and encouraged to think about his stylistic and intellectual similarities with Emerson, his motivation for promoting Whitman, and the local context of South Place Chapel where he preached. South Place Chapel is now called Conway Hall Ethical Society after its famous nineteenth-century American minister. It is still functioning and thought to be the oldest surviving freethought organisation in the world. Students can access the current website at <www.conwayhall.org.uk> and browse the archive catalogue online to find out more about Moncure Conway and his congregation.

WHITMAN

Conway introduced Whitman to English readers in the *Fortnightly Review*. In an article published in October 1866, he quoted at length from *Leaves of Grass*. His characterisation of Whitman drew heavily on the relationship between prophecy, democracy, and national formation. He quoted Thoreau as saying that Whitman was 'apparently the greatest democrat the world has ever seen'.[23] He gave a verbal portrait of the poet in working-man's clothes, at home among the people, who all liked him but didn't have the faintest clue that he had written a book. In Conway's article, we see something of Whitman's desire for international publicity. Conway quotes from one of Whitman's letters, with his permission, defining his ambition as

> to give something to our own literature which will be our own, with neither foreign spirit, nor imagery, nor form, but adapted to our case, grown out of our associations, boldly portraying the West, strengthening and intensifying the national soul, and finding the entire fountains of its birth and growth in our country.[24]

Conway exposed readers of the *Fortnightly* to Whitman's self-styling as a uniquely American prophet-artist, assuming national status and aligning democratic purpose with religious vocation. Conway concluded the piece by saying, '[I]t is understood by his friends that he is writing a series of pieces which shall be the expression of the religious nature of man, which he regards as essential to the completion of his task.'[25] Whitman was known in London in the mid-1860s as one of the only distinctly American voices of the time. An article on recent American poetry published in the *Fortnightly* on 1 March 1867 claimed that only Whitman and Emerson had anything very American about them. It was only now, the author J. Knight claimed, that America was beginning to have a literature of its own. Whitman and Emerson were largely responsible.[26]

In this context, besides tracking authors like Conway across multiple numbers, students can also trace shifts in approaches for representing key authors like Whitman over time. An 1871 article published in the London *Westminster Review* shows that by the end of the decade, this image of Whitman as a distinctly American prophet-artist was accepted in London intellectual circles. The author opens by saying that the British interest in the relationship between literature and broad social and democratic thought has not, up to this point, sought to apply itself to any American literature. He states that Whitman has been said to be the representative of American democracy and that he wants to investigate in more detail what this might mean. The author acknowledges that Whitman is already known to English readers

through Conway's piece in the *Fortnightly Review* and through selections
recently published by William Michael Rossetti, but he claims that critics have
thus far studied him only as a personality, not as a product of contemporary
American society and its infant democracy. He is keen to emphasise that democratic value does not equate with popularity and to locate the prophet within
a paradoxically central and liminal social position. For the author, Whitman's
oddity is entirely in keeping with prophetic character. Moreover, the role of
the prophet seems automatically representative of the most profound national
characteristics:

> The representative man of a nation is not always the nation's favourite.
> Hebrew spiritualism, the deepest instincts, the highest reaches of
> the moral attainment of the Jewish race, appear in the cryings and
> communings of its prophets; yet the prophets sometimes cried in the
> wilderness, and the people went after strange gods.[27]

He continues to explain that Whitman's prophetic and democratic role is part
of national formation, but national formation is part of a global and religious
conception of human commonality: 'the self-celebration of himself as a man
and an American; it is what he possesses in common with all others that he feels
to be glorious and worthy of song'.[28] In this 1871 article, Whitman's vision is
presented as democratically available and valuable to all even as this value
relates largely to his national associations with new America.[29] Through periodical material, which is justifiably contained within nationally based courses,
students can start to map some of the international territory of the relationship
among prophecy, democracy, and nationhood in the second half of the 1860s.
Like the *Fortnightly*, the *Westminster Review* is also available through *British
Periodicals Online*. Students could take this example of Whitman's reputation
in England and use it to think about cross-pollination between periodicals.
The *Westminster Review* article was written in the knowledge that Conway had
already made Whitman familiar to readers, and it overtly referred to his article.
They could be asked to investigate other possible common areas of transatlantic interest or to discover journalists and literary contributors who wrote for
both periodicals.

SWINBURNE, WHITMAN, AND BLAKE

Students might also be encouraged to think about Swinburne's homage to
Whitman in his own emergent democratic poetic. In 1868 Swinburne published his major work of art criticism, *William Blake: A Critical Essay*.[30] It was
fundamentally concerned with the democratic application of the prophetic

mode. Two years earlier, Swinburne had written to Conway, who was already promoting Whitman's reputation in England, that Blake was a 'republican under the very shadow of the gibbet . . . a lover of America, of freedom, and of France from the first and to the last'.[31] In other words, Conway claims that Blake was not afraid to stand up for freedom and democracy even when it put him in personal danger. One year earlier he had been recruited by Mazzini to aid Italian Unification. Swinburne's 1868 *Essay* provides evidence of his growing desire to marry aesthetic and political purpose. Students might be asked to consider the resonance that Swinburne's words have in this mid-nineteenth-century transatlantic context of prophetic and democratic debate. Whitman was brought in at the end of Swinburne's book in order to emphasise Blake's contemporary democratic relevance. The passage is on the website associated with this volume, and students could be asked to think about the way Swinburne capitalises on Whitman's associations with new America in order to claim Blake's revolutionary spirit for the present day.

Swinburne's book was reviewed by Conway for the *Fortnightly* immediately after its publication. Conway picks up on Swinburne's mystical sense of a 'transfusion of spirits' between Blake and Whitman and comments on a more general Blakean legacy in America in the form of Transcendentalism among cultivated people and Spiritism in more vulgar circumstances.[32] He quotes the full passage containing Swinburne's comparison of Blake and Whitman and claims that to readers familiar with both poets the claim might even seem understated. Conway's review made the prophetic connection between Whitman and Blake familiar to a much wider audience than would have been available for Swinburne's book. The timeliness of prophecy is central to Conway's argument. He writes, 'Neither the times at which the great mystics appear, nor the forms of their oracles, are accidental.'[33] Conway takes Swinburne's 'transfusion of spirits' a step further, calling Whitman the 're-appearance' of Blake in America.[34] Both prophets further the spirit of democracy, enacting the revelation from within, rather than simply widening the political franchise.

Morley, the current editor of the *Fortnightly*, was, at this moment, particularly disillusioned with British political efforts to widen the franchise. In an editorial entitled 'The Chamber of Mediocrity', published on 1 December 1868, he denounced the state of contemporary politics and implied that the literatus had more radical potential and constituted more of a threat to the status quo than a whole host of bickering, nervous, and ultimately tame politicians, whether Tory or Whig: 'It was a little clique of ingenious literary men which was shaking France to its foundations a hundred years ago, while the nobles and the court were busy with their diversions.'[35] Likening the British Parliament to the late eighteenth-century French court, Morley implies that it is undemocratic, outdated, and guilty of failing the public. He clearly feels that his own contributors and his group of friends are about to have their moment.

One of the things students might do with this is to investigate the extent to which Morley's contributors enacted his wishes. Morley warned against timorousness and cant. Students could be asked to think about the temperament and tone of contributions as well as the arguments they put forward. They would discover that Swinburne began to be published more frequently in the magazine from around this point and could think about the role played by poetry in forming a sense of community and widening democratic involvement.

The greatest irony is that while Morley's contributors were keen to capitalise on American associations with new beginnings in the late 1860s, Whitman was haunted by the knowledge that he wasn't early enough. The civil war clearly left him disillusioned. In *Democratic Vistas*, he calls again and again for the literatus who will lead America into futurity, but the turgid nature of the text makes it hard to believe such a figure is more than a phantom, a haunting reminder of his own failure to achieve the celebrated prophetic character of *Leaves of Grass*. There is no freshness and sweet-smelling air in *Democratic Vistas*. The body of youthful vitality and sexual appetite has become cankered, experienced, and old. *Songs of Parting* is equally filled with lamentation. Like Moses, condemned only to lead his people to the edge of the Promised Land, Whitman laments:

O book, O chants! must all then amount to but this?
Must we barely arrive at this beginning of us? – and yet
it is enough, O soul[.][36]

But Swinburne clearly still associated Whitman with freshness, newness, and sexual energy:

Sweet-smelling of pine-leaves and grasses
[...]
Prophetic
Lips hot with the bloodbeats of song.[37]

In *Democratic Vistas*, Whitman declares a necessary solidarity with Europe. In *Songs of Parting*, he imagines America as a player on 'the world's stage': 'I see not America only, not Liberty's nation but other nations preparing'.[38] But his tone was no longer the tone that Swinburne praises. A spectator rather than an agitator and a retrospective singer of the past, Whitman lacks the early energy that Swinburne wants.

CONCLUSIONS

The transatlantic context for debates surrounding prophecy, democracy, and nationhood in the mid-nineteenth century is far larger than I have managed to detail here. The relationship troubled thinkers from Emerson, Carlyle, Whitman, and Emily Dickinson to Mazzini, Swinburne, John Ruskin, and George Eliot. I have shown how periodicals such as the *Fortnightly Review* provide an international lens through which we might teach the interaction, reception, and distinction between major European and American figures. With the enormous amount of nineteenth-century periodicals now available as digital archives, this strategy has the potential to invigorate and fundamentally alter our capacity for teaching transatlantic currents, especially within nationally defined courses. I have shown that the idea of new America and Whitman's associations with freshness and newness feature in the pages of the *Fortnightly* and provide a way into thinking about the importance of space and time in the democratisation of the prophetic mode. I have also indicated some of the poetic comparisons and historical ironies that might result from this kind of work and provided a pedagogical model for identifying and analysing key sites, modes, and recurring themes associated with the transatlantic exchange of prophet-artists through localised print culture.

NOTES

1. For example, John Holloway, *The Victorian Sage: Studies in Argument* (London: Macmillan, 1953), and John Stephen Mack, *The Pragmatic Whitman: Reimagining American Democracy* (Iowa City: University of Iowa Press, 2002).
2. See also Linda Freedman, 'Walt Whitman and William Blake: The Prophet-Artist and Democratic Thought', in Robin Peel and Daniel Maudlin (eds), *Transatlantic Traffic and (Mis)Translations* (Durham, NH: University Press of New England, 2013), pp. 133–55.
3. Holloway, *Victorian Sage*, p. 15.
4. Robert Weisbuch, *Atlantic Double Cross: American Literature and British Influence in the Age of Emerson* (Chicago: University of Chicago Press, 1986), p. 22; see also Camille R. LaBossière, *The Victorian Fol Sage: Comparative Readings in Carlyle, Emerson, Melville, and Conrad* (Lewisburg: Bucknell University Press, 1989).
5. Walt Whitman, *Leaves of Grass*, 4th edn (New York: William E. Chapin, 1867).
6. William Michael Rossetti (ed.), *Poems by Walt Whitman* (London: John Camden Hotten, 1868).

7. Whitman, *Democratic Vistas* (New York: Redfield, 1871).
8. Whitman, 'Songs of Parting', *Leaves of Grass*, 5th edn (New York: Redfield, 1871–2), p. 375.
9. William J. Goede, 'Swinburne and the Whitmaniacs', *Victorian Newsletter*, 33 (Spring 1968), 19.
10. Algernon Charles Swinburne, *Songs before Sunrise* (London: Chatto & Windus, 1875), p. 143.
11. Francis Lawley, 'The Last Six Days of Secessia', *Fortnightly Review* (hereafter *FR*), 15 August 1865, pp. 1–10.
12. Moncure D. Conway, 'Personal Recollections of President Lincoln', *FR*, 15 May 1865, pp. 56–65.
13. George Henry Lewes, 'Public Affairs', *FR*, 1 June 1865, p. 242.
14. J. Cotter Morrison, 'Religious Utopias in the US', *FR*, 7 March 1867, p. 290.
15. W. Hepworth Dixon, *New America* (London: Hurst & Blackett, 1867).
16. Morrison, 'Religious Utopias', p. 292.
17. John Morley, 'Young England and the Political Future', *FR*, 7 April 1867, p. 496.
18. Conway, 'Modern Times, New York', *FR*, 1 July 1865, p. 427.
19. Ralph Waldo Emerson, 'Self-Reliance', in Joseph Slater, Jean Ferguson Carr, and Alfred Riggs Ferguson (eds), *The Collected Works of Ralph Waldo Emerson*, vol. 2 (Cambridge, MA: Harvard University Press, 1979), p. 27.
20. Conway, *Autobiography: Memories and Experiences of Moncure D. Conway* (London: Cassell & Co., 1904), p. 55.
21. Ibid., p. 55.
22. C. A. Bayly and Eugenio F. Biagini (eds), *Mazzini and the Globalisation of Democratic Nationalism* (Oxford: Oxford University Press, 2008), p. 3.
23. Conway, 'Walt Whitman', *FR*, 15 October 1866, p. 546.
24. Ibid., p. 535.
25. Ibid., p. 548.
26. J. Knight, 'Recent American Poetry', *FR*, 7 March 1867, pp. 382–3.
27. Edward Dowden, 'The Poetry of Democracy', *Westminster Review*, 40 (July 1871): 37.
28. Ibid., 51.
29. Ibid.
30. Swinburne, *William Blake: A Critical Essay* (London: John Camden Hotten, 1868).
31. Deborah Dorfman, *Blake in the Nineteenth Century: His Reputation as a Poet from Gilchrist to Yeats* (London: Yale University Press, 1969), p. 159.
32. Conway, 'William Blake: A Critical Essay by Algernon Charles Swinburne', *FR*, 3 February 1868, p. 218.

33. Ibid., p. 216.
34. Ibid., p. 217.
35. John Morley, 'The Chamber of Mediocrity', *FR*, 4 December 1868, pp. 683–4.
36. Whitman, *Leaves of Grass*, 5th edn, p. 373.
37. Swinburne, *Songs before Sunrise* (London: Chatto & Windus, 1875), p. 143.
38. Whitman, *Leaves of Grass*, 5th edn, p. 373.

PART V

Envisioning Digital Transatlanticism

CHAPTER 16

Transatlantic Mediations: Teaching Victorian Poetry in the New Print Media

Alison Chapman

How does popular serial print participate in the culture of exchange between Britain and America during the Victorian period? How are our teaching practices mediating transatlanticism for the students? And what place has poetry in popular transatlantic print culture? These questions emerged during my graduate class in winter 2010 on 'Victorian Poetry and the New Print Media' at the University of Victoria. The main learning outcome of the course was to deepen the students' understanding of poetry in mass print culture through research projects on print copies of a wide variety of periodicals (by which I mean a variety of serial print, including annuals, magazines, newspapers, quarterlies and weeklies). Unexpected outcomes of the course for me were numerous: the challenge to my pedagogical approaches and disciplinary definitions following the students' periodical discoveries; the idea for the creation of the *Database of Victorian Periodical Poetry* (after a promise rashly given to the students that their fascinating index work would be put on the web); questions about the place of transatlanticism within the dramatic expansion of digitised Victorian print; concerns about the relationship between print (or analogue) media and digital media; and an interest in the kinds of digital tools that uncover Victorian poetry's transatlanticism. I had embarked on digital (or hybrid) pedagogy, which has emerged as a response to digital humanities initiatives, embracing 'flexible expectations of our end product'.[1] Working with the digital prompts a different kind of teaching and a different kind of Victorian poetry syllabus.

Fundamental to this essay is the doubled concept of mediation, of print media performing transatlanticism and a vehicle for transmitting and disseminating transatlanticism, in other words print media as an agent producing meaning and an intermediary circulating meaning (as defined by the *Oxford English Dictionary*). This is particularly true of digital versions that constitute another kind of mediation, between analogue and digital. The media studies term 'remediation' is important to conceptions of the dissemination of print, both through the practice of widespread reprinting in the nineteenth century and the transformation from print to digital formats. As defined most influentially by David Bolter and Richard Grusin, remediation is 'the way in which one medium is seen by our culture as reforming or improving upon another' and 'repurposing earlier media into digital forms'.[2] The mediation of transatlanticism thus also implies remediation, the generative and iterative production of the concept of transatlanticism and its literary culture across the boundaries of nations and media. In particular, as a remediation, the shift from print text to digital object is not the production of a simple substitution or simulacrum. In the crossing of media, the literary text alters both its form and its interpretative framework. A poem read in a print periodical is not only different visually and materially from a poem read through clicking a link on a database search results list that takes the reader to either a jpeg of the poem or a link to the poem within the entire digitised book (such as the *Database of Periodical Poetry* or the *Periodical Poetry Index*), but in the process of remediation into a digital object, the poem is embedded explicitly and implicitly within an entirely new interpretative schema. For example, a poem in a print volume is fundamentally different from a poem in a hypermedia archive that offers a non-linear and non-hierarchical model of reading. But, to date, rather than exploring the knotty pedagogical and methodological issues arising from digitisation, nineteenth-century scholars who write on teaching with digital media mostly celebrate its democratic potential, 'transform[ing] classrooms into archives'.[3] That may indeed be the case, but the tools used need also to be the focus of critical inquiry, as James Mussell argues in *Nineteenth-Century Print and the Digital Age*. This digital approach reconfigures transatlanticism, through the print mediations that constructed it for the popular imagination, into a categorical incoherence.[4] Transatlantic mediation, through periodical print, is the performance of estrangement and instability.

DIGITAL TRANSATLANTICISM

Julia Flanders comments on the 'rhetoric of abundance' that dominated discussions of digital resources in the last decade, resulting in the sudden visibility of a massive corpus of texts, because 'storage is cheaper than decision-making'.[5] In particular, full nineteenth-century periodical runs that were often tucked away in major research libraries are now available to anyone with Internet access. A student researching nineteenth-century poetry will find multiple digital manifestations in a variety of print media, not all of them belonging to the poet's national affiliation. For example, a student researching Christina Rossetti's sonnet 'Vanity of Vanities' through a Google keyword search will find (currently at the bottom of the first page of hits) the poem's reprinting in *Harper's* for June 1870 (p. 48). Its first appearances in the privately printed *Verses: Dedicated to Her Mother* (1847), and then in *The Prince's Progress and Other Poems* (1866), are not currently ranked higher than the American reprint in the Google search, which of course does not in itself rank according to bibliographical chronology, but which nevertheless reveals other kinds of surprises. The mass digitisation of American and British periodicals offers a wealth of new information on the crisscrossing of poems across the Atlantic.[6] How does this digital explosion of serial print, from the ephemeral dust of the analogue archive into the (questionably permanent) archive of the cloud, change pedagogy?

The digital explosion challenges the conception of transatlanticism, usually understood as a matrix of Anglo-American relations.[7] The digital revolution has both expanded the term 'transatlanticism' and also undermined any unified meaning, as digitisation reveals the extent that British and American print travelled promiscuously across the Atlantic.[8] Bob Nicholson, for example, argues that the common editorial 'scissors and paste' practice 'created a space in which . . . the two cultures became increasingly entangled'.[9] Widespread literary piracy, the pervasive culture of reprinting, and the absence of an American copyright law until 1891 meant that British authors had no protection in America. British popular print also routinely republished American periodical contributions. Digitisation now allows the movement of print to be traced.

Digital copies of nineteenth-century newspapers reveal the wholesale reprinting of periodical contributions in both countries. The penny illustrated weekly, the *London Journal* (1845–1928), for example, regularly lifted material from American writers, while the popular American *Harper's New Monthly Magazine* (1850–) prided itself on the rapid 'transfer' of material from the British press (as outlined in the first issue).[10] The first contribution in the first issue of *Harper's*, 'A Word at the Start', emphasises the cultural value of periodical publication to Britain, France, and America: '[t]he wealth and freshness of the Literature of the Nineteenth Century are embodied in the pages of its periodicals'.[11] Periodical contributions interweave 'these sources of instruction and interest' with 'merely local and transient interest', and the mission of the magazine is to bring forth the best pickings from international periodicals.[12] Not only was periodical material from the other country reframed for a different national readership, but also some periodicals took advantage of improvements in communication technologies (for example the 1858 cross-Atlantic telegraph cable) to publish simultaneously in Britain and America, such as *All the Year Round* (1859–95). In addition, copies of periodicals circulated internationally and had an important readership afterlife through 'distribution networks'.[13] Some periodicals, such as *Chambers's (Edinburgh) Journal*

(1832–1956), shifted their publication schedule in line with shipping timetables. The transatlantic mediation of periodical literature was both a piratical reprinting and the distribution of titles across national boundaries.

Tracking the mediations between Britain and America questions the stable category of national literatures, even as this was a booming period for their formation through print culture. But 'Victorian' literature usually means Victorian British, which in turn usually means Victorian English literature, or literature in English, produced by authors born and/or living in England. How do we teach Victorian poetry after the recent massive digitisation, and how do we situate periodicals as important, alongside single-authored volumes of original poetry?[14] How would American poets be taught alongside their British contemporaries? Currently, for example, a search in the *Database of Victorian Poetry* (in progress) reveals nine poems by William Cullen Bryant, one by Edgar Allan Poe, and four by Lydia Sigourney. A search in the *Database* for all poets identified as American, out of the current dataset of over 5,200 poems and over 500 poets in sixteen British periodicals, finds fifty-four (including Sarah T. Bolton, Kate Putnam Osgood, W. O. Peabody), surely a low estimate given the practice of unsigned and pseudonymous poets, as well as the challenges of identifying poets who did not publish volumes of poetry and who are not featured in the Library of Congress catalogue, bibliographies, and biographical databases. Searching the *American Historical Newspaper* database with the limits 'poetry' and the date 1843–89 results in 11,796 hits, although there is no way to search for a poet's nationality (I did count six poems by Tennyson). This is a reminder to check the dataset of any database to understand the parameters in which it operates, as Mussell argues, for searches of digital material will inevitably leave an incomplete record. *The Broadview Anthology of Victorian Poetry and Poetic Theory*, which I often adopt for teaching, includes no American poets, under the implied assumption that 'Victorian' denotes British. Richard Cronin's *Reading Victorian Poetry*, however, makes the trenchant point that 'the British poets of the nineteenth century recognised their debts . . . to their American contemporaries'.[15]

The national segregation was underlined by anthologist Edmund Clarence Stedman, whom Michael Cohen terms the 'inventor of Victorian poetry'.[16] Although his popular anthologies create a Victorian American poetry through a 'transatlantic interdependence', Stedman's anthologies nevertheless keep distinct British and colonial poetry from emerging American national traditions. Thus, although Stedman relies on a model of transatlantic literary exchange, the national literary tradition was still a paradigm he maintained. Meredith McGill remarks of recent criticism on American literary traditions that 'despite strong efforts to think beyond the nation, most of these studies leave national literary histories more or less in place'.[17] To what extent does the transatlantic exchange of poetry in the Victorian era challenge the false unity, or unstable category, of national literature, even as transatlanticism was used in this period to establish and define national literature?

Colonial, transnational, international, indeed even global literatures in English from the Victorian era, are challenging Anglo-centric canonical assumptions.[18] Students have got there before us as they navigate the new world of mass digitisation. My 2010 graduate class on Victorian periodical poetry frequently produced periodical volumes that fascinated them, such as the American annual *Magnolia* (1836–55) or the magazine *Harper's*, asking if they 'counted' as Victorian. They also found reprints of British poems in American periodicals, and American poets in British periodicals, and asked if this 'counted' too. Transatlantic literature belongs of course neither to the British nor Americans proper, allowing some pressing questions about national boundaries, canon formation, and the circulation of periodical print culture. After all, *Harper's* is included in the *Waterloo Directory*, an editorial note explains on the database, despite being an American publication, 'because it heavily re-printed British periodical excerpts'.[19] My students' repeated requests – 'does this count as Victorian' – pointed to the fundamental problem with periodical print and the culture of crossing national boundaries in print circulation, including but not limited to the promiscuous culture of reprinting. As the course developed, the important question 'does it count' was modulated into 'how does it circulate', because constructing periodical poetry research along national lines was both unworkable and unhistorical.

DIGITAL TOOLS

What would happen if the blind spot in Victorian poetry studies, transatlanticism, was put into focus in a graduate course on Victorian periodical poetry, foregrounding the circulation of periodical print while retaining the student-centred discovery of material? A course responding to digital initiatives both quantifies and analyses periodical poetry, yet also charts poetry's movement across titles and national boundaries. Thus I adapted my course, which evolved into a new one on popular Victorian poetry (for fall 2013), asking what it means to create a canon of poems that were most read (anthologies, gift books, volumes, periodicals), while addressing problems of quantifying popularity.[20] The course constructs a provisional canon of the most read Victorian poems, and investigates how popular poetry is related to canonical book-based poetry.

Since I taught 'Victorian Poetry and the New Print Media', it is easier to trace a poem's circulation and also to curate, analyse, and collaborate on findings with ready-made software. For example, using WordPress or Omeka builds a digital exhibit of poetry, a WordPress plug-in such as PressBook creates a flexible e-anthology of the material, and adopting the Neatline suite of add-on tools for Omeka (developed by the Scholar's Lab at the University of Virginia) creates spatial and temporal maps of the relationships between poems and periodical titles. The research-intensive focus of digital humanities scholarship is changing in response to digital pedagogy, a field that has a dedicated journal (*Hybrid Pedagogies*), conferences, and academic studies. This movement aims to counter the tendency to put pedagogy as secondary or, in Hirsch's words, in 'parenthesis'.[21] Recent discussion of digital pedagogy has focused on the growing number of user-ready tools that curate, annotate, visualise, or map, and the danger that they represent merely instructional technology, limiting the classroom experience rather than challenging old pedagogical practices. Paul Ffye comments that technology can only improve the classroom with a change in pedagogy: '[h]ow do we break the thrall to tools and technologies which may limit the horizon of our pedagogical creativity?'[22] Natalie Houston, Lindsy Lawrence, and April Patrick suggest that analysis of digital tools belongs in a digital humanities course.[23] It is my contention that critiques of digital platforms, tools, and methods belong in every higher education literary course to nurture students' digital literacy.

Digital pedagogy is changing teaching at a structural level.[24] Firstly, learning is not just an experience documented by the summative result of a high-stakes essay or exam, but is a process of reflection through various low-stakes assignments. For example, Jentery Sayers proposes the adaptation of the 'change log', a format that gives the students structure to map out their changes in thinking and writing, a technique likened to digital 'versioning' tools.[25] Process is valued as much as product, aided by digital tools that allow students to share their learning process and to collaborate on exercises and projects such as blogs and wikis.[26] Also valuable are tools such as Storify, which collates, publishes, and shares material gathered from media across the web (such as a student twitter stream discussing a text or a seminar). Blog posts can be grouped, edited, and transformed into a PDF with a tool such as Anthologize, a useful way to present the process of learning through blog posts as an assignment in itself. Of course, there are other analogue methods to documenting learning processes, such as a reading journal, but the digital tool's value is that collaboration and adaptability are highlighted as classroom competencies, and the tool is not just a supplement to classroom activity but fundamental to its structure.

Secondly, learning outcomes in digital pedagogy embrace making and playfulness. For Sayers, 'tinkering' is an apt term for the digital classroom, connoting 'inexpert, tactical, and situational experimentation', forcing both teacher and student to be adaptive and open to uncertain outcomes.[27] Learning is not focused on a final summative project, but rather emphasises a 'commitment to process' and a 'sense of play'.[28] The classroom is a dynamic space in Jesse Stommel's definition of digital pedagogy, 'less a field and more an active present participle'.[29] Ultimately, the power relation between student and teacher becomes radically student-centred.

Such openness to discovery, collaboration, and making, however, still needs to be specifically framed in terms of learning outcomes. While a digital classroom requires adaptability and an embrace of the unexpected, it is important not to romanticise digital pedagogy as merely a productive shift of power between student and teacher or a blue-sky approach to the vastness of digitisation. The 'Victorian Poetry and the New Print Media' course relied on the students' finding and sharing of poems as the basis of constructing the course. Students were required to engage deeply with the material, both in a big tent fashion (by indexing poetry in a run of periodicals and then analysing any patterns quantitatively) and on a micro-scale (by requiring students to find and present on periodical poems, as well as write a close reading on a poem found in a particular subset of periodicals identified for that week).

Students were expected to base their research on the analogue poems in Special Collections, enhanced by digital versions where necessary. With the expansion of digitisation and poetry indexing, however, it is now possible to mix advanced searching and data mining of digitised material (such as nationality or gender of poets contributing to a periodical, or whether a set of periodical poems is illustrated or not) with analysis of analogue material. A future course on periodical poetry would take advantage of expanding 'out-of-the-box' tools for collation and analysis by seeking a deeper understanding of the relationship between print and digital media. In particular, students can be asked to examine the digital tools they might otherwise see as a shortcut to finding the print material they want, such as quantifying the American periodical reprints of British poems. There is nothing wrong with search engine queries, which allow a vast amount of data to be processed quickly. But thinking about what it means to digitise a poem, how the digital environment is different from the original print context (where the paratextual material such as decorative wrappers, heading banners, and advertisements are often omitted), what the print context of an issue or volume or series tells us about patterns in periodical poetry and its relationship to contributions in other genres, allows the very tools that students use to be put into question.

Studying analogue and digital versions requires investigation of their relationship. Is one version a supplement to the other? A replacement of the other? Which has primacy? What happens when a serial run is digitised by different organisations?[30] *Harper's*, for example, is available through *Periodicals Archive Online*, but the material is organised by volume and alphabetically by contribution title. The same magazine is available through the *Making of America*, with the digital objects organised by its placement in the magazine (helpful when tracking the place of poetry in an issue, and when looking for editorial comments, such as the inaugural issue's crucial essay 'A Word to the Readers', which is immediately apparent in *Making of America*, but which is not even included in *Periodicals Archive Online*). The digital version is not a perfect replica of the print version, but only a (sometimes imperfect) scan of one version of the print poem, and organised in a particular way. Digitised copies do not capture what Stauffer terms the 'human traces' of print copies, such as annotations and inscriptions. The digital, Stauffer contends, is not a replacement for the print text but a simulacrum.[31] The question of what has been digitised, and what is available in the library, leads to fertile class explorations about the politics of collecting, the making of the canon, the benefits of close reading alongside what Moretti terms 'distant reading', and the cost of losing print copies forever.[32] As Alan Liu comments, 'even apparently workaday digital tools older than the Web itself – for example, Microsoft Word – can be used against the grain to defamiliarise what we thought we understood about the way humanities discourse works'.[33] As more tools become available, with little or no coding required of the user, putting the tool itself up to the light for examination is crucial.[34]

A course on transatlantic print culture needs to ensure that the students do not lose sight of the value of print copies in this brave new world of massive digitisation. The digitised copy offers up wonders through keyword searches, for example, but exactly *which* lone copy of the print material now stands synecdochically for all versions of the analogue text? How might other print copies give different information about the periodical? In the case of a database, what does the dataset include? Does it (can it) identify all the authors? Does it indicate the author's gender, nationality, education, and class? Does the database allow searches of material by illustrator, by date, by nationality? Certainly the emphasis on many databases, such as my own *Database of Victorian Periodical Poetry*, is on the identification of authors (which is no easy feat given the preponderance of unsigned and pseudonymous poets). While I am committed to the scholarly value of discovering authorial identity, reading the analogue text privileges the deep embeddedness of the poem in its print context and (except arguably in the case of the celebrity poet) displaces the author-function in favour of the rich print environment of the poem. Thus, while indexing periodical poems demonstrates the intermeshing of British and American literature and low and high culture through identifying the poets, reading analogue copies of periodicals frequently challenges the cult of the author and forges a different reading experience of the poem in its relationship to the material around it, creating a seriality of poems and poetics that interrelate forwards and backwards through a periodical title. The other important analysis of the database is how periodical poetry is defined. Does it include translations? Songs with musical scores? Poems in a language other than English? Poems embedded into prose fiction and book reviews? Sometimes these distinctions can be tricky to maintain, for example when a cumulative volume index lists a poem that is actually found in the middle of a book review. Thus the digital tools lead back to the print object, where a copy is available, and the tool itself is a construction rather than a transparent window into some textual truth.

TRANSATLANTIC DIGITAL PEDAGOGY

Models for assignments in an upper-level undergraduate or graduate Victorian transatlantic periodical poetry course can benefit from our new digital expansiveness with an emphasis on discovery, play, experimentation, flexibility about outcomes, and collaboration, as well as the conventional humanities skill sets such as library research, academic writing in its various formats, presentations, and critical thinking. In transatlantic literary studies, giving students the skills to put poetry in its rich print contexts is crucial so that they can position poetry as part of the interpretation, re-packaging, and dissemination of another nation's culture. Assignments crafted with digital pedagogy in mind would, firstly, emphasise the students' centrality in finding and making a teaching canon of periodical poetry. This approach asks the student to identify what kinds of poem might make a canon, how popular serial poetry intersects with more canonical poetry, how a canon could be constructed that is less author-based than print-context based. Curating and interpreting a canon of transatlantic periodical poetry through collaboratively authored platforms such as WordPress or Omeka privileges process over product, and allows the student to think through the implications of a print culture anthology, such as how to represent the poetry's embeddedness in its periodical environment. A collaborative wiki can work the same way but also allow students to include a range of material in addition to information on a collection of transatlantic periodical poems, such as the numerical and geographical circulation of specific periodicals, and contextual posts on key topics such as copyright law and the Atlantic telegraph. One of the benefits of a wiki is its student-centric approach and the ability to log edits and corrections. The potential for collaboration within the classroom, between different cohorts of the same course, and between different institutions, has exciting potential, although my experience as the general editor of the *Victorian Poetry, Poetics and Contexts* wiki is that teachers experience a tension between the wiki philosophy of author-autonomy and speedy evolution and editing of material, and the need for scholarly protocols (for example on the kinds of research references that are appropriate). The anthology of a student-authored, collaborative teaching canon of this poetry can also fruitfully include the e-publication as a final project through PressBook or another PDF generating tool, and a self-reflexive exercise documenting and reflecting upon the process of working with periodical material.

Secondly, a digital pedagogical approach would craft assignments that involve a critique of the digital tools used to find, curate, and interpret periodical poetry. This assignment might be a list of questions related to finding the material that the students are invited to consider, such as the relationship between digital and analogue texts, the parameters of the dataset embodied in a specific database, the potentials and limitations of a particular search engine, and articulating the mutually beneficial relationship between digital tools and non-digital analytical approaches. Thirdly, a digital approach leads to assignments requiring comparison between the quantitative interpretation of large data sets and the close analysis of a small section of text (such as a short poem). As the tools available rapidly change, compendiums (for example, *BambooDiRT*) are essential.

Pressing students to write in a variety of formats, for e-publication (like blog posts, wiki posts, change logs) as well as conventional analogue formats, not only challenges and diversifies writing skills but also expands seminar discussions into the difference in (and protocols for) writing in a public digital forum and writing essays only for the instructor. In my experience with the wiki, students found it challenging to write in a factual, encyclopaedic way, with strict referencing to reliable sources. But the end result was a more profound understanding of the difference between description and analysis, and writing for a public/social audience and an individual professor.

All these suggestions work with any kind of course based on digital and analogue texts, but they are particularly appropriate to transatlanticism because that term is so invested in mediation. Like the tensions between analogue and digital, transatlantic texts work within different categories (of the nation), unsettling unitary definitions and emphasising dynamism and context. Let me provide a final example. A student in a transatlantic periodical poetry course is asked to analyse the differences between print and digital versions of the *Anglo-American*, published in New York from 1843 to 1847 and available through Google Books and partially in my institution's library. Examining a list of poems from the volume index of the digitised version gives students a sense of the poems, although in the case of this volume such an index is missing. Even so, an index that distinguishes the poetry contributions will not give an indication of the cultural presence of poetry in other forms, such as in the advertisements and reviews. For example, the issue for 3 January 1846, rather than beginning with poetry, which was customary, starts with a review of the 1846 *Fisher's Drawing-Room Scrap Book*. This annual is distinguished from other expensive titles that are tainted by overwhelming emphasis on its engraved plates, or by 'scraps and alms' from the editor's fashionable friends.[35] The review laments this evidence that 'good literature, like every other good or useful commodity, in our hard-fisted times – the times, however of Byron, and Scott, and Southey – must be paid for, and well paid for, or not obtained at all'. The review then quotes at length several poems by Caroline Norton and ends with giving all of her 'Invocation of death', claiming that it 'will almost bear comparison with kindred strains of the elder English poets'.[36] Canonical poets and popular poets jostle for space in the proliferating transatlantic culture of reprinting. Other paratextual information from the *Anglo-American* gives important information about its mission, such as the decorative banner illustration placed between the words 'Anglo' and 'American' of the title, that displays a lion and an eagle side by side with shafts of sunlight emerging from behind the British crest and American flag. The implication is clear: national literatures are separate yet connected. This message is underlined with the Latin tag beneath the title *audi alteram partem* (hear the other side), a major legal principle of natural justice but also a call for communication between nations. The digital version (in this case the scan of a copy from Indiana University Library) encourages a linear, chronological reading, offering no sense of print's tactility (the paper quality, page size, illustration quality). Typing 'poem' into the search for this Google book renders an incomplete list of poetry. Extracting information about the culture of poetry in the digital volume has its limitations, and the digital version is in the end only a partial version of the analogue text. But examining the relation between analogue and digital yields important information, not just as part of the student's digital literacy, but also as part of the deep mediated structure of transatlanticism.

Periodicals are part of the dynamic performance of transatlantic mediations, and also a way of disseminating concepts of Anglo-Americanism. But periodical poems are also fundamentally mediated by their print contexts and digital environments. Transatlantic periodical poems unsettle concepts of nationhood, literary traditions, and cultural value. As an incomplete, mediated cultural event, transatlanticism is performed and represented through popular serial print. Although digital versions and tools seem to amplify the print material in its detail as well as its expansive range, both the complex enmeshing of British and American literary traditions and the incompleteness of the mass digitisation yields a transatlanticism (in Giles's phrase) as telesthesia, performance at a distance. Digital pedagogy offers the tools to examine the telesthesia of transatlantic print as a circulation of texts, seen artificially and yet illuminatingly up close through the constructed lens of the digital object and the digital tool.

NOTES

1. Monica E. Bulger, Jessica C. Murphy, Jeff Scheible, and Elizabeth Lagresa, 'Interdisciplinary Knowledge Work: Digital Textual Analysis Tools and Their Collaborative Affordances', in Laura McGrath (ed.), *Collaborative Approaches to the Digital in English Studies* (Logan: Utah State University Press, 2011), p. 259.

2. David John Bolter and Richard Grusin, *Remediation: Understanding New Media* (Cambridge, MA: MIT Press, 2000), p. 59.

3. Bob Nicholson, 'Digital Detectives: Rediscovering the Scholar Adventurer', *Victorian Periodicals Review*, 45: 2 (2012), 222.

4. Compare Paul Giles: '[i]n this digital age, telesthesia's repositioning of a discrete object of analysis in terms of "relationality and mobility" threatens to introduce instability into what have traditionally been self-enclosed systems'. By telesthesia, Giles means 'performance at a distance'. See *Virtual Americas: Transnational Fictions and the Transatlantic Imaginary* (Durham, NC: Duke University Press, 2002), pp. 19–20; see also James Mussell, *The Nineteenth-Century Press in the Digital Age* (Basingstoke: Palgrave, 2012).

5. Julia Flanders, 'The Productive Unease of 21st-Century Digital Scholarship', *Digital Humanities Quarterly*, 3: 3 (2009). Available at <http://www.digitalhumanities.org/dhq/vol/3/3/000055/000055.html > (last accessed 17 June 2013).

6. In addition to Google Books, prominent examples are the *British Newspaper Archive*, the *Nineteenth-Century American Newspapers*, *Nineteenth-Century British Library Newspapers*, *Nineteenth-Century UK Periodicals*, and *Nineteenth-Century Serials Edition*. In addition, see the following poetry indexes and databases: *Database of Victorian Periodical Poetry*, *Index to British Annuals*, *The Local Press as Poetry Publisher*, and *The Periodical Poetry Index*.

7. See the introduction of Paul Giles, *Transatlantic Insurrections: British Culture and the Formation of American Literature, 1730–1860* (Philadelphia: University of Pennsylvania Press, 2011).

8. For a historical account of the relationship between British and American newspapers, see Joel H. Weiner, *The Americanization of the British Press, 1830s–1914: Speed in the Age of Transatlantic Journalism* (Basingstoke: Palgrave Macmillan, 2012).

9. Bob Nicholson, ' "You Kick the Bucket; We Do the Rest!": Jokes and the Culture of Reprinting in the Transatlantic Press', *Journal of Victorian Culture*, 17: 3 (2012), 274.

10. 'A Word at the Start', *Harper's New Monthly Magazine*, 1: 1 (1850), 1. Available at <http://ebooks.library.cornell.edu/h/harp/harp.1850.html> (last accessed 27 June 2013).

11. Ibid.

12. Ibid.

13. Matthew Taunton, 'Distribution', in Laurel Brake and Marysa Demoor (eds), *Dictionary of Nineteenth-Century Journalism in Great Britain and Ireland* (Ghent and London: Academia Press and the British Library, 2009), p. 171.

14. For a groundbreaking essay on the importance of periodical poetry, see Linda K. Hughes, 'What the *Wellesley Index* Left Out: Why Poetry Matters to Periodical Studies', *Victorian Periodicals Review*, 40: 2 (2007), 91–125.

15. Richard Cronin, *Reading Victorian Poetry* (Oxford: Blackwell, 2012).

16. Michael Cohen, 'E. C. Stedman and the Invention of Victorian Poetry', *Victorian Poetry*, 43: 2 (Summer 2005), 166. See especially Edmund C. Stedman (ed.), *A Victorian Anthology, 1837–1895: Selections Illustrating the Editor's Critical Review of British Poetry in the Reign of Victoria* (Boston: Houghton Mifflin, 1895); and Edmund C. Stedman (ed.), *An American Anthology, 1787–1900: Selections Illustrating the Editor's Critical Review of American Poetry in the Nineteenth Century* (Boston: Houghton Mifflin, 1900).

17. Meredith L. McGill (ed.), *The Traffic in Poems: Nineteenth-Century Poetry and Transatlantic Exchange* (New Brunswick, NJ: Rutgers University Press, 2008), p. 2.

18. See, for example, Mary Ellis Gibson, *Indian Angles: English Verse in Colonial India from Jones to Tagore* (Athens, OH: Ohio University Press, 2011); Caroline Levine, 'World Literature as Victorian Literature', *Performance and Play*, NAVSA Conference, 3–6 November 2011; Patrick Vincent, *The Romantic Poetess: European Culture, Politics and Gender, 1820–1840* (Durham, NH: University of New Hampshire Press, 2004).

19. John North (ed.), *The Waterloo Directory of English Newspapers and Periodicals: 1800–1900*. Online database.

20. There is no one definitive source for circulation figures. Indeed here too parameters need to be carefully distinguished to produce meaningful comparisons (for example, for book sales figures); are first edition numbers compared [as well as speed of sale?], and what about reprints and circulating library figures? For newspaper circulation, see Graham Law, 'Circulation', in Brake and Demoor (eds), *Dictionary of Nineteenth-Century Journalism*, p. 120.

21. Brett D. Hirsch, '</Parentheses>: Digital Humanities and the Place of Pedagogy', in Brett D. Hirsch (ed.), *Digital Humanities Pedagogy: Principles, Practices, and Politics* (Cambridge: Open Book Publishers, 2012), pp. 1–6.

22. Paul Fyfe, 'Digital Pedagogy Unplugged', *Digital Humanities Quarterly*, 5: 3 (2011). Available at <http://www.digitalhumanities.org/dhq/vol/5/3/000106/000106.html> (last accessed 17 June 2013).

23. Natalie M. Houston, Lindsy Lawrence, and April Patrick, 'Teaching and Learning with the Periodical Poetry Index', *Victorian Periodicals Review*, 45: 2 (2012), 227; see also Mussell, *Nineteenth Century Press*.

24. For a definition of tools and their importance to literary studies, see also

John Bradley, 'Text Tools', in Susan Schrelbman, Ray Seimans, and John Unsworth (eds), *A Companion to Digital Humanities* (Oxford: Blackwell, 2004), pp. 505–22. Available at <http://www.digitalhumanities.org/companion/> (last accessed 27 June 2013).

25. Versioning is a digital tool that allows differences in electronic texts, marked-up according to TEI guidelines, to be highlighted and displayed, for example with the software *The Versioning Machine* and *Juxta*. For an example, see *The Modernist Versions Project*, available at <http://mvp.uvic.ca/> (last accessed 17 June 2013).

26. For an example of a student-authored, collaborative, and cross-insti-tutional wiki, see *Victorian Poetry, Poetics and Contexts Wiki*. Available at <http://victorianpoetrypoeticsandcontext.wikispaces.com/> (last accessed 28 June 2013).

27. Jentery Sayers, 'Tinkering Classrooms', in Laura McGrath (ed.), *Collaborative Approaches to the Digital in English Studies* (Logan: Utah State University Press, 2011), p. 284. Available at < http://ccdigitalpress.org/cad/> (last accessed 17 June 2013).

28. Bulger et al., 'Interdisciplinary Knowledge Work', pp. 257–8.

29. Jesse Stommel, 'Decoding Digital Pedagogy, pt. 2: (Un)Mapping the Terrain', *Hybrid Pedagogy*, 5 March 2013. Available at <http://www.hybridpedagogy.com/journal/decoding-digital-pedagogy-pt-2-unmapping-the-terrain/> (last accessed 25 March 2014).

30. See Hughes for a survey of student's experiences with digital and ana-logue media, whose results showed a distinct preference for digital forms. She concludes with the hope that pedagogy will evolve to 'spur on-going exploration of the ways that our medium of investigation shapes not only what but *how* we can know, conceptualize, and theorize.' Linda K. Hughes, 'Wilde Pedagogy: Digitized Resources and Gender Analysis of Periodical Visuality', *Victorian Periodicals Review*, 45: 2 (2012), 234.

31. Andrew D. Stauffer, 'The Nineteenth-Century Archive in the Digital Age', *European Romantic Review*, 23: 3 (2012), 339–40.

32. Ibid., pp. 338–9.

33. Liu's response is included in Bulger et al., 'Interdisciplinary Knowledge Work', p. 274.

34. For an example of the growing number of digital tools available, see *BambooDIRT*, available at <http://dirt.projectbamboo.org/> (last accessed 18 June 2013).

35. 'Fisher's Drawing-Room Scrap Book', *The Anglo-American*, 3 January 1846, p. 1.

36. Ibid.

CHAPTER 17

Digital Transatlanticism: An Experience of and Reflections on Undergraduate Research in the Humanities

Erik Simpson

In the summer of 2004, I worked with a group of six advanced undergraduate students at Grinnell College to produce a website called *The Transatlantic 1790s*.[1] This essay will describe that experience and offer some thoughts about the uses of small-scale digital humanities projects for teachers of the humanities and particularly for scholars of transatlantic studies. I mean to outline a model of undergraduate pedagogy in the digital humanities that draws on multiple generations of practices in humanities computing during the web era, spanning the 1990s to the present. The ability of online projects to create visual models of interconnectedness makes humanities computing an especially fruitful area for transatlantic studies.

To reflect on the recent history of humanities computing (an older and broader phrase than 'digital humanities'), I will look backwards and forwards from the 2004 summer project, which came about in the context of Grinnell's Mentored Advanced Projects (MAP, pluralised to MAPs) initiative, then a new programme at the College. Developed as a way of regularising and compensating the supervision of summer research then mainly done by students in the sciences, the MAP programme sought to extend the idea of closely mentored capstone projects across the curriculum.[2] The MAP programme requires students to do advanced work that moves beyond regular curricular offerings; to be supervised regularly and closely by the instructor; and to produce results that are shared beyond the audience of the instructor and fellow students. Many MAPs in the humanities resemble theses: they are individually crafted research projects organised by a proposal driven by a student's research interests. My version instead used a seminar model, in which the students worked in a predetermined subject area by pursuing their varied interests in a shared space with a common set of core readings.

I divided the schedule of my course into two blocks. The first was essentially an undergraduate seminar on transatlantic literatures of the 1790s that took advantage of students' full-time attention to the course by moving rapidly through primary texts. I chose the transatlantic content of the readings in part to reflect my own scholarly interests; after working mainly on British and Irish literature in graduate school, I was then in the early stages of a book project on transatlantic literature.[3] The course texts were organised in clusters including political writings of the Revolution-era United States; literary and polemical works of the Joseph Johnson circle in London (William Blake, William Godwin, Mary Wollstonecraft); British reactions to the French Revolution; and gothic and sentimental novels such as Matthew Lewis's *The Monk*, Ann Radcliffe's *The Italian*, Charles Brockden Brown's *Edgar Huntly*, William Hill Brown's *The Power of Sympathy*, and Susanna Rowson's *Charlotte Temple*. *The Interesting Narrative of the Life of Olaudah Equiano* provided a crossing point, a text bridging the generic and geographical divides separating many of the other works. We also read a small number of secondary materials, both in history and in literary criticism, but we reserved most of those works for the second half of the course.

In the second block, we departed from the seminar model as the students designed and executed digital projects based on our shared readings. We began this part of the course by exploring other humanities projects on the Internet, discussing what we found useful and attractive in those sites as well as what would and would not be realistic to attempt. (For one obvious example, we were not going to undertake the kind of archive creation that might develop over years or decades in a digital humanities institute at a research university.) I told the students that I planned to have us ground our work in an online, searchable, customisable annotated bibliography, but beyond that collective enterprise, I hoped they would apply their work and imagination to making and sharing projects that interested them and would, if all went well, interest a niche audience on the Internet as well.

At its base, this approach to building web projects came from the ethos and practices I absorbed in the early days of the World Wide Web, when my graduate training included an enthusiastic exploration of the new ways of sharing pedagogical and research materials on the Internet. Before the widespread adoption of commercial content management systems, making course websites (for example) publicly accessible by writing basic HTML was easier than crafting a password-protected secure environment. Although creating one's own public web pages is now even easier than it was then, content management systems and institutional training have combined to make closed environments the default location of online course materials.

In asking my students to learn a bit of code and use the web as an environment for serious creative play, therefore, I sought to recapture the kind of experience I had as a student in graduate school at the University of

Pennsylvania, where in 1995 I took Stuart Curran's Electronic Literary Seminar, an undergraduate and graduate course that gathered students of literature and computer science, introduced them to what was then the cutting edge of humanities scholarship online, provided some lessons in HTML programming, and invited them to explore and create digital environments. The course's commitments to fostering students' initiatives were reflected in its 'Rules of Engagement': one rule read, 'If you don't know something you need to know, ask someone who knows it. And ask again, until you really know it. Ignorance isn't the bliss it's cracked up to be.' And the last was this: 'If the class seems too easy, it's your fault.'[4] Even at that early stage, when having photographs on the web was still largely a novelty, the students in the seminar were able to create projects reflecting many of the enduring concerns of humanities computing and the digital humanities, from digital archives to textual analysis tools and electronic literature.

Curran's course inspired many of the guiding principles of my summer MAP and subsequent work in the pedagogical digital humanities, but its most important short-term effect on my work came from Curran's decision to have students do their own programming – helping one another when necessary, to be sure, but fundamentally taking control of their code. For me, the acquisition of basic web programming skills led to developing them further, in part by qualifying me for part-time jobs that allowed and required me to continue programming in non-profit and corporate settings. Once I had those skills, I looked for ways to apply them to my academic work, and such applications have become increasingly central to my scholarship and pedagogy, most clearly in my teaching website, which integrates course syllabi, assignments, and instructional materials on literature, research, and writing.[5] I hope to create similar possibilities for students who learn basic coding skills in my digitally oriented classes, though I handle the construction of each site's structural components.

Even for students who will not continue to write computer code, the process of co-designing an online project and learning the basic processes of web programming (creating and uploading a page, using tags and links, and so forth) opens up what Matthew Kirschenbaum calls programming as 'a kind of world-making, requiring one to specify the behaviours of an object or a system from the ground up'.[6] Even websites with simple structures – made from the classic web programmer's tools of pages, images, links, style sheets, and navigational apparatuses – involve creating connections in multiple directions and modelling a reader's experience of reading and interacting with the site. For many of my students, being able to produce a 'Hello, world!' message in raw HTML still provides an excitement beyond that of posting photo albums to Facebook, and I hope that excitement leads to other ways of resisting the prefabrication of today's social web.

In the 2004 summer course, we organised much of the site's content in a MySQL database, which allowed our web pages to use PHP to call information from the database into the website. In non-technical terms, this process would enable, for instance, the bibliographical information about a given scholarly resource to be stored in the database and retrieved for use in any number of contexts. For instance, a student's annotation of Pamela Clemit's book *The Godwinian Novel* could become part of a customised bibliography of criticism from the 1990s, or a bibliography of scholarship on Charles Brockden Brown, or a topical bibliography generated by searching for the keyword 'Priestley' – and the varied locations of the citation would illustrate its relevance to American, British, and transatlantic frames of analysis. This dynamic generation of a page's content in response to a user's requests gave our site a flexibility that had been out of reach for most websites a decade previously.

The use of databases in humanities computing is nothing new, and literary scholars have productively attended to the implications of database technologies in pieces such as Stephen Ramsay's essay in the *Companion to Digital Humanities* titled 'Databases', which describes the architecture and design of relational databases, or Ed Folsom's 'Database as Genre: The Epic Transformation of Archives'.[7] These pieces theorise the database's power to organise information, such as archival sources and metadata, so that the critical analysis may subsequently benefit from that organisation. As Ramsay puts it, 'after we have designed and implemented relational systems, and reaped the benefits of the efficiencies they grant, we consider the role they may play in the varied pursuits which have descended from what was once called – appropriately – the higher criticism'.[8] In adapting relational databases to undergraduate pedagogy, I mean in part to undo that sequence by placing the products of students' analytical work in the database itself. When a student's detailed annotation of a theoretical piece or a student's analytical essay becomes part of the content of the database, it becomes adaptable and reusable by a website's users and, crucially, by other students. Giving access to such a database through a web interface enables two important processes. First, it creates a visual representation of the students' participation in the academic conversation about literary texts; and second, it transforms students' writing into the object as well as the output of students' analysis.

In 2004, the students decided to create three interlinked sections for our own site. These were, first, the annotated bibliography I had suggested; second, a detailed chronology of the transatlantic 1790s, divided into categories such as literature, history and politics, and science and technology but also keyword-searchable; and six projects, one by each student, that would build on the bibliography and chronology but otherwise allow for nearly complete autonomy.[9] These sections, two collaboratively written and one consisting of individual projects, constitute the site as it exists today.

The students produced a large amount of material in their ten weeks together. Their final chronology includes more than 850 entries, all of which include basic details such as a date, essential facts, identification of the student who authored the entry, and a bibliographic citation; some also add a more substantial explanation of the described event. The bibliography comprises many dozens of entries, most with substantial annotations as well as basic citations. The individual projects reflect the range of the students' interests. The lone history major in the group, Elizabeth Braverman, created 'Conversations in Politics', focusing on Thomas Paine and his critics and followers in England and America. Sarah Cornwell wrote 'Daughters of Misfortune: Anatomy of the 1790s Seduction Novel', which surrounds a modern recasting of *Charlotte Temple* ('Lily, or Virtue Confused') with short academic essays on key concepts such as coquetry, consent, and the seducer. Sara Millhouse wrote 'Loyalists: Spies, Defense from Sedition, and the "swinish multitudes"', analysing the relatively under-examined movements in support of British institutions during this revolutionary era. In writing 'Revolutionary Nuptials', Betsey Blanche investigated debates about marriage in the 1790s to illustrate the centrality of marriage to other conversations about the roles of religion, education, slavery, and revolution. Elisa Lenssen wrote 'Everybody Matters: Science and the Corporeal in 1790s Literature', working with physiognomy, figurations of the eye, and diagnoses such as hysteria in the discourse of the day. Justin Wallace used narrative theory, particularly the concepts of narrative tracing and narrative embedding, to undertake a comparative analysis of some of the course's novels in 'Gothic Narratives'. All of the projects draw on the digital bibliography extensively, allowing readers the choice to click on references for more information about source texts, often including library accession information.

These projects showed me the particular value of this application of the digital humanities to transatlantic studies, a value that arises precisely from the ability of the projects to represent a transatlantic approach explicitly or implicitly. The juxtaposition and interconnection of the collective bibliography and individual projects imply the streams that merge to form transatlantic scholarship: criticism that addresses literature of any subset of Britain or the Americas, criticism that already employs a transatlantic framework, theoretical texts about the concepts of transatlantic or Atlantic studies, and general literary theory that readers can apply to transatlantic issues. The bibliography does not aspire to complete coverage of transatlantic studies, even as applied to the 1790s, but it does provide something between the bibliography of a monograph and a library's catalogues and databases: a curated collection of resources drawing on multiple scholars' perspectives and allowing for future expansion.

I did have some subsequent students add to *The Transatlantic 1790s*, but in a limited and short-lived way. Now, I see that additive process as a central goal in my digital pedagogy because it enables the passage of classroom culture from one generation of students to the next. It seems strange to me that every time I teach the same novel, for instance, to a new group of students, they have no sense of how my students have discussed that text in the past. Although I appreciate the pleasure of insights that feel new repeatedly – for instance, seeing class after class discover their own ways of talking about the narration of *Wuthering Heights* as a function of Lockwood's relationship to Ellen Dean – I still want to resist the convention that the writing of every group of students disappears into file folders when a semester ends. I wonder whether our courses can, like the speaker of Keats's 'On First Looking into Chapman's Homer', recognise the wonder of 'first looking' while also prizing the community implied by appreciating what has come before. Capturing the work of a group of students online, and having another group of students augment that work, creates place-based, semi-virtual communities that can accomplish more than any one group can in a single semester.

Working more recently to create new online projects with students, I have developed a set of four goals for digital pedagogy appropriate to my situation at Grinnell.

1. Maintain a core sense of the web as a creative space where academic writing has a live, interested audience.

The most powerful effects of the course came from the combination of giving students simple tools for creating web-specific content, on the one hand, and, on the other, giving them a concrete sense of reaching an audience of interested readers. Mark Sample has written recently about his 'ongoing effort – not always successful – to extend [his] students' sense of audience'; he argues for building and sharing as the means of realising his vision of the digital humanities, whose heart is the reproduction rather than the production of knowledge.[10] In a similar vein, I want to cultivate a sense of audience that has a useful immediacy – they write, read, and edit with their classmates – as well as a useful ambition to reach a wider readership online.

2. Foster the creation of expansive archives.

These online projects create connections between conventional library research (itself increasingly an online activity, of course) and online resources. Far from replacing conventional library-based research, my students' projects rely heavily on it, and their websites allow easy linking among their most creative work and its bibliographical backbone. Writing in a digital environment lets a student curate a kind of expansive archive: a collection of thematically connected materials that points outward to scholarly resources, other web projects, and work inherited from other students. These projects prize archival curation without archival enclosure.

3. Encourage the inheritance of classroom culture and achievement.

This is a pedagogy of remixing as well as making. These experiences have clarified for me how much my other pedagogy, and humanistic pedagogy in general, valorises original writing and research over the skills of collaboration, even when incorporating group exercises and other common forms of 'collaborative' work. My newer assignments therefore strive to use the web to foster the skills of co-creation: intensive editing of other students' work, larger projects that require students to coordinate multiple contributors, and projects that will involve the contributions of future students.

The aspect of this sharing that involves the transmission from one group of students to another does, however, require more structure and management than I initially imagined it would. I have found students less comfortable than I anticipated with incorporating other students' writing into their own. In the past, I have approached the issue by presenting the work of previous students and other (published) scholars simply as two kinds of contributors to 'inventory', in the sense Mary Carruthers articulates:

> Having 'inventory' is a requirement for 'invention.' Not only does this statement assume that one cannot create ('invent') without a memory story ('inventory') to invent from and with, but it also assumes that one's memory-story is effectively 'inventoried,' that its matters are in readily-recovered 'locations.'[11]

My mistake was to assume that once good student work was inventoried, readily recoverable, and presented as the stuff of invention, students would readily merge this inventory with the more conventional materials of published scholarship. In fact, I have found students much more comfortable referring to conventional authorities than to their peers. I will work in future courses to emphasise and guide this process of merging student-produced and conventionally published scholarly inventories.

4. Allow for the addition of new analytical tools to established ones.

This last goal arises from the changing practices of humanities computing – or what we now call the digital humanities – in the last decade. My 2004 students' work reflects little of the quantitative and geographical emphasis of today's digital humanities, and I want my current and future students to explore the analytical power of contemporary practices and their successors. Just as my earlier students' projects augmented library research rather than replaced it, my current students are working to layer GIS mapping, textual tagging, and quantitative analysis onto the bibliographies and research-based analytical projects I have described. I mean for this layering to make visible the interconnections among literary study in a variety of modes, and to allow my students and their readers to evaluate the power and limitations of multiple methodologies. I am currently working on one implementation of a database-backed set of student-written resources about James Joyce's *Ulysses* – I also teach my department's seminar on that book – designed specifically to combine close reading of the novel with computer-aided spatial and quantitative analysis. For example, my transatlantic background will inform a GIS-based section on the 'global Ulysses', which will link to a collective bibliography to engage scholarly work on the intersections of nation, race, and travel in the novel. I hope, in other words, for a pedagogy that stages the engagement or confrontation between literary theory and machine learning. As Ted Underwood has written, if literary theory and computer science 'really approach similar questions in incompatible ways, it will be a matter of some importance to understand why'.[12] Focusing these methodological questions on a specific area of acknowledged contestation, such as the transatlantic, will help undergraduates understand and contribute to the coming debates in literary theory.

   In light of this last goal, I return in closing to the special uses of this pedagogy for transatlantic studies. In that field, the work of combining theoretical sophistication with the newest quantitative and geographical tools will be especially important in the coming years. The techniques of computational 'distant reading' – Franco Moretti's term for analysing literature by searching large archives of texts – increasingly enable the empirical investigation of, for example, the way British periodical journalism was reprinted, clipped, and circulated in American publications.[13] Matthew Wilkens has begun to raise questions about the literary periodisation surrounding the American Civil War; we will similarly be able to unearth stylistic signatures and patterns of allusion and reference that will add new evidence to questions of how much and what kind of borders the Atlantic Ocean created among British, American, and Caribbean literary cultures.[14] In humanities computing, that is, we can construct tools that achieve a kind of transatlantic perspective unavailable to scholars whose academic world is shaped by the conventional boundary marker of the Atlantic: a perspective that can generate new readings by, as a starting point, not knowing where authors were born or what genealogies generally contain them. We can also create online environments that place these new insights in the context of transatlantic theory and (less conventionally) vice versa. Doing so will allow teachers and students to co-create the means of understanding the compatibilities of, and confrontations between, the methods of close and distant reading.

NOTES

1. Available at <http://www.cs.grinnell.edu/1790s/> (last accessed 18 October 2013).

2. To clarify what may and may not be transportable from my context, I will note that the MAP programme involves stipends for summer students' living expenses and partial course releases for participating faculty; the students' stipends allow the programme to require full-time work of forty hours per week on the MAP, for ten weeks. I detail the institutional support for the MAP programme in part to make explicit the resources required by the kind of project I describe in this essay. Although the project required very little funding compared to many kinds of summer research that require laboratory equipment or group travel, it did require funding from the college and could not have worked as a full-time summer project without that funding. I hope that some of the general goals I describe later in this essay will apply to other institutional situations, though I recognise the barriers to digital projects for many teachers and scholars that Katherine Harris has eloquently described. See Katherine Harris, 'In/Out, DH, Pedagogy, or Where it all Started (MLA 2011)', *triproftri*, 1 March 2011. Available at <http://triproftri.wordpress.com/2011/03/01/inout-dh-pedagogy-or-where-it-all-started/> (last accessed 18 October 2013).

3. See Erik Simpson, *Mercenaries in British and American Literature, 1790–1830: Writing, Fighting, and Marrying for Money* (Edinburgh: Edinburgh University Press, 2010).

4. Stuart Curran, 'A Decalogue for Computer Classes'. Available at <http://www.english.upenn.edu/~curran/205-505/rules.html> (last accessed 18 October 2013).

5. Erik Simpson, 'Connections: A Hypertext Resource for Literature'. Available at <http://www.cs.grinnell.edu/~simpsone/Connections/> (last accessed 18 October 2013).

6. Matthew Kirschenbaum, 'Hello Worlds', *The Chronicle Review*, 23 January 2009. Available at <http://chronicle.com/article/Hello-Worlds/5476> (last accessed 18 October 2013).

7. Stephen Ramsay, 'Databases', in Susan Schreibman, Ray Siemens, and John Unsworth (eds), *A Companion to Digital Humanities* (Oxford: Blackwell, 2004), pp. 177–97; Ed Folsom, 'Database as Genre: The Epic Transformation of Archives', *PMLA*, 122 (2007), 1571–79.

8. Ramsay, 'Databases', p. 196.

9. In other courses subsequent to the MAP, I have continued to look for ways to divide the attention of students doing shared readings, so that each student develops a specialised interest which then becomes part of a collaborative reading in the classroom. Cathy Davidson has recently theorised the value of this kind of division: discussing recent scientific developments in the study of attention and 'attention blindness', she writes: 'Where [many neuroscientists] perceive the shortcomings of the individual, I sense opportunity for collaboration. If we see selectively but we don't all select the same things to see, that also means we don't all miss the same things.' See Cathy Davidson, *Now You See It* (New York: Viking, 2011), p. 2.

10. Mark Sample, 'Building and Sharing (When You're Supposed to be Teaching)', *Sample Reality*, 19 October 2011. Available at <http://www.samplereality.com/2011/10/19/building-and-sharing-when-youre-supposed-to-be-teaching/> (last accessed 18 October 2013).

11. Mary Carruthers, *The Craft of Thought: Meditation, Rhetoric, and the Making of Images, 400–1200* (New York: Cambridge University Press, 2000), p. 12.

12. Ted Underwood, 'Interesting Times for Literary Theory', *The Stone and the Shell*, 4 August 2013. Available at <http://tedunderwood.com/2013/08/04/interesting-times-for-literary-theory/> (last accessed 18 October 2013).

13. See Franco Moretti, *Graphs, Maps, and Trees: Abstract Models for a Literary History* (London: Verso, 2005). Ryan Cordell, Elizabeth Maddock Dillon, and David Smith presented their techniques for performing this kind of analysis in 'Uncovering Reprinting Networks in Nineteenth-Century American Newspapers' at the Digital Humanities 2013 conference in Lincoln, Nebraska.

14. See Matthew Wilkens, 'Canons, Close Reading, and the Evolution of Method', in Matthew K. Gold (ed.), *Debates in the Digital Humanities* (Minneapolis: University of Minnesota Press, 2012), pp. 249–58.

CHAPTER 18

Twenty-First-Century Digital Publics and Nineteenth-Century Transatlantic Public Spheres

Tyler Branson

This brief chapter has two main claims: the first is that modern developments in public sphere theory are useful in reflecting on and articulating the collaborative methods we have been using to build a digital commons on the *Teaching Transatlanticism* website. The second is that public sphere theory can also help us look at nineteenth-century transatlanticism with a refreshed academic curiosity. In their introduction to this collection, Linda Hughes and Sarah Robbins note that 'bidirectional literary exchanges between British and American authors' are examples of how transatlantic scholarship 'has increasingly admitted and probed the dynamic currents of literary production and exchange', which is 'opening up ever-larger questions about where, exactly, the boundaries of transatlanticism start and stop'.[1] During my work as the web designer, editor, and manager of the *Teaching Transatlanticism* website, several of these 'ever-larger questions' surfaced most notably as we actively built what we hope to be a vibrant online space for anyone interested in transatlantic pedagogy. The methods our team employed as we implemented plans for the website illuminated questions about how public spheres form and operate. For example, as scholars and teachers interact with the site from various countries and institutions, will these transatlantic exchanges constitute the formation of a public? If so, how does that change the way we conceive of nineteenth-century transatlantic exchanges? If we relinquish the ideology of the nation-state as the arbiter of cultural development, as transatlantic studies urges us to do, does that change the way we understand how publics are formed? These questions, which arose in a very twenty-first-century context, allow us to look backward at nineteenth-century transatlantic public spheres with renewed interest.

PUBLIC SPHERE THEORY AND *TEACHING TRANSATLANTICISM*

The concept of the public sphere has a long and complicated history which cannot be fully detailed here. However, I will highlight several important concepts around the public sphere to show the potential connections of these ideas to the formation of our digital presence and our conceptions of nineteenth-century transatlantic publics. Many modern conceptualisations of the public sphere are based on Jürgen Habermas's *Structural Transformation of the Public Sphere*, which, first published in 1962 in German and finally in English in 1989, outlines the rise and fall of the bourgeois public in seventeenth- and eighteenth-century print culture Europe.

One of the key elements of this public sphere, Habermas notes, is the capacity of private citizens to come together, bracket their differences, and engage in rational-critical debate about issues of public concern. Paralleling the rise of the modern state, the bourgeois public sphere represented a new sociability within which, for the first time, public opinion could circulate unfettered in salons and coffee houses, separate from church or state apparatuses. The rise of market economies, long-distance trade, and the spread of print culture also helped give substance to a new kind of 'public' discourse. In other words, the historical and social circumstances in the seventeenth and eighteenth centuries allowed for a distinctive public sphere based on rational-critical debate to emerge and flourish.[2]

Nancy Fraser, Seyla Benhabib, Michael Warner, and others have critiqued Habermas's vision, questioning if the democratic potential of the public sphere was ever even possible. Habermas's idealistic and gender-blind public sphere, they argue, mutes the impact of women and other oppositional publics. This critique asserts that assuming a monolithic public ignores the multiplicity of public discourse. Fraser, for instance, proposes that there are multiple and oppositional 'subaltern counterpublics', or 'parallel discursive arenas where members of subordinated social groups invent and circulate counterdiscourses' that in turn shape public discourse.[3] Benhabib similarly argues that Habermas's model ignores the issue of difference and 'the differences in the experiences of male versus female subjects in all domains of life'.[4] Warner critiques Habermas's vision even further, highlighting the danger of universalising *the* public, stressing instead that there are multiple *publics* organised by discourse circulated among strangers. In Warner's theory, discourse circulates not in contestation to the state, as Habermas argues, but in a kind of *poïesis*, or 'poetic world making'. Any discourse addressed to a public, Warner writes, works *poetically* to 'characterize the world in which it attempts to circulate, projecting for that world a concrete and livable shape, and attempting to realise that world through address'.[5] According to Warner, public discourse is not just political debate among private citizens, but the circulation of discourse that recreates a social world through address.[6]

In the early processes of working on the website that supplements this book, we frequently referred to it as our 'public' site, inadvertently invoking a Habermasian notion of a wide-sweeping 'public' stretching beyond the confines of our institution and classrooms – a kind of social entity that means everyone and nobody at the same time.[7] But as we confronted challenges constructing the site, especially after deliberately reflecting on the decades of critique on Habermas's theories, we began to realise that our broadly defined public space was actually comprised of multiple publics – addressees with different vested interests and discursive 'moments of attention'.[8] As we collaborated on design, layout, and the vetting of contributors, we began to ask: what kinds of publics were we formulating? Were we hailing other transatlantic scholars? Graduate students? Secondary teachers? Undergraduates? How did the organisation of the topics prioritise some of these discourses while deprioritising others? Is that hierarchy desirable? Moreover, if we take into account Warner's theory that publics not only circulate discourse but also create and circulate social worlds, we had to ask: What kind of social worlds were we creating and circulating through the creation of our website? As we mapped out the different topics under 'Teaching Resources', for example, we struggled to define who we were calling forth with those options. Did we want to include comprehensive exam lists for graduate students? Were we stressing materials of interest only to those in institutions of higher learning? What about independent researchers or high-school teachers? Reflecting on these questions, we realised that these varying degrees of publicity in our act of public-making pushed up against the Habermasian ideal of a public space where everyone can bracket their differences and openly engage in rational-critical debate. Clearly, as the significant vetting process of both teaching materials and 'public' comments demonstrates, the discussions taking place on our site are far from representing *the* public, if we can even say there is *the* public.[9]

What is represented online is a carefully crafted world of discourse on transatlantic teaching which calls forth multiple publics at different times, using this book project as an exigence. In the digital age, though, the kinds of publics that discourse creates are often unknowable or at least fleeting. Warner captures this well when he writes that

> Public Discourse says not only: 'Let a public exist,' but: 'Let it have this character, speak this way, see the world in this way.' It then goes out in search of confirmation that such a public exists, with greater or lesser success – success being further attempts to cite, circulate, and realize the world-understanding it articulates. Run it up the flagpole, and see who salutes. Put on a show and see who shows up.[10]

This site is the culmination not just of a book and digital humanities project on transatlantic teaching, but also a reflective process on how publics form and operate. It is our effort to put on a performance to see who shows up, in the hope that others cite, circulate, and realise the world we are promoting. Moreover, current public sphere theory, which challenges the concept of a universal public in favour of multiple *publics* or *counter*publics, may provide the best explanation of our efforts to create common ground among a diversity of academic publics by extending the content of *Teaching Transatlanticism* online.

PUBLIC SPHERE THEORY AND NINETEENTH-CENTURY TRANSATLANTICISM

Scholarship on the public sphere presents productive questions that not only influenced the content of the website dramatically, but also have potential to impact transatlantic studies more broadly. Several transatlantic scholars have already incorporated more nuanced understandings of public discourse into their work. For example, Paul Gilroy demonstrates the multiple layers of publicity in *The Black Atlantic*. Gilroy argues that nineteenth-century black culture can be thought of as a system of complex transatlantic exchanges connoting a desire to 'transcend both the structures of the nation state and the constraints of ethnicity and national particularity'. These desires, Gilroy writes, 'have always sat uneasily alongside the strategic choices forced on black movements and individuals embedded in national and political cultures and nation-states in America, the Caribbean, and Europe'.[11] Here, Gilroy demonstrates the power of thinking about publics not in terms of nations, borders or '*the* public', but rather through *publics* engaged in complex transnational cultural and intellectual exchanges.

Transatlantic studies naturally lends itself to a critical approach to public spheres, particularly through the lens of technology. Tom Standage writes in *The Victorian Internet*, for example, that nineteenth-century telegraphy technology allowed for instantaneous global connection, a communication revolution that resembles many twenty-first-century issues like mediation, access, and complex networks.[12] Similarly, in his essay from the collection, 'Making Anglo-American Oratory Resonate', Tom Wright argues that the nineteenth-century rise in print culture did not erase oral literacy practices, as some scholars initially argued, but instead enriched the dynamic and layered nature of public culture. Wright shows that embedded in this 'age of mass print' was a resurgence of public oratory. This 'loquacious age', Wright demonstrates, presents teachers and scholars with 'a range of critical, linguistic, conceptual and contextual tools'. We can benefit, Wright asserts, from studying how a period very much defined by massive media shifts also generated a 'fresh fascination with human presence'.[13] Here Wright is highlighting the dynamic and layered nature of public culture in the face of technological change. It is not the case that technological shifts created a new kind of consciousness in which orality was completely subsumed by print. Rather, orality and print thrived simultaneously, often in conflict, sometimes in cohesion, but always in a dynamic public discursive arena. Similarly, as we constructed the *Teaching Transatlanticism* website, we noticed how the materials and the conversations we hope to start may invoke multiple, overlapping publics, or that these texts may spark oral, person-to-person exchanges in transatlantic classrooms in addition to digital exchanges through the interface of the website.

CONCLUSION

In her 2004 Conference on College Composition and Communication (CCCC) address 'Made Not only in Words: Composition in a New Key', Kathleen Blake Yancey argues that new technologies signal 'the creation of a writing public that, in development and in linkage to technology, parallels the development of a reading public in the nineteenth century'.[14] She writes:

> Like 19th-century readers creating their own social contexts for reading in reading circles, writers in the 21st century self-organize into what seem to be overlapping technologically driven writing circles, what we might call a series of newly imagined communities, communities that cross borders of all kinds – nation state, class, gender, ethnicity.[15]

Yancey uses nineteenth-century public culture to reflect on the ways public discourse circulates today on the Internet. Matthew Rubery similarly documents the increase in the speed of communication between America and Britain in 'A Transatlantic Sensation'. The increased use of telegraphy, he argues, contributed to increased transatlantic circulation of the meeting between Henry Stanley and the famous missing explorer David Livingstone in Africa. This event, Rubery writes, was 'one of the most widely read news stories of the nineteenth century'.[16] The encounter between Stanley and Livingstone, perhaps the first news story to go viral, showcases how technologically driven 'reading publics' form meaningful transatlantic exchanges.

Considering Yancey's reflection on the connections between nineteenth- and twenty-first-century reading and writing practices, it is easy to see how scholars can incorporate modern theories of the public to better analyse nineteenth-century transatlantic culture. Transatlantic studies more broadly, I argue, can benefit from a closer look at theories of how publics form and operate. As noted above, public sphere theory formulated by scholars like Michael Warner and others helped me better understand the layered, mediated, and collaborative methods we have been using to build a digital commons in the *Teaching Transatlanticism* website, which envisions not an over-generalised public but a collection of overlapping yet distinctive human teaching voices from all over the world. But thinking about the dynamic, layered, mediated, and poetic nature of public discourse is also helpful for scholars studying transatlantic culture, as Gilroy, Rubery, Wright, and others have clearly demonstrated.

While public sphere theory can teach us a lot about transatlantic studies, the opposite also is true. Nineteenth-century public culture can teach us a lot about our own historical moment as scholars and teachers. This is not to suggest that we can somehow predict future dilemmas or technological changes by learning the lessons of the past. Nor is it to say that there are no unique cultural and historical moments. Rather, new intellectual shifts compel us to look not just forward, but backward as well, so that we can gain new insights, new theories, and new understandings of how people have anticipated change, dealt with uncertainty, and persevered in efforts to forge a better world. With this knowledge, perhaps we can become freshly inspired to do the same.

NOTES

1. See Linda K. Hughes and Sarah Robbins, 'Introduction', in this collection, pp. 1–17.
2. Jürgen Habermas, *The Structural Transformation of the Public Sphere: An Inquiry into a Category of Bourgeois Society* (Cambridge, MA: MIT Press, [1989] 1991).
3. Nancy Fraser, 'Rethinking the Public Sphere: A Contribution to the Critique of Actually Existing Democracy', *Social Text*, 25/26 (1990), 67.
4. Seyla Benhabib, 'Models of Public Space: Hannah Arendt, the Liberal Tradition, and Jürgen Habermas', in Craig Calhoun (ed.), *Habermas and the Public Sphere* (Cambridge, MA: MIT Press, 1996), p. 92.
5. Michael Warner, 'Publics and Counterpublics', *Public Culture*, 14: 1 (2002), 81.
6. Ibid.
7. One reason behind our use of the term public arose from our actually building and using another website to facilitate collaboration throughout the early stages of our work. This password-protected webspace posted draft versions of the essays that would eventually appear in print in *Teaching Transatlanticism*. Students in Linda Hughes and Sarah Robbins's fall 2013 graduate seminar, as well as various participants in

and 'friends of' the ongoing writing project, posted responses to drafts to support the chapter writers' revisions and to encourage rhetorical links-building across the collection. Though this website might best be characterised as semi-public, given the rather large number of people who used the password to join in, we tended to invoke a 'private' and 'public' dichotomy when referencing either of those online spaces, since the initial building of both took place around the same time.

8. Warner, 'Publics and Counterpublics', 61.
9. Contributions submitted to the *Teaching Transatlanticism* website are vetted significantly by our web team before being posted permanently to the site. This vetting process, while vitally important for maintaining a professional and scholarly ethos, also highlights the dynamic nature of the word 'public', for it is not 'public' in the sense that anyone can contribute, but 'public' in the sense that the rhetorical strategies are consistent with the social world we are attempting to create.
10. Warner, 'Publics and Counterpublics', 82.
11. Paul Gilroy, *The Black Atlantic: Modernity and Double Consciousness* (Cambridge, MA: Harvard University Press, 1993), p. 19.
12. Tom Standage, *The Victorian Internet: The Remarkable Story of the Telegraph and the Nineteenth Century's On-Line Pioneers* (New York: Walker, 1998).
13. See Tom Wright's chapter, 'Making Anglo-American Oratory Resonate', in this collection, pp. 151–63.
14. Kathleen Blake Yancey, 'Made Not Only in Words: Composition in a New Key', *College Composition and Communication*, 56: 2 (2004), 298.
15. Ibid., 301.
16. Matthew Rubery, 'A Transatlantic Sensation: Stanley's Search for Livingstone and the Anglo-American Press', in Christine Bold (ed.), *The Oxford History of Popular Print Culture* (Oxford: Oxford University Press, 2011), p. 515.

PART VI

Afterword

CHAPTER 19

Looking Forward

Larisa S. Asaeli, Rachel Johnston, Molly Knox Leverenz, and Marie Martinez

In the first transatlantic seminar co-taught by Linda Hughes and Sarah Robbins, students who had previously self-identified as either 'British' or 'American' specialists – or in some cases as working within composition/rhetoric – came together in 2010 to launch an enterprise that also led to this *Teaching Transatlanticism* collection. By 2013, as the essay anthology was unfolding with input from new students, four alumnae from the initial seminar reflected on their earlier experiences, their writing process echoing the collaborative spirit of the first seminar, as seen below.

LARISA S. ASAELI: TRANSATLANTIC REFLECTIONS AND REFORM

Although I label myself an Americanist and my current scholarship focuses on American topics, I have been an Anglophile for many years. My personal reading list has always been transatlantic. As a teen I read what appealed to me from the family book shelf; I devoured *Pride and Prejudice* and *Jane Eyre* alongside *Little Women* and *Caddie Woodlawn*. As an undergraduate at Brigham Young University-Hawai'i, I focused on British literature and wrote about Jane Austen as a proto-feminist for my senior project. In my master's programme at Brigham Young University I switched to contemporary American literature due to excellent course offerings. As a doctoral student it was logical for me to enrol in the transatlantic seminar with Linda Hughes and Sarah Robbins. Now, as a doctoral candidate in American literature, I realise how my fondness for both literary fields was enriched as I developed analytical lenses for thinking about these literary relationships.

Early in the semester it was easy for me to accept the field's shifting notions about literature, place, and culture since I already considered myself a transatlantic reader. It became a pleasure to trace and analyse intertextuality and exchanges, for example contrasts and similarities between the working poor in the England of Elizabeth Gaskell's *Mary Barton* and the enslaved Americans in Harriet Beecher Stowe's *Uncle Tom's Cabin*. Harriet Martineau and Harriet Beecher Stowe became multi-faceted celebrity authors as I read about their travels in the United States and Great Britain respectively. Canadian and Caribbean authors such as Susanna Moodie and Olaudah Equiano were added to my reading lists. We learned about the intersectionality of identity and nationality with race, class, and gender. We discussed imperialism in the United Kingdom and the United States. My lenses for literary analysis expanded with every meeting.

I was most inspired by the unit on transatlantic abolition and anti-slavery movements. I had recently seen the film *Amazing Grace* and was stirred by the tireless work of Thomas Clarkson and William Wilberforce.[1] As a result, I believed I knew a lot about the topic. However, when we read the Voyages website[2] about the transatlantic slave trade, the content shocked and intrigued me. I discerned that the slave trade was not limited to the Southern United States; rather, it was a multinational network rigidly entrenched in numerous economies and cultures. The horrors of the slave trade came into vivid focus as our course work progressed from the website to the transatlantic exchanges between authors in the US and UK. In particular, I was riveted by the heart-breaking and entertaining memoir *The Interesting Narrative of the Life of Olaudah Equiano*. I marvelled that he became part of British society and was not ostracised due to his skin colour, a narrative very different from those of free African and African-American women and men in the US. Equiano's account was a fascinating counterpoint to other readings in this unit, such as Elizabeth Barrett Browning's 'The Runaway Slave at Pilgrim's Point'. Her powerful adaptation of an enslaved woman's voice and experiences stunned me. I had always pictured EBB as a demure poetess who wrote extraordinary love sonnets. Instead, I encountered a poet whose depictions of rage, hatred, and despair gave voice to thousands of enslaved women. Alongside EBB's poem, we read Marjorie Stone's article about transatlantic exchanges among the poem, the poet's life, and American print culture.[3] Stone's work has since found a place in my dissertation on nineteenth-century social reform. One aspect of my project is a close examination of a transatlantic publication site, the abolitionist gift book *The Liberty Bell*, as a venue supporting the anti-slavery movement. Putting that transatlantic abolitionist culture in dialogue with my study of national civic identity, as linked to gendered social reform, has enabled me to see US culture as both similar to and distinct from British culture in the nineteenth century.

My future scholarship will include more work on transatlantic nineteenth-century reform causes, specifically the reception of American social reform texts by British readers and vice versa. My work will be organised around two key inquiries: the cultural work based in national identities for the UK and the US, and the connected cultural work shared by reformers via interpersonal relationships. And now that I have the skills and courage to expand my scholarship and teaching even further to embrace transnational themes, I am planning research projects with the literatures of Pacific Rim nations.

Soon after I began the transatlantic seminar, I started thinking about the Pacific (since I self-identify with Pacific Island peoples and cultures). I wondered about how New Zealand and Hawai'i were, and continue to be, affected by transnational exchanges. While living in New Zealand, I had seen American fast food, clothing, and TV shows; I had also been asked disturbing questions about America's aggressive military policies and racist attitudes. While living in Hawai'i, I learned about the overthrow of the monarchy by American businessmen and the decimation of native peoples by colonial diseases. But I also learned about the rich literary traditions of Pacific Islanders. And while many of their texts are written in English, few are anthologised or taught in American universities. This oversight needs correcting. I can shift my scholarly gaze back to the Pacific Rim, to a geopolitical space and peoples that I identify with now that I see Anglophone literary studies decentred from the Atlantic Rim. I no longer feel bound to focus only on New (and Old) England. This shift in thinking has led me to more questions. For example, how were Pacific Island people entangled in European slave-trade networks? What were the impacts of disease and the transmission of disease on Pacific Islander material culture production? What texts of resistance did native and colonial women produce? And were there any abolition or anti-slavery societies in Hawai'i, Australia, and New Zealand? This transatlantic course has given me the lenses for approaching these questions while validating my stance as an American scholar with transnational connections.

RACHEL JOHNSTON: TRANSATLANTIC ANECDOTES

I attended a graduate student recruitment 'meet and greet' the March prior to beginning my PhD in literature. Even with a theatre/costume/literature/women's studies/composition/writing centre/rhetoric background, I unquestioningly identified as an eighteenth-century British literature scholar. At lunch I took an open seat with several students, nervous to share my area of study because it rarely incites much excitement. But the problem this time was not my century – I had joined a table of Americanists! And I, normally comfortable anywhere, felt inched out of the conversation because of my ignorance of American poetry and US Civil War history.

With the poetic balance of a TV sitcom, we next attended a presentation by Linda Hughes and Sarah Robbins, who discussed their upcoming team-teaching. We were all motivated by the excitement both had for the possibilities of transatlantic collaboration. Many of us ended up attending TCU, and most of us took the class – packed in the seminar room elbow to elbow because of the interest it generated – and all semester I sat next to the student who joked I had 'sat among Americanists' at that March luncheon. Soon the American literature and British literature students became friends and even collaborated outside the course. We realised that our fields actually had everything in common: slavery issues, women's rights, wars, social disturbance, industrialisation, colonisation, art, travel, medicine, religion, marriage, domesticity. Whether studying British or American texts, we had been reading transatlantic literature all along – we simply didn't know it. We had been placing boundaries around our knowledge, assuming difference and singularity where they did not exist, and failing to find connections simply because we were not looking for them. The class offered a new lens, allowing us to 'purge our critical prose of the gobbledygook of stale theoretical platitudes' as Gilbert and Gubar call for in their introduction to the second edition of *Madwoman in the Attic*.[4]

Two years after the revelations of the transatlantic course and while reading transatlantically for my doctoral exams, I discovered Frances Smith Foster, an author who purges her critical prose of 'stale theoretical platitudes' by researching outside the canon and across oceans, borders, and centuries, just as we did in the transatlantic course. Foster reminded me that it is 'the stories that reveal the multiplicity of conditions and experiences', rather than those which reinforce dominant perspectives, that 'will be most helpful to us'.[5] I now strive to share multiple experiences and remove constructed boundaries in my teaching while discussing with students why these boundaries and dominant stories exist. Recently, I taught a course focused on world mythology and, like my reaction in the transatlantic course, students were amazed at the connections between the myths of distant countries and their own folklore. Expanding the transatlantic approach to a world perspective helped emphasise for my students the value of studying literature which reveals the multiplicity and connections of human experience.

As Kate Flint argues, 'the Atlantic is a space of translation and transformation, rather than of straightforward transmission',[6] and the connections we discover are often complex. For my own research, this points to a fascinating and unsettled relationship between early America and Great Britain, one simultaneously collaborative, competitive, self-righteous, self-effacing, didactic, dogmatic, judgemental, and sympathetic. These aspects of translation and transformation make transatlanticism a slippery approach to grasp and exemplify the value of a co-taught course with a diverse student population working to guard against one-sided Ameri- or Brit-centric notions. The class mirrored transatlantic literary negotiations as the students of each side strove to understand the other while still asserting our own form of 'national identity'.

The transatlantic conversations we studied in class – like Britain's criticism of early American novels followed by America's prolific literary responses versus the supportive relationship between George Eliot and Harriet Beecher Stowe – illustrate the complexity of transatlanticism. In these examples, the most important connection between nation and transatlanticism is the very thing we teach first-year composition students: audience matters – especially when the audience can respond with texts of its own. Not only were Americans reading British texts and vice versa, both sets of readers/writers were responding and redefining their national identities through the 'active interventions into social and political life' of novels.[7]

Now that I am removed from my transatlantic support group in the lonely phase of writing a dissertation, combining the 'multiplicity of conditions and experiences' as Foster describes is my greatest challenge – and the greatest value I have found in transatlantic studies. As I work on my dissertation, 'Unions in Crisis: British and American Marriage Anxiety and Nation-Building in Art and Novels, 1660–1860', Foster's charge has ultimately meant avoiding the 'false dichotomy between nationalism and transnationalism' and using multiple experiences to discover the ways 'the nation and transatlantic are deeply implicated in one another'.[8]

As I continue my transatlantic education, I still feel uncertainty in reading 'multiple experiences'. I still strive to avoid generalisations and categories and am part of a writing group of Americanists and British-focused students from the transatlantic course who, thankfully, will not hesitate to point out when I err. Though I still identify myself as an eighteenth-century British scholar, that label means less and less as my internal identifier adds more centuries, countries, and disciplines inspired by transatlantic reading.

MOLLY KNOX LEVERENZ: TRACKING TRANSATLANTIC PERIODICAL CULTURE

I didn't know what to expect when I signed up for Linda Hughes and Sarah Robbins's graduate seminar on transatlantic literature. I assumed we would simply be reading British and American books in the same course – essentially studying texts in terms of topic and time frame rather than national boundaries. And we did do that, as when we studied abolitionist writings from both sides of the Atlantic. We also studied how Britons and Americans wrote about each other, as in Charles Dickens's *American Notes*. Our focus was more complex and challenging than I was expecting, however. We moved beyond surface-level transatlantic exchanges to grapple with the nineteenth century as a transatlantic culture, a network of relationships and texts transported across vast physical and experiential expanses but bound by the world of print. This transatlantic perspective on nineteenth-century print culture has affected the research questions I pose and the methodologies I use to answer them, as well as the frameworks I employ in my teaching.

Although I gained much from the course, at mid-semester I struggled to understand what it meant to examine a text through a transatlantic lens. The timeline of a single course made it difficult to grasp transatlanticism and transatlantic research methods before embarking on a seminar project. A year later, however, I had the opportunity to take another class with Linda Hughes, on research methods for Victorian periodicals. Although the course itself did not have a transatlantic focus, Dr Hughes encouraged us to pursue our own interests, allowing me to develop a transatlantic project. I decided to examine the transatlantic dialogue surrounding the publication of Wilkie Collins's *The Moonstone* in *Harper's Weekly*. In my project (published in *American Periodicals*) I read the novel and its illustrations in dialogue with articles and images throughout *Harper's Weekly* during the novel's serialisation, demonstrating how the serial and other texts comment on British imperialism. This reading allows us to see how the reprinting of *The Moonstone* is part of an ongoing transatlantic discourse within the periodical, one that not only critiques English imperialism but also reflects American desire for globalisation. Although Collins's appearance in an American periodical makes the textual transatlantic exchange evident enough, I would not have been able to grasp the implications of transatlantic discourse and culture without the transatlantic class. That course helped me realise that there are transatlantic (and transoceanic and transnational) contexts and cultures distinctly different from, and yet intrinsically tied to, single-nation contexts.

The seminar inspired me to wonder about more than the American reception of Collins's novel; the methodologies and theories I read pressed me to question how texts such as Collins's create meaning and connection across texts and around the world. As Margaret Beetham argues:

> A periodical is not a window on to the past or even a mirror of it. Each
> article, each periodical number, was and is part of a complex process
> in which writers, editors, publishers and readers engaged in trying to
> understand themselves and their society; that is, they struggled to make
> their world meaningful.[9]

Similarly, in the transatlantic class, I was struck by Barbara Buchenau's description of how print culture functions transatlantically as a method of making meaning for one's nation: 'Comparing British and American literature will make it possible to understand the process of American literary self-definition as an ongoing discussion of Americans with the British, with people from other nations, and among themselves.'[10] Thus, in a transatlantic context, periodical content becomes a significant site of national identity formation. Transatlantic discourses are inherently both outwardly focused and self-reflective.

As I look to the future of both my own scholarship and transatlanticism as a field, I see dynamic opportunities for uncovering the ways texts make meaning for readers. When we understand texts as part of a transnational discourse rather than simply as symptomatic of national ideologies and events, we can see how texts call and respond to both readers and to each other. When we acknowledge the international relationships that inform textual production – everything from the origin and inspiration of content to the economic and political ramifications of (re)printing – we gain a better grasp of the lived experience of nineteenth-century persons and a keener insight into our own relationship to print, discourses, and people in a global economy.

Transatlanticism also gives me a new critical lens to apply to teaching. As a graduate student, I have had the opportunity to teach a broad, lower-level, literature survey course, one not bound by nationality or genre. Instead of seeing the lack of specification for such a course as a grab-all for non-majors, I find in transatlanticism a cogent frame for seeing the threads that connect texts across national boundaries, centuries, and genres. While the connections I have made with my students between, for example, the portrayals of gender, justice, and death in *Antigone* and Suzanne Collins's *The Hunger Games* do not indicate a shared contemporary culture as we see in nineteenth-century periodicals, transatlanticism does allow my students to see how, as readers, we are part of a history of print culture. While *Antigone* and *The Hunger Games* have something to tell us about Greek mythology and contemporary culture respectively, transatlanticism has provided me with a theory of intertextuality that inspires me to teach these disparate texts as significant points in an interconnected literary history.

MARIE MARTINEZ: REFLECTIONS ON TRANSNATIONAL TRANSMISSIONS

Though the 2010 transatlantic seminar initially produced logistical uncertainties for me, it proved to be one of the most significant experiences of my graduate career. Graduate courses often equip students with new lenses for examining literature while exploring new methodologies, but the transatlantic seminar shifted my perspective toward more than a new lens; I discovered a new way of seeing. The course transformed my scholarly interests and informed my pedagogy.

Our first reading assignments helped deconstruct my notions of a so-called British or American text. Dickens's *American Notes*, Meredith McGill's 'Charles Dickens, Reprinting, and the Dislocation of American Culture', and Amanda Claybaugh's 'Toward a New Transatlanticism' illuminated the relationship between Dickens and America.[11] For the first time, I considered Dickens as part of a larger conversation. Resituating his work as unavoidably influencing and influenced by others sparked an interest in uncovering other transatlantic networks through the travels, publications, and reception of additional authors. However, I was still uncertain about how these revelations might impact my research.

I was grasping for definitions and the implications of a transatlantic approach in the second week of the course when I presented on Sofia Ahlberg's 'Transatlanticism'.[12] Her piece helped me remap the nineteenth century, considerably expanding my perception of nineteenth-century culture. Citing Paul Gilroy's image of the ship in motion and the circulation of ideas and activities in *The Black Atlantic*, Ahlberg argues that the Atlantic offers 'a vantage point that is not national, but polynational; not territorial, but relational'.[13] In my limited British focus, the Atlantic Ocean had seemed like a barrier isolating and separating Britain from others, often its own colonised nations, but Ahlberg's essay encouraged me to see the ocean as shared space, more a link than an obstacle.

Two texts in particular further changed my perspective. Reading Susanna Moodie's *Roughing It in the Bush* through a transatlantic lens revealed that nineteenth-century disease and medicine are intrinsically transnational.[14] I was struck by Moodie's descriptions of the 'dreadful cholera . . . depopulating Quebec and Montreal' at the time of her emigration.[15] Realising that Moodie's tale is intertwined with the cholera epidemic of 1831–2 ravaging English and European ports before heading across the Atlantic to North America, I saw links between disease, water, and travel. Moodie uses both sea imagery and disease metaphors to describe emigration in 1830 as a 'great tide' that 'flowed westward'.[16] She refers to a 'Canada mania' that 'pervaded the middle ranks of British society' as an 'infection'.[17] On its own, the fact that Moodie connects travel to both water and disease did not mean much at the time, but it took on new importance later as I contemplated a dissertation on Victorian contagion.

The second text that made a lasting impact was Elizabeth Gaskell's. Like Moodie, Gaskell had first-hand experience with cholera, and her 1848 social problem novel, *Mary Barton*, tackles issues of poverty and sanitation.[18] Transatlantic inquiry led me to a fresh understanding of the novel's resolution.

I began by considering Will Wilson's position as a sailor. Gaskell's characters are fascinated by Will's transatlantic experiences that change him: 'Mary gazed with wondering pleasure at her old playmate; now, a dashing, bronzed-looking, ringleted sailor, frank, and hearty, and affectionate.'[19] Gaskell's treatment of Will suggests that transatlantic travel is valued and transformative. But Will is not the only transatlantic traveller in the novel. The heroine's journey toward resolution is intertwined with her own transformative transatlantic excursion. Mary's attempts to reach Will in time for Jem's trial put her in dangerous, compromising situations and even threaten her health. On the other hand, Mary's eventual emigration with Jem to the 'Indian countries' of Canada, of which they have 'heard fine things', suggests that they can escape the past and start a new life together.[20] I was convinced that the chapters involving Mary's quest to find Will are pivotal, but I could not decide quite how. Transatlantic travel, all at once associated with adventure, danger, despair, and opportunity, made *Mary Barton* fresh. When I began developing my dissertation on Victorian contagion, I realised that Mary's close proximity to water is a marker of her recovery from a dangerous social infection. Gaskell's novel opens with descriptions of an atmosphere consistent with nineteenth-century vulnerabilities then believed to cause cities and neighbourhoods to fall prey to miasmas. Manchester, primed for an outbreak, is threatened by both physical and social disease. Esther, the fallen woman, is one source of infection: Mary Barton's desire to climb the social ladder comes from her aunt Esther, resulting in her flirtation with Henry Carson. Gaskell suggests that Esther's fate may well be Mary's if Mary continues to succumb to the infection. Mary, however, ultimately resists the disease. She realises her error when Jem is arrested and she goes to the docks in search of Will, who alone can provide an alibi for Jem. After the 1831 cholera epidemic in Britain, buckets of water were routinely used to clear out the filth that built up in homes and streets in order to prevent subsequent outbreaks. Similarly, Mary Barton's episode by the sea is representative of her cleansing her life of disease. Her emigration with Jem across the Atlantic is reminiscent of many in the nineteenth century who fled disease-ridden places to escape infection and start a new life. As a result of the transatlantic course, scenes like this now meaningfully resonate with me.

Transnational interests like my study of disease's circulation also inform my teaching. For instance, in an introductory literature course entitled 'Nineteenth-Century Contagion', students read *Mary Barton* and Elizabeth Barrett Browning's 'The Cry of the Children' alongside Edgar Allan Poe's 'Masque of the Red Death' and Elizabeth Stuart Phelps's 'The Tenth of January' in a unit on the politics of contagion. I've come to believe that teaching transatlantically introduces students to texts that can bridge gaps in history and give them a more global perspective as they see writers and characters crucially connected to more than one place.

NOTES

1. *Amazing Grace*, DVD, directed by Michael Apted. USA: 20th Century Fox, 2007.
2. 'Voyages: The Trans-Atlantic Slave Trade Database'. Available at <http://www.slavevoyages.org/tast/index.faces> (last accessed 20 May 2014).
3. Marjorie Stone, 'Elizabeth Barrett Browning and the Garrisonians: "The Runaway Slave at Pilgrim's Point", the Boston Female Anti-Slavery Society, and Abolitionist Discourse in the *Liberty Bell*', in Alison Chapman (ed.), *Victorian Women Poets* (Woodbridge: Brewer, 2003), pp. 33–55.
4. Sandra Gilbert and Susan Gubar, 'Introduction to the Second Edition: Madwoman in the Academy', in *Madwoman in the Attic*, 2nd edn (New Haven, CT: Yale University Press, 2000), p. xlii.
5. Frances Smith Foster, *'Til Death or Distance Do Us Part': Love and Marriage in African America* (Oxford: Oxford University Press, 2010), p. 123.
6. Kate Flint, quoted in Brigitte Bailey, 'Transatlantic Studies and American Women Writers', in Beth L. Lueck, Brigitte Bailey, and Lucinda L. Damon-Bach (eds), *Transatlantic Women: Nineteenth-Century American Women Writers in Great Britain and Europe* (Hanover, NH: University Press of New England, 2012), p. xiv.
7. Amanda Claybaugh, *The Novel of Purpose: Literature and Social Reform in the Anglo-American World* (Ithaca, NY: Cornell University Press, 2007), p. 36.
8. Colleen Glenney Boggs, quoted in Bailey, 'Transatlantic Studies', p. xxiv.
9. Margaret Beetham, 'Towards a Theory of the Periodical as a Publishing Genre', in Laurel Brake et al. (eds), *Investigating Victorian Journalism* (New York: St. Martin's Press, 1990), p. 20.
10. Barbara Buchenau, '"Wizards of the West"? How Americans Respond to Sir Walter Scott, the "Wizard of the North"', in H. C. MacDougall (ed.), *James Fenimore Cooper: His Country and His Art* (Oneonta: State University of New York College at Oneonta, 1997), pp. 14–25; *James Fenimore Cooper Society Website* available at <http://external.oneonta. edu/cooper/> (last accessed 11 October 2010).
11. Charles Dickens, *American Notes* (New York: St. Martin's Press, 1985); Meredith McGill, 'Charles Dickens, Reprinting, and the Dislocation of American Culture', *American Literature and the Culture of Reprinting, 1834–1853* (Philadelphia: University of Pennsylvania Press, 2007), pp. 109–40; Amanda Claybaugh, 'Toward a New Transatlanticism: Dickens in the United States', *Victorian Studies*, 48: 3 (2006), 439–60.

12. Sophia Ahlberg, 'Transatlanticism', in Andrew Maunder and Jennifer Phegley (eds), *Teaching Nineteenth-Century Fiction* (Basingstoke: Palgrave Macmillan, 2010), pp. 196–209.

13. Ibid., p. 196.

14. Susanna Moodie, *Roughing It in the Bush*, ed. Michael A. Peterman (New York: W. W. Norton, 2007).

15. Ibid., p. 14.

16. Ibid., p. 9.

17. Ibid., p. 12.

18. Elizabeth Gaskell, *Mary Barton*, ed. Thomas Recchio (New York: W. W. Norton, 2008).

19. Ibid., p. 130.

20. Ibid., p. 312.

Index

AASS (American Anti-Slavery Society), 107, 112

abolitionist movement, 107–17
  and 2010 transatlantic seminar, 246
  anti-slavery writings, 36, 98, 111
  Box Brown's 'guerrilla memorialisation', 90–1
  and oratory, 155
  origins, 114
  in sensation literature, 189–90
  see also Chapman, Maria Weston; Douglass, Frederick; Martineau, Harriet; transatlantic slave trade

AFASS (American and Foreign Anti-Slavery Society), 112

African Atlantic agency, 89–91

African Canadians, 109

African slave traders, 86–7

Aguilar, Grace, 34

Ahlberg, Sofia, 252

Ainsworth, William Harrison, 183

Alcott, Louisa May, 191

All the Year Round, serial instalments, 36–7

Allen, Walter, *Transatlantic Crossing*, 3

America *see* Canada; North America; United States

American Anti-Slavery Society (AASS), 107, 112

American Civil War *see* Civil War, American

American and Foreign Anti-Slavery Society (AFASS), 112

American Historical Newspaper (digital database), 214

American literature
  American romance and European realism, 40–1, 42–3

  cultural earliness, prophecy and poetry, 196
  poetry, in relation to British, 172–5
  separate from British literature, 2–4, 252
  see also British literature

American Revolution, impacts of and nation-building, 125, 126–8

American Studies scholarship, 2–4, 40–3
  Anglo-American literary relations, 47–8, 49–50
  transnationalism, 43–6

'Americanness'
  gender and American literary criticism, 24–5
  in *Portrait of a Lady*, 136, 137–44

analogue (print) media, and digital media, 211–12, 217–19, 220–1

analytical tools, digital humanities, 231–2

anarchism, 160–1

Anderson, Benedict, 6

Andrews, William, 108

Anglo-African Magazine (journal), 76

The Anglo-American (journal), 220–1

Anglo-American literary relations, 47–8, 49–50

Anglo-Jewish literature, 34

annotated bibliographies, online, 226, 228–9

anonymity, in nineteenth-century periodicals, 198

anthologies, 55–60
  definitions and uses, 56–7
  of Romanticism, 59–60
  and transatlantic Romanticism, 55–66
  of Victorian poetry, 214

anti-Catholicism, 26

Calhoun, John, 'Slavery, A Positive Good'
 (speech), 155
Canada
 African Canadians, 109
 British emigration to, 100–2, 252
 Canadian identity, nineteenth century,
  96–7, 98–9
 French Canadians, 96–7
 immigrants as Canadian writers, 48, 97–8,
  100–2
 and transatlantic Romanticism, 61–2
Canadian transatlanticism, 95–105
 class formats, 97–9
 concepts of Canadianness, 104–5
 final questions, 103–4
 Pauline Johnson, 98–9, 102–3
 presentation and discussion, 99–100
 Susanna Moodie, 97–8, 100–2
Capilano, Joe (Squamish), 99
Caribbean, as transatlantic setting, 74
Carlyle, Thomas, 151, 196
 Sartor Resartus, 1
Carruthers, Mary, 231
Cattaneo, Carlo, 201
'change log', 216
Chapman, Maria Weston, 36
Chapman, Maria Weston, and transatlantic
 abolitionism, 107–17
 correspondence and reports, 107–8, 110,
  112–13, 114–16
 and Douglass, 110, 115–17
 Martineau's 'portrait' of, 115–16
 Pinda (novella), 117
 Right and Wrong in Massachusetts, 114
 'The Times That Try Men's Souls'
  (poem), 117
Chase, Richard, 42
Chee Dimock, Wai, 6
Chesnutt, Charles, 'The Wife of His Youth'
 (short story), 79–80
Child, Lydia Maria, 'The Quadroon' (short
 story), 76–7
cholera epidemic (1831–2), 252, 253
Chopin, Kate, The Awakening, 187
The Christian Recorder (African Methodist
 Episcopal newspaper), 77
chronologies, online, 228–9
Civil War, American
 African American literary references to, 74
 impacts of and nation-building, 198–202
'civilisation', and settlers in North America,
 101–2
class
 cricket and popular culture, 44

difference and behaviour in North
 America, 101
Putnam's and middle-class conservatism,
 125
and sensation novels, 183, 190–1
Claybaugh, Amanda, 4, 252
Cohen, Daniel, 184
Cohen, Michael, 214
Coleridge, Samuel Taylor
 'Christabel' (poem), 58
 and William Wordsworth: Lyrical Ballads,
  58, 165, 167
collaborative learning, 248
 digital projects, 216–17, 225–33
Collins, Suzanne, The Hunger Games, 251
Collins, Wilkie, 188
 The Moonstone, 250
 The Woman in White, 190, 191
colonialism
 in British North America, 96, 98
 and synecdochal thinking, 139–40
Colored American Magazine (journal), 33, 79
confessional scenes, and anti-Catholicism,
 25–6
Conrad, Joseph, Heart of Darkness, 161–2
contagion as metaphor, and transatlantic
 emigration, 252–3
Conway, Moncure, 198, 199–200, 201
 and Mazzini, 200–1
 and Swinburne, 204
 and Whitman, 202–3
Conway Hall Ethical Society (formerly South
 Place Chapel), 201
Cornhill Magazine (journal), 37
Cornish, Samuel, 107
Cornwell, Sarah, 229
cosmopolitan perspectives, 138–9
counter discourse, 236–8
course packs, anthologies and transatlantic
 Romanticism, 55–6
courses, seminars and syllabi, 27–8, 32–3,
 34–5
 2010 transatlantic seminar, 5–9, 245–53
 anthologies and transatlantic Romanticism,
  55–6, 59–66
 Atlantic abolitionist networks, 109–10
 black Atlantic, a dramatic tableau, 84–91
 Canadian transatlanticism, 97–105
 Electronic Literary Seminar, 227
 oratory, 153–62
 poetic genre and nationality, 164–5
 race, appropriation and print culture,
  70–80
 sensation literature, 182–4, 189, 190–3